The Reverb series looks at the connections between music, artists and performers, musical cultures and places. It explores how our cultural and historical understanding of times and places may help us to appreciate a wide variety of music, and vice versa.

reverb-series.co.uk
Series editor: John Scanlan

Already published

The Beatles in Hamburg
Ian Inglis

Brazilian Jive: From Samba to Bossa and Rap
David Treece

Nick Drake: Dreaming England
Nathan Wiseman-Trowse

Remixology: Tracing the Dub Diaspora
Paul Sullivan

Tango: Sex and Rhythm of the City
Mike Gonzalez and Marianella Yanes

Van Halen: Exuberant California, Zen Rock'n'roll
John Scanlan

REMIXOLOGY

TRACING THE DUB DIASPORA

PAUL SULLIVAN

REAKTION BOOKS

Published by Reaktion Books Ltd
33 Great Sutton Street
London ECIV ODX, UK
www.reaktionbooks.co.uk

First published 2014

Printed and bound in Great Britain by Ashford Colour Press, Gosport, Hants

A catalogue record for this book is available from the British Library

ISBN 978 1 78023 199 0

CONTENTS

INTRODUCTION

People get warped by dub . . . and they never recover.[1]

– Ian Penman

Ethereal, mystical, conceptual, fluid, avant-garde, raw, unstable,
provocative, transparent, postmodern, disruptive, heavyweight,
political, enigmatic . . . dub is way more than 'a riddim and
a bassline', even if it is that too. Dub is a genre and a process,
a 'virus' and a 'vortex'; it draws the listener into a labyrinth,
where there are false signposts and 'mercurial' trails that can
lead to the future, the past . . . or to nowhere at all. It is apposite
that the etymology of this so-called aural magic realism lies in
the tricknological process of manipulating sound on film; that is,
doubling or dubbing and the ghoulish habit of re-recording voices
onto a soundtrack. And there is a neat coincidence too, perhaps,
that the Jamaican patois word for 'ghost', taken from the Obeah
(a set of beliefs and practices developed in the West Indies), is the
similar-sounding duppy.

In Kingston, the capital of Jamaica, where dub was first
created, 'dubplate' was the term used for acetates on which
instrumental versions of popular tunes to be tested out on sound
systems were pressed. These dubplate versions were initially
instrumentals of roots reggae songs, which became popular on
the Kingston circuit after sound system operator owner 'Ruddy'
Redwood cut an acetate of 'On the Beach' by The Paragons
(1967) at Duke Reid's Treasure Isle studio, and engineer Byron
Smith accidentally left the vocals out.[2] Redwood decided to play
the 'mistake' anyway, thereby paving the way for his deejay

(Wassy) – and a bemused but excited crowd – to fill in the gaps with their own voices. Engineers and producers took the concept of the instrumental a step further by not only removing the vocals, but using multitrack technology to delete, add or rearrange other elements (drums, guitars, bass) and adding further studio effects such as reverb and echo.

Dub versions were a boon for record producers and labels looking for B-sides for their 7-inch (45-rpm) records. Recording new songs for this purpose was costly and using the rhythm track of the A-side not only saved money but allowed the sound system selectors to talk over the track. While the concept of version, i.e., mainly instrumental takes on pre-written songs, has a history prior to dub (specifically in African-American and Caribbean music forms like jazz, blues and salsa), its Jamaican variant was unique, owing to the levels of modification involved.

Although technology had been used to 'open up' and rearrange music before, by musique concrète artists, for example, and Western music producers, like George Martin and Teo Macero, the concept of the mixing-board-as-instrument (and its corollary, the engineer-as-artist) was fully realized in Kingston. The way in which the dub pioneers (with Lynford Anderson, Errol Thompson, Augustus Pablo, King Tubby, Keith Hudson, Lee 'Scratch' Perry among them) began deconstructing songs into their constituent parts then rebuilding them into alternative compositions – literally turning them inside out to reveal their 'seams' – made the music simultaneously avant-garde and hugely popular with the sound system crowds.

The importance of the sound system cannot be understated in the development of dub, not only because of the dissemination of the music, but also because of its role in the music's creative evolution. This reduction of songs to shadow and suggestion prefigured the concept of the remix, as well as laying the foundations for the birth of rap and the phenomenon of the MC, when the sound system deejays filled in the absences with their hype. Sound system selectors and operators, meanwhile, were the first incarnation of the modern DJ where the voice was contained in a studio. They broke through the 'remoteness' of radio broadcasts to provide a physical conduit between the playing of pre-recorded music and the audience.

Although dub was, and is, a more or less fluid process with no rigid rules, certain sonic tropes are recognizably consistent when tracing its development. Chief among them are reverb and delay (echo). Although they are often confused as the same thing, there is a slight technical difference. 'Reverb' can be defined as repetitions of a sound that occur within a few milliseconds of the sound being made, and which the brain perceives as originating from the same location. Singing in the shower is an example of reverb. 'Delay' / 'echo' carries a more distinctive repetition than reverb as it clearly comes from a different place than the source material. Shouting into a cave is an example of echo.

Reverb and echo have been used in various forms of music, from rhythm and blues and country music (Muddy Waters's or Elvis Presley's recordings on Chicago's Chess Records or for Sun Records in Memphis, for example), to Western classical music, where studios have employed these techniques to simulate acoustic settings such as churches and cathedrals.[3]

But dub's originators, most of whom were engineers, used echo and reverb to reunify fragmented songs as well as to disorient the listener, as though pulling the rhythmic 'rug' from under their feet. Such an approach often produced psychedelic results, and gave the music a 'trippy' reputation that persists today. As Erik Davis memorably put it, 'good dub sounds like the recording studio itself has begun to hallucinate'.[4]

Since echo is also related to human memory (the human brain codes the remnants – the echo – of a memory), it can be used as a tool to transport listeners to the past. Jamaica's dub pioneers used echo in combination with the sentiments and spirituality of roots reggae to provoke a sense of Jamaica's ancestral African roots, while at the same time invoking the infinity of the cosmos – and the future – by creating cavernous spaces within the music.

Another major characteristic of dub is its emphasis on bass. Early dub mixes were also known as 'drum and bass' mixes, referring to their stripping down of the music to its bare rhythmic components. The bassline occupied an increasingly foregrounded role and was subsequently intensified.

In *Dub in Babylon*, Christopher Partridge points out how

the heavier [the bass] is, the more it communicates what might be described as 'dread culture' . . . bass and dub and reggae necessarily references all that is meant by the term 'dread', often including masculinity and notions of transcendence. . . . Bass is, to some extent, gendered, being indicative of masculinity. As in many cultures, this is largely because the vocal register is gendered. As the typical male gets older, so the tone of his voice lowers and, consequently, the more masculine it is understood to be.[5]

Backing up this idea of bass as masculine is its 'penetrative' aspect; the way it can be felt as well as heard – vibrating through the body, shaking the ribcage, bothering vital organs – especially in the context of the dance hall, with its powerful speakers. At the same time, a case can be (and has been) made for dub's maternal nature.

Music listeners such as Simon Reynolds have noted dub's ability to take us back to the 'amniotic sea of the womb . . . the lost paradise before individuation and anxiety'.[6] Bassist and all-round dub aficionado Jah Wobble has similarly argued that bass

tends to be a feminine power, but it can be a male power as well. It's a feminine power insofar as it comes from earth and it's all pervasive. It also has male qualities, it can penetrate and it can also be very dynamic. But the main thing for me is that it's all supporting. It's very much the quality of the Divine Mother.[7]

Another fairly consistent production trope is the overdubbing of effects and non-musical sounds onto recordings, and non-musical sounds too. From Kingston producers, like Errol Thompson and Lee Perry, to British 'second wave' luminaries, like Mad Professor and Adrian Sherwood, engineers have maintained a penchant for utilizing everything from film and television dialogue to the sounds of animals and crying babies to help create atmospheres that are both entertaining and eerie. As a genre (or perhaps sub-genre, since it developed out of roots reggae), dub was fairly short-lived in Jamaica, peaking in the mid to late 1970s and already winding down in the early 1980s. But its creative strategies and associated rituals – the sound system, the deejay, the remix – have continued far beyond its island of origin.

Closely following the Jamaican diaspora, Remixology charts this journey, and looks at dub's role as a 'meta-virus'. It considers how dub has infiltrated and informed a host of mutant 'strains' and hybrids – from punk, jungle and dubstep to hip hop, trip hop and techno – and even, in the case of dub poetry, shaped linguistic culture. I hope you enjoy the ride.

1 THE KINGSTON CONTEXT

THE RISE OF THE JAMAICAN SOUND SYSTEM

Dub emerged in Jamaica, just like reggae, its 'significant other', as part of a broader musical, social and political context that included the rise of sound system culture, the establishment of a national sound, and the founding of a local music infrastructure that incorporated record labels, studios and producers. Before sound systems, the main source of broadcast entertainment in Jamaica was through radio, which had been around since the early 1930s. Given that radios were still prohibitively expensive in the 1940s, poorer Jamaicans would often gather around a shared radio, especially in the evenings.

The first national radio station (Jamaica Broadcasting Corporation, or JBC) was not founded until 1959. However, those who did have access to radio sets could pick up commercial stations such as Radio Jamaica and Rediffusion Network (RJR), owned by the British Rediffusion Group, as well as transmissions from abroad. In the right conditions, short-wave transmissions could be picked up from the BBC, and medium-wave stations from Cuba and America such as Nashville's WLAC, Miami's WINZ and New Orleans' WNOE. Most of these stations were playing rhythm and blues – the sound that fuelled the early sound systems.

Home systems such as radiograms (or 'radiophones', radios that had the capacity to connect to a phonograph or electric turntable externally) were also developed around this time, but were equally scarce. In 1950 a modest turntable system cost the average Jamaican an entire year's wages, and even if such a purchase could be afforded, there was still the problem of how to secure records for it since the rhythm and blues records popular with younger (poorer) Jamaicans mostly had to be imported and were therefore expensive.[1] As was the case with radios, so with radiograms: those fortunate enough to own one often held listening parties in their homes too. These systems also became a useful way for shops – particularly those selling alcohol – to boost sales: by stringing up speakers above their doors, establishments could attract more customers. It was in this way that two of the principal sound system pioneers – Arthur 'Duke' Reid and Clement 'Coxsone' Dodd – started out.

It was not long before rudimentary ready-to-go systems could be rented from stores like that of Stanley Motta, one of Kingston's leading producers of mento, which was the prevailing style of local folk music. In Norman Stolzoff's *Wake the Town and Tell the People*, Hedley Jones, a band leader who built his own cello (a popular instrument with mento bands) at the age of fourteen as well as the first ever solid-body electric guitar in 1940, before moving to the field of electronics, claims that by the 1940s there were already two men in Kingston who

> had two small sound systems that they would buy records [for] and go out and play for parties. The first one was Count Nicholas. And the one that followed was called Count Goody. Both used small RCA amplifier sets made for PA systems that used to be sold by Stanley Motta.[2]

Stolzoff also quotes an interview with Bunny 'the Mighty Burner' Goodison, who ran the Soul Shack sound system, in which he mentions a man called Roy White. The latter was booked to play records on a portable PA system between speeches at political rallies to 'keep the crowd involved and attentive'. Soon the likes of

White, Goodison, Nicholas and Tom 'The Great Sebastian' Wong, another early soundman, were hiring out their musical services for parties.

After the Second World World War, Hedley Jones started up a radio repair shop where he began building amps. On realizing that demand for records was growing, he also began selling imported jazz records for a new vinyl section called 'Bop City', named after the New York jazz club. In order to promote this new business to the public, he designed his own special amp known as the 'Williamson form'. According to Stolzoff, this amp was the first of its kind in Jamaica, and was not only more powerful than other commercially available amps of the time, but also came with a major technological innovation in the shape of a 'splitter' that could manipulate the treble, mid-range and bass frequencies. After hearing the power and quality of the amp, other sound system owners, such as Tom Wong, began commissioning Jones for their own amps, and they quickly became a standard among the growing sound system community.

As wattage also started to increase, more emphasis began to be placed on lower frequencies and a whole new scale in speaker design emerged. In early 1950, Jones constructed an amp for aspiring soundman Roy Johnson, whose system featured speaker cabinets that were literally the size of wardrobes. Nicknamed 'the House of Joy', Johnson's system became a prototype for the larger type of sound system that emerged soon after.

Hedley and his apprentices, Fred Stanford and Jacky Eastwood, were at the forefront of constructing this next phase of systems which would dominate Kingston nightlife throughout the 1950s. Jones and Eastwood built a system for former policeman and liquor-store owner Arthur 'Duke' Reid (which he called 'The Trojan'), as well as for Coxsone Dodd (called 'Downbeat'). Stanford would go on to work for Reid, servicing his equipment and building new sets for his friends. Dodd and Reid not only became Kings of the Dancehall (along with Wong), but were the first to go into the studio to record exclusively for the sound systems.

The sound systems soon grew into sonic powerhouses that literally could be heard for miles around. Initially, the soundmen played in a variety of informal venues (for example in empty yards, community halls and private homes) but outgrew these spaces and began to organize events in enclosed open-air areas known as 'lawns', and later 'dance halls' – a slightly misleading name, given that there were neither walls nor roofs, let alone a hall. Most of the key dance halls were located in downtown Kingston, around the central area known as 'Beat Street', where larger venues with names like 'King's Lawn', 'Chocomo Lawn' and 'Forrester's Hall' drew ever-burgeoning crowds.

The sounds were generally controlled by two people: a deejay, who introduced and sometimes spoke over the records to keep the audience's interest piqued, and a selector ('selecta'), who chose and played the records and, when technology enabled it later on, sometimes mixed the singer's or the deejay's voice.

Each sound was associated with an area and usually had its own set of followers. 'Dances' became important social, cultural and even political events, as Jamaicans gathered not only to listen to the trending music of the day, but to discuss community topics, flirt and socialize.

As more systems emerged, competitions known as 'clashes' began to take place. These were a partial continuation of the competitive performance traditions of many West African cultures such as those in Trinidad and Brazil. Here, though, the larger clashes could feature up to eight systems on one lawn, each trying to outdo each other and become the 'Champion Sound'.

An important component in these musical battles was the specific records each sound system owned and played. Given the paucity of records in Kingston in the 1950s and '60s, sound operators largely depended on the imports that started flowing into local shops, or were available through mail order or obtained on personal trips to Florida and other southern u.s. states, where shoppers would sometimes pick up technology as well as music.

So crucial was having exclusive records for a system's success that operators quickly developed stealth strategies: buying up all available copies of a new record was not unheard of, nor was the retitling of a record, or scratching off labels (or sticking on fake ones) to try to confuse the 'spies' who began cropping up at dances. One particularly memorable anecdote involves Dennis Alcapone and Lloyd Daley hiding under the speaker boxes of leading sound systems like those of Duke Reid and Coxsone and recording their specials directly onto a Grundig machine for clandestine airings on Daley's Matador set. These so-called survival strategies also periodically erupted into violence and even sparked gang warfare. Reid, a former police officer and professional marksman, was well known for firing shots into the dance to keep the crowd hyped – as well as for roughing up competitors and sabotaging rival sound systems, as, indeed, were many others.

Among the most famous competitive stories of the era, related in Lloyd Bradley's *Bass Culture*, is that of Willis 'Gatortail' Jackson's song 'Later for the Gator' (1950), nicknamed 'Coxsone's Hop', which Coxsone used as musical ammunition against his rival Reid and other systems for years, fiercely protecting its identity. Some seven years later, word got out that Reid had not only worked out what the song was, but had got hold of a copy. Coxsone visited Reid's Trojan Sound system with Prince Buster to see if the rumours were true. Buster maintains they were at the bar:

> We wait. Then as the clock struck midnight we hear 'Baap . . . baa da dap da dap, daa da daaap', he have a glass in him hand, he drop it and just collapse, sliding down the bar. I had to brace him against the bar. The psychological impact had knocked him out. Nobody never hit him.[3]

In the 1960s, Kingston's new rude boy scene would usher in a new, aggressive mood to the dance hall; this was a consequence of the escalation of political violence and gang warfare that would engulf sound system culture.

SYSTEM TO STUDIO: THE CREATION OF A JAMAICAN SOUND

The choice of music played on the sound systems was restricted to the kinds of recordings accessible at any given time. Initially, this meant a mix of locally produced mento and imported rhythm and blues. Before R&B, other types of imported music had been popular in Kingston such as big band jazz and swing. This was mainly due to the U.S. occupancy of the island during wartime. Live jazz groups were especially popular amongst the upper echelons of Jamaican society, while mento – the nation's first indigenous music – was increasingly disparaged as a rural or 'redneck' sound. The sound systems, with their reliance on recorded music rather than on musicians, played a large part in killing off a local live music scene that had already been greatly diminished by the war. As Prince Buster memorably put it,

> So the promoter never mek no profit – dem did prove too expensive fi the dance promoter. Den alone eat a pot of goat! So when sound come now, the sound no tek no break. When these few sound system come, it was something different.[4]

As the U.S. moved away from rhythm and blues towards rock-and-roll, the supply of the former started to dry up in Jamaica, causing something of a crisis for the sound systems, which needed fresh supplies of exclusive R&B tunes to survive. It was for this reason that in the late 1950s soundmen – fed up with being charged extortionate prices by specialist dealers – began hitting the studios with the aim of recording local singers and musicians. The island's recording facilities at this time were limited to those belonging to mento producer Stanley Motta and radio stations like RJR, JBC and Federal. The latter was run by Ken Khouri, who had managed to acquire a cutting lathe as early as 1949 and recorded people at parties and homes. By producing their own takes on the R&B sound – Motta's studio recorded Derrick Harriott's 'Lollipop Girl' in 1969, as well as some of Laurel Aitken's first tunes – these studios aimed to compensate for the lack of so-called authentic product coming in from the States.

Pressed onto dubplates as one-off exclusives, these early recordings were meant for the dance halls rather than for commercial consumption. A normal press would hence usually consist of around 100 records, usually without labels. Dubplates would grow to become an essential factor in the unique system-to-studio process that developed around this time. Made of soft wax coating over a metal core, acetates were created specifically to provide a limited number of performances before decaying. They allowed new tracks to be previewed inexpensively in the dance halls to gauge how crowds responded before being cut on (expensive) vinyl.

Dubplates therefore became an exclusive currency, given to sound system operators by studios for previewing unreleased songs, which in turn fed into the competitive nature of the systems. It did not take long for producers to realize that the more successful dubplates offered a means of building up demand for a potential commercial release.

Lloyd Bradley has claimed that Duke Reid was the first major soundman to 'dip his toe into recording when he began producing his own sessions in 1957'; but there is evidence to suggest that Coxsone Dodd, who was making frequent record buying trips to the U.S. in the 1950s, had already begun making his own recordings at Federal by 1956.[5] Either way, the music began to morph from derivative R&B into something more distinctly Jamaican as local bands fused their attempts with local styles such as mento and other Caribbean sounds. This mixture was initially known as 'bluebeat' – a name taken from the record label run by Emile E. Shalit, who began to import these early Jamaican releases into the UK.

Bluebeat became more popularly known as 'ska', whose signature rhythmic thrust is alleged to be based on a beat invented by Memphis pianist Roscoe Gordon. Its emergence coincided almost directly with Jamaican independence on 6 August 1962, though curiously, there seems to be no evidence of any conscious effort to create a 'national sound'.[6] The music took a definitive leap forward in the early 1960s when Prince Buster (Cecil Bustamente Campbell) started making records for his own Voice of the People system (and later for the Bluebeat label). A former boxer who had previously worked as 'security' for Dodd, Buster was one of the principal forces in fusing local styles such as mento and buru with jazz horns and shuffling R&B. Ska's infectious melodies, upbeat rhythms and African-American vocal harmonies made it hugely popular not only in Jamaica but beyond too, especially in Britain, which by then already had a large Jamaican population following the post-war influx of the Jamaican diaspora. The sound provided the perfect catalyst for Jamaica's nascent music industry, with producers such as Motta and Khouri rapidly incorporating it into their repertoire. The arrival of the jukebox in the late 1950s, as well as a large increase in the ownership of radio sets, helped disseminate ska to an even wider public.

The growth of the Jamaican recording industry was very much connected with global and local technological developments. A watershed moment, for example, was the installation of the island's first two-track mixing desk at Federal studios in 1963. Not long afterwards, the first ever complete operation of mixer and recorder by MCI (Music Center Incorporated) was installed at Federal's main rival, WIRL (West Indies Records Limited) – whose studio changed its name to 'Dynamic Sound' to underscore its new multitrack prowess. This new technology began to spread to other studios and it was not long before soundmen including Duke Reid and Coxsone Dodd were muscling in on the action too. Dodd employed Hedley Jones to build his now legendary Studio One (officially 'Jamaica Recording and Publishing Studio') in a former nightclub in 1963.

Not only did Jones and Dodd record ska's first and only all-star group, the Skatalites, but Studio One was the first to split the channels, recording the band on one track and the vocals on the other, creating what was known as 'Jamaican Stereo', a significant element in the later emergence of dub. Reid opened his own independent two-track facility called 'Treasure Isle' in 1965 on the fourth floor of his liquor store, while around the same time Randy's four-track Studio on The Parade, set up by Vincent 'Randy' Chin and his wife Patricia, became the most significant facility after Studio One.

By the mid-1960s, most of the earlier set-ups had progressed from one-track (mono) recorders to two-track, and then on to the four-track recorders by the turn of the decade. This was a little behind the u.s. which had eight-track machines by then. Many of Kingston's first commercial studios were fitted out by Bill Garnett, who had started out as Federal studios' technical engineer during the tenure of Australian radio technician Graeme Goodall. Garnett was responsible for installing innovative technology such as API mixing consoles, tape machines and MCI high-pass filters into studios like Randy's, Joe Gibbs's, Harry J's and – a little later in the early '70s – Channel One, while Goodall would go on to train future Jamaican music (and dub) pioneers like Lynford Anderson and Sylvan Morris (who would in turn bring through Errol Thompson).

As imported vinyl became a distant memory, the shift to a purely local circuit of production was complete: locally produced sounds – still mostly issued as exclusive dubplates – played by local

selectors to local crowds. As the 1960s wore on, the jaunty, stac-
cato riffs of ska were replaced with the slower, moodier grooves
of 'rocksteady', which utilized deeper melody lines propounded
by the newly prominent electric bass. Named after the title of a
song released by Alton Ellis, rocksteady was built around the
'one drop' drum beat – typified by a heavy accent on the second
and fourth beat of every bar and often played by the bass drum
and the snare together. While many producers claim to have
pioneered the rocksteady groove, it was Duke Reid who capitalized
on it, recording and releasing vocal harmony groups such as The
Gaylads, The Maytals and The Paragons.

Known initially for its balladeers and their lyrical tropes of
lost love, the music grew more ominous as it soundtracked the
emergence of the rude boys, Jamaica's first youth subculture.
Characterized by young, sharp-dressed 'yoots' who wore porkpie
hats and suits, rude boys emerged following independence in 1962.

Randy's Records store, Kingston.

They came to Kingston (and other cities) in search of work and found unemployment rates as high as 35 per cent. Frustrated, poor and inspired by the rebellious characters in American gangster films, the rude boys – and so-called slack girls or skettels, their female counterparts – ran in gangs and changed the mood of the dance halls with their aggressive style. As politica tensions rose throughout the country, gun violence grew rife, and some of the more middle-class soundmen such as Winston Blake and Bunny Goodison started playing dances in clubs rather than outside in potentially lethal dance halls. They even started calling their sounds 'discoteques', causing a virtual split between uptown 'discos' and downtown sound systems.[7] Coxsone's Downbeat and Duke Reid's Trojan also ceased to operate on the road, leaving the studio as the primary site for musical creativity.

As a musical form, rocksteady innovated many techniques that would become popular in Jamaica's next big new sound, reggae, which would look to the emerging Rastafarian movement for lyrical inspiration as well as for solutions to the violence in Jamaican society. Indeed, it was not long before films like *The Harder They Come* (Perry Henzell, 1972) and the rise of Bob Marley – a former rude boy himself (his street-fighting skills earned him the nickname 'Tuff Gong') – would bring reggae and the Rastafarian movement to the world.[8] Meanwhile, the slow rhythms and extra sonic space of both rocksteady and reggae would prove essential in unleashing a parallel universe of sonic experimentation known, also known as 'dub'.

INSTRUMENTALS, VERSIONS AND DUBS

It was the culture of the dubplate that led directly to the development of the first 'proto-dub' instrumentals. The story goes that in late 1967 Ruddy's Supreme Ruler of Sound operator Rudolph 'Ruddy' Redwood was getting a dubplate of the rocksteady track by The Paragons called 'On the Beach' (1967) cut at Treasure Isle's studio. Engineer Byron Smith (allegedly assisted by King Tubby) was having difficulty dropping in the vocal track and wanted to stop cutting, but Redwood insisted that Smith continue to the end.[9] When the miscued dubplate finished cutting, Redwood apparently pronounced it 'art' and played it at his next dance, where the crowd went wild. Of the event, Bunny Lee recalls that

> the dance get so excited that them start to sing the lyrics over the riddim part and them have to play it for about half an hour to an hour! The Monday morning when I come back into town I say, 'Tubbs, boy, that little mistake we made, the people them love it!' So (King) Tubby say, 'All right, we'll try it.' We try it with some Slim Smith riddim like 'Aint Too Proud to Beg.' And Tubby's start it with the voice and [then] bring in the riddim. Then him play the singing, and them him play the complete riddim without voice. We start a call the thing 'version'.[10]

The concept of the instrumental B-side was already part of the U.S. recording industry, especially in the soul scene. Archie Bell's 'Tighten Up' (1968) and Bill Moss's classic 'Sock it to 'em Soul Brother' (1969) both had instrumentals, with the other side of the Fantastic Fours' 'I Love You Madly' (1968) even coming with a slightly dubbed up instrumental. The use of rhythm tracks for more than one purpose was not without precedent in Jamaica either. At Studio One in 1965 Roland Alphonso had played sax on a song called 'Rinky Dink', using the rhythm from Lee Perry and the Dynamites' 'Hold Down' (1965) with the vocals removed.[11]

Yet Redwood and Smith's seminal moment at Treasure Isle was certainly a major catalyst for what would quickly become standard practice of putting what became known as 'versions' on B-sides. Following the positive response to his 'error', Redwood lost no time in cutting instrumentals of other popular Duke Reid tracks to play at his dances. Although most of these were straight-up instrumentals with just the vocals removed, they soon started to feature extra reworkings – new melody lines, the replacement of one instrument with another. These modified instrumentals were sometimes continued as 'versions', but also as 'dubs' or 'dub versions', owing to their distribution on dubplates around the systems.[12]

It soon became clear that these 'dub versions' had an economic advantage, insofar as they allowed different 'songs' to be created with the same rhythm at no extra cost. Since musicians were generally paid by the session or song back then, producers remained primary copyright holders. 'Before versions we had double A-sides', Clive Chin recalls:

> I remember one big hit was a rocksteady tune called 'Hold Me Tight' by Johnny Nash [1968], which had a version of Sam Cooke's 'Cupid' on the other side. Both of them were big hits, but labels and producers weren't benefiting from that in terms of sales, which is partly why the use of rhythm tracks and versions came about . . .

From the off, the Jamaican recording ethos was keenly economical: bands, musicians and sessions were all efficiently (hurriedly) organized to get the most out of them commercially. Initially, the studio techniques of the Anglo-American studios – for example, tape editing – were not picked up by the ska producers, who tended to leave mistakes in, often recording several takes and then choosing the best one. However, some creative techniques did develop locally. The Ethiopians' 'Headache' (1967) had an innovative repeat echo on the drums during the instrumental break; 'Cool Night' by The Jamaicans (1968) and 'Right On Time' by The Sensations (1968) employed echo on their rhythm tracks

– as did Prince Buster's 'Rock & Shake' (1967) – though these techniques were not yet indicative of a trend.

In 1969, engineer–producer Lynford Anderson (Andy Capp) became one of the first to begin taking 'versions' into uncharted territory. Along with musician, producer and founder of The Dragonaires, Byron Lee, he combined an R&B rhythm from Derrick Morgan's 'Fat Man' with a well-known reggae guitar riff (played on the organ by Lloyd Charmers and some vocals borrowed from a Canadian soft drinks commercial to make 'Pop a Top'. This tune became a hit, along with other Andy Capp productions such as the equally infectious 'The Law' (also made with Lee in 1970), which employed more than the usual echo and reverb. Soon, studios all over Kingston began to produce acetate 'versions' for the systems, which started to carry the name 'specials' or 'one-offs' to increase their value (which was some-what ironic, given that they only lasted around a dozen plays). Adding to the exclusivity of these acetates was the fact they were cut directly from the master tape and mixed live at the same time, ensuring their uniqueness (mistakes were left in), and saving producers time and money in the process.

The commercial appeal eventually became too strong to resist and 'versions' began to be sold to the public, leading to a vogue for system-specific specials that featured specially recorded vocals that bigged up a particular sound system. Although 'dub versions', like instrumentals, often carried traces of an original song, they had the pivotal difference of going much further in manipulating sound in post-production. Real dub begins at the point where engineers and producers did not just subdue or remove a vocal, but stripped a song to its naked skeleton of drums and bass – hence one of the original names for dubs was 'drum and bass mixes'.

This wilful deconstruction provided the impetus for yet more sonic experimentation, such as the adding of effects, dramatic pauses or 'breakdowns' and more dynamic bass courtesy of local talent like Aston Barrett, Errol Walker, Boris Gardner and Robbie Shakespeare. These pared down experiments also paved the way for another unique Kingston phenomenon: the deejay.

BIRTH OF THE DEEJAY

The history of the sound system deejay can be traced back to the 1950s when the majority of systems only had one turntable. Operators had to be particularly deft at removing a finishing record while simultaneously replacing it with (and cueing up) the next one, and to kill any dead time, in the late 1950s selectors began to use a microphone to chat or announce the next record. Clearly influenced by American 'jive talking' radio disc jockeys (the African American Douglas 'Jocko' Henderson was especially influential), Jamaican deejay/selectors began to creatively expand their repertoire into other verbal interjections, mostly intended to create drama or excitement in the dance, an approach captured nicely in the phrase 'a quick tongue and a good time'.[13]

Deejaying became something of an art form in its own right, with each individual developing a style and character of their own. Duke Reid and Prince Buster, for example, were well known for shouting out their favourite catchphrases over the mic, while Count Matchuki, initially hired for Tom The Great Sebastian's sound and later a regular at Coxsone's Downbeat and Prince Buster's Voice of the People set, worked extra hard to become an entertainer in his own right.

Matchuki was the first deejay to make a name for himself. Helped along by the fact that his mother owned two record players (a rare privilege) and his penchant for American publications like the Harlem-based *Jive Magazine*, Matchuki went further than talking between records, working his verbal injections into the music itself, mixing up Harlem street talk and Jamaican slang. According to Prince Buster, he was the first to actually go along with the track instead of just talk on top of it, he knew how to do it so you could still appreciate the tune, you're not just listening to him. Matchuki devise that technique and so many others who come immediately after him learn from it, because nothing exist like that before.[14]

Along with deejay contemporaries like King Stitt and Sir Lord Comic, Matchuki set a trend that would inspire other MC-related music forms from hip hop in the U.S. to grime in the UK. In addition to dropping jokes and making social commentary, Matchuki was famous for producing a percussive 'chick-a-took' sound with his mouth and chatting away in bits of Spanish, the 'Queen's English' or cockney, depending on his mood.

It was not until 1967 that anyone tried to make recordings in the new 'talkover style', when Skatalites co-founder Lester Stirling produced 'Sir Collin's Special', in which he spoke over the rhythm. Other DJs such as Sir Lord Comic and King Sporty tried too (as did Prince Buster, with his 'imaginarium' of characters from judges to tour guides); King Stitt also had hits with 'Fire Corner' and 'Herbsman Shuffle' (produced with Lynford Anderson). However, the first to make a major splash was U-Roy (Ewart Beckford).

U-Roy started out spinning records in the early 1960s for the Doctor Dickies set. He stepped properly onto the deejay scene in the mid-1960s. His strange, rambling monologues and yelps and screeches likened to 'a hundred severely ruptured parrots', but his melodic 'singjay' style proved massively popular.[15] One of his major inventions was to insert his own lyrics into songs in combination with the original vocals, treating the crowds to what were basically live remixes of popular tunes.

'When I was at school I would ask my grandma if I could go to the dance', he recalls. Indeed,

Sometimes she would agree, sometimes not. At the
beginning the sounds played all American music. Even
Tubby's played funk and soul and jazz like James Brown,
Fats Domino, Aretha Franklin in the early days. Then it
changed to ska and rocksteady and reggae. I remember the
versions coming about while I was deejaying with Tubby's.
The dubplate versions then were like an album, you'd have
the original song first and that would run right into the
riddim instrumental. People thought we were cutting the
vocal out in the amp at the time; they didn't realise it was
done in the studio.[16]

U-Roy's first recordings, such as his 'Old Fashioned Way', a take
on Ken Boothe's 'Old Fashioned Way' (recorded by Keith Hudson
in 1971) and 'Earth's Rightful Ruler' (recorded with Peter Tosh and
cut under Lee 'Scratch' Perry's direction in 1969), bewildered radio
programmers and initially failed to capture the public imagination.
But after a while his recorded work started to garner huge success,
especially classics like 'Wear You to the Ball', 'This Station Rule
the Nation' and 'Wake the Town' (1969), with its much-quoted
introduction: 'Wake the town and tell the people . . . 'bout the
musical disc coming your way!'

These tunes and others, bolstered by his regular appearances
on King Tubby's sound (which was also hugely popular), helped
propel U-Roy to superstardom. It wasn't long before others
followed in his footsteps, such as the two friendly 'feuders' I-Roy
(a huge emulator of U-Roy) and Prince Jazzbo (a reggae and
dance hall deejay and producer) and spiritual chanters like Big
Youth and Prince Far I.

Another very popular deejay was Dennis Alcapone, who,
inspired by the Reid, Dodd and Buster sound systems of his youth,
formed the El Paso sound. Alcapone's 'Forever Version' (1971) –
engineered by Sylvan Morris at Studio One – is a classic proto-deejay

recording, not least because Morris left parts of the original vocal tracks in the mix, so that Alcapone could 'answer back'.

U Brown (Huford Brown) was part of this second wave and was directly inspired by U-Roy. He took over U-Roy's role on King Tubby's sound in the mid-1970s, following U-Roy's accident, and eventually released his own hit records like 'Satta Dread' (1976) and 'Weather Balloon' (1977). He was introduced to sound system culture by an older friend who encouraged him to sneak out and join the dances at a young age. At first the deejays were just introducing and toasting between the songs, but then U-Roy started to be 'more present in the version', as he recounts.

> The first sounds I started listening to was Tubby's and Tippatone. I started deejaying on the Silver Bullet sound, then moved to Tubbys later on for a while when U-Roy had an accident. As far as I'm concerned, U-Roy is a big brother to me in every department of life, from when I first met him around 1970 to now. He always carried himself well and dressed respectably. When I first spoke to him, he was recording for Bunny Lee at Tubby's, and he came out and just asked me how it sounded.[17]

It has been estimated that by the early 1970s there were around 50 or 60 deejays operating in Kingston. They were joined in the dance by other excitement-inducing innovations such as the sudden rewinding of records (backspins), the dropping out and reintroducing of basslines (via channel-splitting amps), and sound effects like air horns and gunshots (which were sometimes real). These strategies to 'nice up the dance' leaked into recordings as dub's producers grew more imaginative and the interplay between sound system and studio grew stronger.

2 KINGSTON'S DUB PIONEERS

THE FIRST DUB RECORDINGS AND PRODUCERS

It was the advent of multitrack recording that made dub possible. Before then, engineers had recorded the whole band session onto one track, usually using the 'final take' (as good as it was going to get) as the final product. Multitrack meant that engineers could record different parts of the song onto different channels, and even at different times; for example, a vocalist or a saxophone could be added onto a separate track and added (dubbed) onto the final mix later.

Four-track recording was especially influential in Kingston. The extra two tracks meant that engineers could not only remix the music track underneath the main vocal, but the vocal and horn phrases could be emphasized, or cut in or out as needed. Another factor was the equalization (tone control) on the mixing desk, which could be used to alter the sound of the instruments during a mix (King Tubby famously built his own high-pass filter for this, which has never been replicated).

The complex and competitive nature of Kingston's studio and sound system scene, combined with the predominantly oral nature of its history, makes it difficult to form a chronology of Kingston's early dub recordings that is wholly accurate. However, there are some commonly agreed milestones, such as the fact that one of the earliest dub protagonists was Lynford Anderson (Andy Capp), former apprentice of WIRL studio engineer Graeme Goodall.

Through Goodall, Anderson became an integral part of WIRL, and had a hand in mixing some of the more interesting 'versions' to come out of the studio. In 1968, his work coincided with the deejay trend – with the infectious pro-ganja hit 'Herbsman Shuffle', for example, which featured King Stitt chatting lines like 'take a draw' while doing an impression of a spliff being inhaled, and the previously discussed hits 'Pop a Top' (1969) and 'The Law' (1970), were also early examples of 'versions' being pushed into interesting territory.

Producers like Lee 'Scratch' Perry, who would become one of dub's premier protagonists, were taking note of Anderson's work (Perry worked with him between his time at Studio One in 1966 and establishing The Upsetter Records label in 1968). Indeed, Perry's song 'Clint Eastwood' (1970) employs many of the same techniques used by Anderson (from riddim to the use of echo, and reverb on the drums and vocals). It is likely that other early 'versions', such as the stripped down B-side of Clancy Eccles's 'Phantom' (1970) and Little Roy's 'Hard Fighter' (1971), produced by Lloyd Daley and described as the first vocal record with a full dub version on its flip side, were also mixed by Anderson.[1]

Another generally under-recognized dub protagonist is Sylvan Morris. Best known for his work at Studio One in the 1960s, Morris was a Trenchtown native who built his first tube amplifier at the age of twelve, and became an electronics repair guy in the local area. He was still a teenager when he arrived at Byron Lee's Dynamic Sounds in 1965, and over the next twenty years he went on to work at Reid's Treasure Isle, Dodd's Studio One, and Harry J's Studio, before finally returning to Dynamic Sounds and producing a slew of commercial reggae classics by the likes of Peter Tosh, Dennis Brown, Black Uhuru and the Mighty Diamonds. Like Anderson, Morris also trained with Goodall, who had been drafted into Dynamic Sounds to facilitate the changeover from a two- to a three-track studio (which was

almost immediately upgraded to a four-track studio). Originally
hired as a maintenance engineer, Morris gradually moved to
mastering and eventually became a mixing engineer under the
guidance of Goodall and Carlton Lee. He worked on seminal
songs such as 'Judge Dread' by Prince Buster (1967) and Errol
Dunkley's 'You're Gonna Need Me' (1967).

Studio One became famous in the 1960s for its 'stereo mixes',
which separated vocals and instruments into left and right channels.
This meant the balance control on the playback system could
be shifted to one side, eliminating the vocal tracks entirely and
presenting a pure instrumental track, a development aided the evolution of instrumentals in Jamaica. While Studio One was not known
for producing dub, Morris laid some significant foundations for its
development, not least the creation of a signature bass sound borne
mostly from Leroy Sibbles's influential playing, which, according to
authors Barrow and Dalton, added 'a new meditative emotional
weight to the lower frequencies, augmented further by the studio's
beautifully idiosyncratic bass-capturing capabilities'.[2]

Morris's other innovations included creating a box with two
holes and a mic at the back of certain speakers to achieve a louder,
heavier bass sound, rebuilding broken ribbon microphones with
random parts to get unique sounds, and 'dreamy' echo effect
heard on cuts like the Eternals's 'Queen of the Minstrels' (1969)
and Jerry Jones's 'Still Water' (1970).

Morris was also an early adopter of delay effects, thanks to the
Sound Dimension, a freestanding tape-based echo unit built by
British technician Ivor Arbiter.[3] The Sound Dimension was popular during the late 1960s with British rock musicians, even when
tape systems were replaced by newer technologies. Its effects
included single echo repetitions with variable delay, multiple
'flutter' echoes and simulated reverb – all of which found their
way into Studio One's repertoire because of Morris (Coxsone
Dodd even named one of his session bands the 'Sound Dimension').

As a recording and mixing engineer, it is not exactly clear what Morris worked on at Studio One, thanks to Dodd's tradition of crediting himself for the work of his engineers. But during his later residency at Harry J's, which started around the mid-1970s, Morris released two full dub albums under his own name, in which he 'versioned' a number of classic Studio One rhythms. He also mixed many influential dub albums such as Augustus Pablo's *East of the River Nile* (1977), parts of Burning Spear's two-volume *Living Dub* (1980) and the first volume of Bunny Wailer's *Dubd'sco* (1978).[4]

In early 1969 another influential engineer, Errol 'E.T.' Thompson, started working at Studio One under Morris. One of the first sessions Thompson mixed at Studio One was the voicing of Max Romeo's risqué 'Wet Dream' (1968), produced by Bunny Lee. Morris and Thompson did not get on too well, however, and the latter moved to Randy's Studio 17, which he helped rebuild later that year. Along with Federal, WIRL, Studio One and RJR, Randy's Studio 17 was one of the most popular studios in its day, responsible for many reggae classics including some of Bob Marley's early (and some might say best) works. Randy's Studio came into existence through Clive Chin's father, Vincent Chin, who had begun maintaining jukeboxes around the island in the late 1950s. Seeing an opportunity to re-sell the old records instead of throwing them away, he opened his first record store at the corner of Tower Street and East Street in downtown Kingston, followed by a second location, called Randy's Record Mart at 17 North Parade in 1962. The studio was built upstairs in 1968.

As chief engineer at Randy's, Thompson recorded some of the most successful Jamaican music that followed over the next few years, including hit material by Lee 'Scratch' Perry, Bunny Lee and Winston 'Niney' Holness. Thompson's experiments were partially aided by a partnership with his old school friend, Clive Chin. Many of the instrumentals that Chin and Thompson recorded, such as Augustus Pablo's monumental hit 'Java' (1971), were created because of Clive's dissatisfaction with the original voicing of the tune. In 1972 the pair teamed up to form the 'Impact All Stars' and crafted one of the very first full-length dub albums, *Java Java Java Java* (commonly referred to as *Java Java Dub*), which was issued in a limited pressing of around 200 copies that were mainly given to the sound systems. Clive Chin recalls that 'We bought an Ampex 4-track from the UK in 1972 and started experimenting on the tracks':

Thanks to the four channels, we could lay out drums and bass, vocals and the other instrumentation all separately. Errol's mixes at Randy's stripped everything down and added reverb and delay. We used to do these for the sound systems . . . I had a sound called Black Moses and Errol's uncle has a sound called El Gong. It was when people started calling the shop or coming in physically that we realised there was a demand for these *versions*.[5]

While not as revolutionary as the dub albums that would soon follow, *Java Java Dub* nonetheless showcases several techniques considered innovative at the time, such as the modest use of reverb, reducing vocals to snippets, and peeling songs back to just bass and drums before slowly fading the instruments back in. On 'Ordinary Version Chapter 3', a version of Lloyd Parkes's 'Ordinary Man' (1973), certain elements are run backwards and the vocal track is slowed down. The album also featured the first public recording of Augustus Pablo's melodica on 'Java Dub', alongside musicians who made up the in-house band, the Impact All Stars.

'I can tell you that this album was the first dub album, before (Herman Chin Loy's) *Aquarius Dub* and Scratch's *Cloak and Dagger* and all them', asserts Clive Chin.

Clive Chin at the mixing board.

When we mixed the track 'Java Dub' in 1972, we mixed it in all different kinds of ways. It was supposed to be a vocal song at the beginning, sung by my old schoolmate, but he wasn't up to scratch so it became an instrumental. After that one we did more in the way of sound effects, rewound tapes etc., but for *Java* it was just about raw dub.[6]

At Randy's Studio, Clive Chin also oversaw seminal recordings by The Wailers, Alton Ellis, Gregory Isaacs, Lee Perry and Black Uhuru, among others. His first hit, however, was with Pablo, for whom he also produced his debut album *This is Augustus Pablo* (1974), which was commissioned by Chin's stepmother, Patricia. The son of an accountant, Pablo was largely a self-taught musician (although his mother had taught him piano). He followed his successes with Chin and Thompson with his own productions, including 'Rockers Dub' and 'Cassava Piece', both of which showed that 'Java' was by no means a one-off.

Pablo's 'Far East sound', inaugurated on the single 'East of the River Nile' in 1971, was a continued presence on the dub scene, especially with King Tubby, with whom he recorded albums like *Ital Dub* (1975), *King Tubby Meets Rockers Uptown* (1976) – only ever released outside Jamaica – *East of the River Nile* (1977), *Original Rockers* (1979) and *Rockers Meets King Tubby in a Firehouse* (1980). He also produced Hugh Mundell's extraordinary debut, recorded when Mundell was just 16, called *Africa Must Be Free by 1983* (1978), which was re-released with associated dub versions in 1989.

Other notable dub albums of this early era are Prince Buster's 1972 *Message Dubwise*, mixed by Carlton Lee, who eschewed abundant effects to focus on a raw drum and bass mix. This is along with Herman Chin Loy's *Aquarius Dub* (1973), produced and mixed by Loy at Dynamic studio, and featuring innovative use of Echoplex and reverb-heavy dub.

Equally influential in terms of innovating dub production techniques was Errol Thompson, who went on to work at Joe Gibbs's new sixteen-track studio in 1975. Together with Gibbs, he formed the Mighty Two, also known as 'Joe Gibbs & The Professionals', and helmed three celebrated 'chapters' of their *African Dub* series (1973, 1974, 1978), which helped dub reach a wider audience during the 1970s. This was particularly the case with the latter two albums, which sold in large numbers in both Jamaica and the UK. Gibbs gave Thompson a more or less free reign at the desk, and his mixes of updated Studio One and Treasure Isle riddims laid down by Gibbs's house band (which featured Sly Dunbar and Robbie Shakespeare) became increasingly marked by his exploration of sound effects such as car horns, barking dogs, ringing telephones and running water. After his active years as an original dub engineer, Thompson moved out of the music industry into Kingston retail before passing away in 2004.

Keith Hudson, a dentist by profession, funded his musical explorations (and his Imbidimts Furnace label) with the money from his day job. He started working with rocksteady rhythms before joining the ranks at Studio One, where he produced Ken Boothe (whose 'Old Fashioned Way' was his first hit), Delroy Wilson and Alton Ellis, as well as being one of the first to record U-Roy ('Dynamic Fashion Way' in 1969) and other deejays such as Big Youth ('S90 Skank') and Dennis Alcapone ('Spanish Omega').

In 1974 Hudson began to produce albums featuring his own (controversially distinctive) vocals, such as *Entering the Dragon* (1974), *Flesh of My Skin, Blood of My Blood* (1974) and *Torch of Freedom* (1975), which convey a unique vision and militant consciousness. But it was his *Pick a Dub* record (1974) that really stood out. Considered by some to be the first purposefully thematic dub album, with tracks specifically dubbed to appear together on the album, the record featured melodica from Augustus Pablo and the power rhythm section of Carlton (drums) and Aston 'Family Man' Barrett (bass), as well as vocals by Horace Andy and Big Youth. Foregoing avant-garde effects in favour of a sparse, skeletal sound, the result is a classic drum and bass workout.

Hudson was signed to Richard Branson's Virgin Records, though the resultant album, the funk-influenced *Too Expensive* (1976), was a commercial and critical flop. He moved to New York, where he produced the far superior (and 'rootsier') *Rasta Communication* (1978), followed by the murky-but-great *Playing it Cool* (1981), released through a collaboration with Lloyd 'Bullwackie' Barnes, which featured a number of songs followed by their dub versions.

Another active dub creator of the era was 'Yabby You' (Vivian Jackson). Following the popularity of his 'Conquering Lion' single in 1972 (the introduction of 'Be-you, yabby-yabby-you' earned him the 'Yabby You' moniker), Jackson had further success with the 1975 album *Conquering Lion* (mixed by King Tubby) and the dubbier full-length 1976 *Chant Down Babylon Kingdom* (aka *King Tubby Meet Vivian Jackson*). Jackson made his name as a producer recording deejays such as Dillinger, Tappa Zukie and Jah Stitch, and by producing several key dub albums including *Prophecies of Dub* (1976) and *Yabby You & Michael Prophet Meet Scientist at the Dub Station* (1981). Without a definitive affiliation to one studio, Jackson used Kingston's leading recording facilities including Channel One, Joe Gibbs, Tubby's, Dynamic Sounds and Harry J.

LEE 'SCRATCH' PERRY

Born and raised on the edge of a sugar plantation near the rural town of Kendal, Jamaica, Lee 'Scratch' Perry arrived in Kingston in the early 1960s after working on a construction site in Negril in the mid-1950s. According to David Katz's biography *People Funny Boy*, Perry spent his time playing dominoes and attending dances, before making his way to the sound system and studio circuit.[7]

Perry worked first at Duke Reid's Treasure Isle, delivering dubplates to sound systems and monitoring their reaction on the dance floor. But Reid and Perry had a somewhat awkward relationship. Although Reid let Perry record at the studio, the relationship came to an abrupt end when the Treasure Isle boss allegedly punched him after a complaint by Perry over a lack of payment and credits.[8] Perry then worked for Reid's rival, Coxsone Dodd, who employed him as an errand boy. It was at Coxsone's Studio One that Perry met Lynford Anderson and got involved in producing ska records, of which 'Chicken Scratch' (1961) was one of the earliest – it also gave him his nickname – and also became a hit on Coxsone's set. In the same year Perry signed a five-year contract to record exclusively for Dodd.

Following the Emperor of Ethiopia Haile Selassie 1's visit to Jamaica in 1966, Perry began to explore Rastafarian ideas in his work. However, this was a religion that Dodd did not care much for. Perry voiced over 30 tunes for Dodd, about 24 of which were licensed for pressing in the UK; but despite Perry's successes, Dodd continued to doubt Perry's singing ability and did not give him proper credit.[9] In the last year of his contract, Perry told Dodd he was going to the country for a holiday, but sneaked into the studio to record the revenge track 'Give Me Justice' (1966) for Carl Johnson (aka 'Sir JJ'). The song became a big hit on the systems and on radio, and Perry spent the pivotal year of 1967 trying to establish himself independently, or at least create a new partnership. He made a series of one-off recordings with various producers. The biggest success was 'Judge Dread' (1967), made with fellow Coxsone defector Prince Buster, who would become one of Perry's closest collaborators.

Perry then aligned himself with Joe Gibbs (another former rival) and set up the Upsetter Records label with Lynford Anderson, through which he released 'Honey Love' (1968), a cover of The Drifters' tune by an obscure artist named Burt Walters. The vocal version was decent enough, but it was the B-side, 'Evol Yenoh' ('Honey Love' spelt backwards) that first showcased Perry's experimental tendencies. Using the same instrumental backing as the original, Perry ran the entire vocal track backwards. This was a technique that was then in vogue with overseas pop and rock bands such as The Beatles (*Sgt Pepper's Lonely Hearts Club Band*, 1967) and Jimi Hendrix (*Axis: Bold as Love*, 1967), but hitherto unknown in Jamaica.

In 1968 Perry also recorded 'The Upsetter', another anti-Dodd tune set to an infectiously chugging rhythm. In need of his own studio band, he approached The Hippy Boys (the Barrett brothers on bass and drums, Alva Lewis on guitar, Glen Adams on keyboards and Max Romeo on vocals) and renamed them 'The Upsetters' to record 'People Funny Boy' (1968). The song sold 60,000 copies on its first pressing and established Perry's name in the local music industry for good. (It was this tune that persuaded the British label Trojan Records, which had been releasing Perry's work in the UK, to launch its own version of the Upsetter label.)

More importantly, 'People Funny Boy' heralded the arrival of a new sound: reggae. Perry would go on to develop not just the rhythms and melodies of nascent reggae but its religious content too, particularly when he started writing and recording songs with Bob Marley and The Wailers. Initially part of Studio One, The Wailers started as rude boys covering American soul tunes. But by the late 1960s, Marley and his band were turning towards the Rastafarian movement. Perry produced some of The Wailers' earliest and most powerful songs, including 'Small Axe' (1970), 'Duppy Conqueror' (1970) and 'Don't Rock My Boat' (1971). At the same time as he was inventing the most internationally mainstream music Jamaica had ever produced, Perry remained keenly experimental.

Perry grew particularly obsessed, like his previous collaborator Errol Thompson, with the use of sound effects. This can be seen on 'People Funny Boy' (produced with Lynford Anderson), which famously contained overdubs of a baby crying (a dig at Dodds), and on his cover of Bob Dylan's 'Blowin' in the Wind' (1968), the B-side to 'People Funny Boy', which used overdubbed wind effects throughout the entire song. Earlier Perry tracks such as 'Kimble' (1968) had also featured the sounds of breaking bottles and cracking whips.

Perry's more formal attempts at dub started around 1973, with his instrumental album *Cloak and Dagger*, of which two different versions were pressed for the UK and Jamaican markets. While the majority of the UK edition is made up of instrumentals, it introduced many of the ideas that would be developed to great effect with the 1974 album collaboration with King Tubby called *Blackboard Jungle Dub* (in full, *Upsetters 14 Dub Blackboard Jungle*). As David Katz points out in his biography of Perry, a track like 'Caveman Skank' was a

thoroughly experimental and ironic dance number featuring
toasting and vocal noises from Perry, along with running
water, crashing cars, and voices lifted from an American
sound effects record; the number opened with a Native
American chief reading a portion of the Bible in Cherokee,
and finished with the bustle of a public auction.[10]

By this time, Perry had started recording in his own four-track
studio, the 'Black Ark', which he set about building after the
success of 'People Funny Boy'. These years were some of Perry's
most legendary thanks to a creative streak he hit at the Ark. His
dubs there grew ever more wild and unpredictable, featuring
musical fragments mixed together in mysterious and compelling
ways. With wiring installed by Errol Thompson (and some extra
help from King Tubby), the Black Ark initially included a quarter-
inch four-track Teac 3340 to record new material and a quarter-
inch two-track to mix down. Perry pushed this equipment to the
limits, filling up the four available tracks and then 'bouncing them
down' to a single track on another machine, thereby freeing up
three tracks to add even more effects and percussion.

Furthermore, Perry was also one of the first to use a drum
machine in reggae music, for the quirky Upsetters' track 'Chim
Cherie' (1974). Programmed by Aston 'Family Man' Barrett for
Bob Marley to voice – although he never did – it instead stayed as
an instrumental rhythm and grew popular in the dance halls. It
was rediscovered in the 1980s, and in 1984 was voiced by UK deejay
Shinehead, who transformed it into a cover version of Michael
Jackson's 'Billie Jean'.

As more equipment was added to the Ark – including a Roland
Space Echo drum machine (with loads of reverb), a recording
booth for drums and a Soundcraft mixing-board – Perry achieved a
layered yet decayed sound. This sound has variously been described
as 'swampy' and 'aquatic'.

Perry attained his commercial peak between 1974 and 1979, releasing albums including *Double Seven* (1974), which was the first reggae album to overdub synthesizers, Max Romeo's *War Ina Babylon* (1976) and The Congos' *Heart of the Congos* (1977). These are in addition to *Super Ape* (1976), which is commonly reckoned to be one of the best dub albums ever made, and its sequel *Return of the Super Ape* (1978). He also scored massive hits in Jamaica and the UK, with singles such as 'Police and Thieves' (featuring Junior Murvin) in 1978, and even produced with international stars including Robert Palmer and the McCartneys.

'When he set up Black Ark he was already ahead of himself', says Clive Chin, who recorded with Perry at Randy's and was also a visitor to the Black Ark studio:

He used to invite me up there . . . he knew that to have young people around him gave him a chance to advance more, and he liked new ideas. He wasn't the most technical person, but he had an ability and love for the music, and boy did he knew what he want and how to get it. Since he couldn't write music scores, he would dance and wiggle around in front of, say, the bass player, to try and physically show what sound he wanted. He wasn't a man who was stuck in the old ways. He was open to different sounds and his ideology was beyond its time. I personally rate 'Scratch' as a genius and an innovator.[11]

It was during the late 1970s that Perry became just as famous for his 'madcap' persona as for his music. Descriptions of him tend to be of the 'sonic sorcerer' and 'eccentric futurist' type; released video footage shows him behind his Soundcraft mixing board, blowing ganja smoke directly onto the recording reels, and there are rumours of him running a studio microphone from his console to a nearby palm tree to record the 'living African heartbeat', 'blessing' his recording equipment and cleaning the heads of his tape machine with the sleeve of his T-shirt.[12] Chin remembers him splashing white rum into all four corners of the studio when he was recording The Wailers.

The Ark's control room was simultaneously transformed into a virtual art installation with photos, random objects, scrawled words and other items that served a talismanic function for Perry's creative energy. In an interview with David Toop, Perry discussed the Black Ark in extraterrestrial terms:

> It was like a spacecraft. You could hear space in the tracks. Something there was like a holy vibration and a godly sensation. Modern studios, they have a different set-up. They set up a business and a money-making concern. I set up like an ark . . . You have to be the Ark to save the animals and nature and music.[13]

But by the end of 1978, Perry's creative streak was coming to an end. Under pressure from outside influences and suffering from exhaustion, he had reached breaking point. Having resisted using old Treasure Isle or Studio One rhythms for his songs, he had effectively removed his music from the sound system / dance hall mainstream. A major turning point came when Island Records inexplicably refused to release albums such as *Heart of the Congos*, *Roast Fish Collie Weed & Cornbread* and *Return of the Super Ape*.[14] Perry reacted with an entirely new phase of erratic and bizarre behaviour like performing linguistic exorcisms and, eventually, destroying his studio. In 1983 a blaze tore through the Black Ark in what Perry later called 'a return blessing through fire'. Perry was held in Hunt's Bay lock-up for several days while they launched an investigation into the cause of the fire, only to release him without charge due to a lack of evidence.

KING TUBBY

Perry started working with King Tubby (Osbourne Ruddock) around the end of 1972. Though both are regarded as masters of the dub genre, their approaches, like their respective personalities, were wildly different. Where Perry was the 'surrealist magician' who blew marijuana smoke into his equipment, got into scraps and made exquisite pop reggae for everyone from Max Romeo to Bob Marley, Tubby was a polite, fairly reserved and clean-cut figure who did not allow weed in his studio.

Tubby had been an electronics enthusiast from a young age. When he left school, he began to take courses in the subject, but stories abound of his early interest in recording sound. Glen Brown, for example, relates how the young Tubby once constructed a special device for his motorbike: 'King Tubbys always build some little speaker, he always have a little [motor]bike, so King Tubby's build a little thing on the bike. Sometimes you're talking to him and he'll record you.'[15] Niney the Observer also remembers Tubby recording songs from late-night radio broadcasts and playing them back over his sound system at the dance.

In the late 1950s, Tubby worked as a radio technician and repairman. By 1961 he had built his own radio transmitter and briefly ran a pirate radio station, playing mostly ska and R&B. By 1962 he had built his first 25-watt amplifier that allegedly sounded so good his friends urged him to build a full sound system and start playing at dances. Shortly afterwards he constructed his famous 'Home Town Hi-Fi' sound system. 'Hi-fi', short for 'high-fidelity sound reproduction', was a well-chosen name. What Tubby's system lacked in terms of heavyweight power, it made up for with clarity and brightness. According to Dennis Alcapone, Tubby's sound literally spread further than most, as he would place steel horns in the tops of the trees, so the high frequencies would carry the sound over Kingston. He would balance this with speakers beneath the trees playing the mid-range and bass.

Tubby kitted the system out with a custom-built reverb and echo facilitator, employed separate tweeter boxes, and also used embryonic transistor technology and custom-built filters to split his frequencies between two different amplifiers (one of which was a custom-built KT88 that gave him special 'round' bass frequencies).[16] This technology enabled him to create studio-style effects while playing live, which looped directly back into his production work.

Tubby's deejay, U-Roy, was crucial to Home Town Hi-Fi's success. Arguably one of the great pairings in musical history, Tubby provided U-Roy with the best dubs around (which helped to make both their names), while Tubby benefited greatly from U-Roy's toasting skills in the dance. Together, they pushed the parallel innovations of deejaying and dub to entirely new levels.

By the late 1960s, Tubby was engineering at Treasure Isle studio (where he had previously worked as a disc cutter). Byron Lee had witnessed Ruddy Redwood dropping the accidental first 'version' at his dance and explained to Tubby the need to make more instrumental tracks as 'them people love them'. The next day he began work with Bunny Lee on creating more instrumentals and 'decorating' them with reverb, delay and other effects.[17]

Tubby set up his own small studio in a spare bedroom of his mother's house, at 18 Dromilly Avenue in the Waterhouse district. Since it was not equipped to record live musicians, it became used more for 'versions', and the recording of vocals thanks to a vocal booth that was set up in the bathroom.

When Bunny Lee upgraded his Dynamic Studios in 1972, Tubby bought their four-track MCI mixing desk. This marked a turning point in his career as a producer, not to mention in the development of dub. The custom built four-track desk enjoyed a new lease of life in Tubby's studio. He further customized the machine by adding a phase shifter and faders that let him slide tracks in and out of the mix smoothly. These faders, which gave a smoother sound to the mix, have been traditionally posited as an example of how Tubby had the edge over Thompson (who used punch buttons), even though both of them approached the mixing desk with fairly equal skill and imagination. Mikey Dread, one of Tubby's many apprentices, claims that 'The man invent a whole heap of things and don't get no credit'.

He made his first echo machine with two old tape recorders. He build spring-loaded switches for his sound effects, so it's pressure-sensitive and he can hit it hard or soft or slowly to get a different sound from each effect . . . in fact, not much of his equipment stayed the way it was when it came out of the factory. Such was his knowledge that if the man don't think a sound is like how he want it, he would go into the circuitry there and then and change it to create the particular effect that he want. His whole studio was custom made by King Tubby himself.[18]

The series of B-sides mixed by Tubby and released between 1972 and 1974 helped to establish dub as a commercial genre and, since he began to be credited on the records themselves, underlined the idea that the engineer could also be an artist in his own right. While he was not alone in pioneering many of the production techniques used, Tubby was the first to use them consistently enough to establish them as recognizable tropes, and was also responsible for pushing some of these techniques into new territory.

Some of Tubby's personal innovations include creating echo delay by passing a loop of tape over the heads of an old two-track machine and applying homemade high-pass filters to snare and hi-hats to make a unique 'splash' sound. Alongside his liberal use of sirens and gunshots (borrowed directly from live sound system performances), Tubby also became famous for his explosive 'thunderclap' effect, a trademark sound that surfaced in his work around 1974. This effect was created by physically striking the reverb coil: the force and speed of the strike determined how loud and severe the crash would sound. Moreover, it could appear at any time in the mix, as much to shock as to enhance percussive elements. Examples abound, including Tubby's versions of Horace Andy and John Holt's 'A Quiet Place' ('A Dub Place', 1975), The Aggrovators's 'Harder Version' ('This a the Hardest Version', 1974) and the explosive introductory section to Horace Andy's 'Skylarking' ('A Serious Version', 1975).

Tubby had mixed some of Perry's work for the Justice League Music and Upsetter Records labels, including many of the 'Skank' series – 'Bucky Skank'', 'IPA Skank', 'Bathroom Skank' and the groundbreaking 'Cow Thief Skank' (which spliced together no fewer than three different Upsetter rhythms several years before samplers were invented).

Although both Perry and Tubby are of equal stature in the history of dub, their working methods were completely different. Tubby worked with a mixing board and vocals, while Perry constantly worked on live rhythms and compositions (in fact, his sessions often started off with recording the studio band). Tubby 'stripped down', whereas Perry's approach was often more additive.

Barrow and Dalton's *Rough Guide to Reggae* points out how Perry took Tubby's sound further by applying 'a layered sonic motif to dub . . . using everyday sounds, harmonies, lead vocals and toasting to create a full blast of sounds.'[19] Perry also applied dub techniques to his vocal productions and placed them in an 'A-side' context, elevating them above their normal B-side status.

Around the same time that Chin and Thompson produced *Java Java Java Java*, Herman Chin Loy produced and mixed *Aquarius Dub* and Prince Buster came through with *The Message Dubwise* (mixed by Carlton Lee), Tubby worked on Lee 'Scratch' Perry's *Blackboard Jungle Dub* (released in 1973). This record used fourteen of Perry's strongest rhythm tracks ('Bucky Skank', Junior Byles's

'Fever' and a handful of Wailers tracks) and was mixed in stereo
with each engineer allegedly working on separate channels
(to avoid repeat of mix). Despite only 300 copies being originally
pressed, it is regarded as one of the best dub albums ever to be
recorded, and certainly one of the first to fully explore the
broader possibilities of dub from the peculiar 'Black Panta' to the
minatory 'Drum Rock'.

By the mid-1970s, Tubby was releasing and producing his own
albums. These include classics such as *Dub from the Roots* (1974),
where, encouraged by producer Bunny Lee, he grew more bold
and spontaneous; *King Tubby Meets Upsetter at the Grass Roots of Dub*
(1974), mixed by Lee Perry; *Surrounded by the Dreads at the National
Arena 26th September 1975* (1976), produced by Winston Edwards with
his Natty Locks acting as backing band; and Augustus Pablo and
Tubby's *King Tubbys Meets Rockers Uptown* (1976). In addition, he cut
dubs for a stream of high-profile producers from Augustus Pablo
and Yabby You to Glen Brown and Bunny Lee.

This period would prove to be one of the creative peaks for
Tubby, as well as for dub in general, as violent politics engulfed the
country and music styles began to change yet again. The album
Rockers Meets King Tubby in a Firehouse (1980), produced by Pablo and
mixed by Tubby and Jammy (Lloyd James), was a reference to the
new nickname given to the Waterhouse district in Kingston, which
had become one of the ghettoized areas for political warfare. This
was a product of the escalating arms race between Manley's PNP (the
centre-left People's National Party) and the rival Jamaica Labour
Party (JLP) led by Edward Seaga (who, as the owner of WIRL, was
also an incredibly important figure in Jamaica's recording industry).

Sound systems stopped travelling between neighbourhoods
as it grew unsafe. Wayne Smith, reggae and dance-hall musician,
whose 1985 recording of 'Under Me Sleng Teng' is generally
regarded as the beginning of dancehall style, lived near Tubby in
Waterhouse. He recalls

That time there, it wicked, wicked. Worst, worst, worst! Even
one time, when me come out of Tubbys and me run, me a see
some people come down a fire gun, a fire gun and a come ina
our turf. One of the persons was a pregnant girl. She was
firing a gun. And some of the man them from over our side
now, shoot, shoot, shoot. And then she get a shot ina fe her
chest. All them a do is take her up and throw her in the truck.
And keep on coming![20]

Tubby was also fatally shot, although not by a political faction. He
was murdered in 1989 outside his own home. However, before
then, Jamaican music would undergo one of its most fundamental
revolutions since the birth of ska and reggae.

SCIENTIST

By the early 1980s, Tubby and Perry had more or less reached
their peak in Kingston, at least in terms of innovation. Perry
burned down his Black Ark studio and went underground, while
Tubby increasingly handed over engineering and production
duties to apprentices such as King (né Prince) Jammy and
Hopeton 'Scientist' Brown.

Dub mixer and producer Jammy replaced Philip Smart when
the latter left for New York and became the mixer of choice for
Bunny Lee. Jammy and Bunny Lee enjoyed a fruitful collaboration
that saw them experiment in the dub tradition with frequency test
tones and machines, plus more Tubbyesque spring reverb slapping.
Known for being more stripped down than Tubby's dubs, Jammy's
cleaner dubs emphasized the groove of the drum and bass, and/or
the riddim. Hence, they were 'a bit busier, less hollow and fatter-
sounding'.[21] Between 1975 and 1983 Jammy collaborated on dub
records with King Tubby on *His Majesty's Dub* (1975); *Scientist on
Big Showdown* (1980) and *Dub Landing Vol. 2* (1982). His reputation

Scientist in 2013.

was enhanced by productions for Black Uhuru's debut album in 1977, for example, and by his move into dancehall in the 1980s. Jammy's biggest production hit, Wayne Smith's 'Under Me Sleng Teng', was one of the first examples of digital rhythm in reggae.

Scientist met Tubby while working in his television and radio repair shop and was given the opportunity to experiment in the recording studio during downtime. Famously, he would play his work to Tubby, who would all but dismiss it in order to encourage his new recruit to hone a more distinctive vision. It worked. Scientist says that 'I was studying electronics in High School when I heard Tubby's *Roots of Dub* album.'

I started using it as a test record for the amplifiers I was
building. It was perfect because it had good frequency
response, good highs and lows. It was this technical aspect
that grabbed my interest in what Tubby was doing, rather
than the production itself.[22]

Scientist began popping into Tubby's shop and studio to buy parts
for his amps. He soon had his own set of keys for the studio and
became Tubby's right-hand man. He recounts that 'I wasn't
thinking of things in terms of music production at first.'

I was still more interested in building consoles and gear and
Tubby's was a good place to learn about that. But after a while
I made Tubby a bet that I would be able to engineer and mix
if he let me access the studio. He lost the bet.[23]

Scientist was responsible for mixing hundreds of records that
passed through the studio, before leaving in 1979 and taking on a
resident engineer role at Channel One.

Channel One and its constellation of musicians, producers
and engineers – not only Scientist but the four Hookim brothers,
Barnabas, Soljie Hamilton and Peter Chemist – were at the forefront of the next major Kingston style: dancehall. The studio also
had its own sound system (also called Channel One), which
worked with deejays like U Brown, Nicodemus and Ranking
Trevor. Channel One's sound was as influential in the 1970s as
Studio One's had been in the 1960s. This was partly due to their
inauguration of the twelve-inch 45 rpm format, which enabled a
better dynamic and heavier bass and treble, and partly because of
the sound Scientist created there alongside the in-house band, the
Roots Radics.

With Channel One's former 'rockers' house band The
Revolutionaries (Sly & Robbie) out of the picture and producing

for Island Records and working as a backing band for international stars like Grace Jones, Peter Tosh, Jimmy Cliff and Black Uhuru, the Roots Radics (bassist Errol 'Flabba' Holt, drummer Lincoln 'Style' Scott and guitarist Eric 'Bingy Bunny' Lamont) became the most in demand session band during this period. Reverting to the one-drop style (leaving one beat out of each bar to create a 'dip' sensation), their sound was reminiscent of rocksteady, but tighter and sparser, proving an especially good match for Scientist's clean, minimal dub sound, all facilitated by Channel One's 24-track mixing desk and use of two-inch tape.

Scientist says that 'I left Tubby's mainly because of the piracy that was happening with labels like Greensleeves putting out my records without permission nor payment.'

But the next biggest reason was that I wanted more experience in recording live music. At Channel One I changed the way reggae was presented and how people recorded instruments in Jamaica. I found how to create a whole new sound by making it clearer, cleaner. This was actually a process I started when I worked at Studio One. At the time, everyone was recording flat with no EQ, and Coxsone got mad when I wanted to use more EQ to make it sound better. But in the end I was proved right.[24]

Early albums such as *Heavyweight Dub Champion* (1980), *Scientist Meets the Space Invaders* (1981), *Scientist Rids the World of the Evil Curse of the Vampires* (1981) and *Scientist Encounters Pac-Man* (1982), helped Scientist create a clean, minimal style or dub that proved highly popular.

The aforementioned albums – and others – were especially popular in the UK, where the large reggae fan base was being supplied by labels like Trojan Records, Virgin Records and Island Records, but whose more underground/sound system scenes were catered for by labels like Greensleeves Records and Fashion

Records. Founded by Chris Cracknell and Chris Sedgwick in 1977, Greensleeves Records started out by releasing the classic deejay LP Dr Alimantado's *Best Dressed Chicken in Town* (1978).

They also imported many of Scientist's dub releases – without his permission, according to Scientist, who at the time of writing is involved in a legal battle with the label – adding colourful, outlandish covers created by Greensleeves Records' graphic artist Tony McDermott, which served mainly as a sales gimmick for the UK market.

Another of the major instigators behind the early dancehall style was producer Henry 'Junjo' Lawes – the man behind the Volcano record label and sound system of the same name. Lawes worked with the Roots Radics and Scientist on some of the earliest dancehall recordings, helping, along with Hyman 'Jah Life' Wright, who had come to Jamaica from his native New York, to establish Yellowman, Barrington Levy, Frankie Paul and Junior Reid as the scene's major stars.

While many regard Scientist's albums as the last 'spasm' of Kingston dub in the early 1980s, Scientist continued applying dub's techniques to dancehall, especially on early albums like those of Barrington Levy, who was one of the first dancehall acts to gain major commercial exposure. In 1979 Levy was only fifteen years old when Junjo, Wright and Jah Life began producing albums like his classic *Bounty Hunter* (1979) and the critically acclaimed *Englishman* (1979), both of which feature Scientist's dub treatments ('If You Give to Me', 'Look Girl') among the mostly sweet and relaxed lovers' tunes.

Volcano's compilation *Jamaican Dancehall Volcano Hi-power* (1983) (along with *A Whole New Generation of DJs* on the Greensleeves label 1981) – co-engineered by Scientist and featuring the Roots Radics – showcased the new wave of deejays who came through dancehall. Ranking Joe, Clint Eastwood, Josey Wales, General Echo and Yellowman all looked to the old guard like U-Roy for inspiration, but sought new directions and styles that would eventually be influenced by u.s. rap and lead to the 'slackness' style.

In 1985, King Jammy – Tubby's other protégé (and Scientist's rival) – produced Wayne Smith's monumental 'Sleng Teng' hit (1985), which transported Jamaican music into the digital era and severed dancehall's connections with its 'rootsy' past. It was the year that both Lawes and Scientist moved to the u.s.; Lawes would later be deported to Jamaica, and eventually (1999) was murdered in London.

It seemed that Jamaica had no more space for roots music, dub or even spirituality. But by then the genie was out of its bottle and there was no way it was going to be pushed back in.

3 LONDON: SOUND SYSTEM CULTURE, DIGIDUB AND POST-PUNK

UK SOUND SYSTEM CULTURE

Not only was Britain, which had claimed Jamaica as a sovereign territory for over 300 years, the first country to begin importing music from Jamaica, it played and continues to play a crucial role in developing and preserving that music, as well as some of Jamaica's wider culture. As Bill Brewster and Frank Broughton put it in *Last Night a DJ Saved My Life*, 'The story of reggae is at times as British as it is Jamaican'.[1]

The migration of Caribbean people to the UK began in earnest following the Second World War. This was mainly due to the UK's high number of war casualties and the government's subsequent desire to fill shortages in the labour market. An 'open-door policy' in the shape of the British Nationality Act of 1948 gave British citizenship to all people living in Commonwealth countries, and full rights of entry and settlement in Britain. During the 1940s and 1950s, inspired by the hope of employment and a better life, many Jamaican men and women saved the £28 and ten shillings necessary to purchase a one-way ticket to Britain. Between 1955 and 1962 over 300,000 migrants came from the Caribbean to live in the UK, of whom 178,000 were from Jamaica.[2] A seminal date was 21 June 1948, when nearly 500 West Indians disembarked the *Empire Windrush* at Tilbury Docks in Essex. The passenger list included many ex-servicemen and -women (for whom the vessel was initially sent to Jamaica), but also a number of professional musicians, band leaders and singers, such as Trinidadians Mona Baptiste and

Aldwyn Roberts. The latter was better known as calypso artist 'Lord Kitchener', who composed his optimistic hit 'London is the Place for Me' during the voyage. Many Jamaican musicians followed.[3]

The promise of a better life was, however, less than a reality for these new arrivals, who more often than not found that employment and housing were denied to them because of their race. Instead of Kitchener's vision of a 'promised land', Jamaicans in the UK generally faced working in positions they were over-qualified for, living in cramped and squalid accommodation and experiencing exclusion from pubs and nightclubs. (Tellingly, Lord Kitchener's follow-up tunes, such as 'Sweet Jamaica', talked about how cold and harsh life in Britain was and included lines about immigrants 'crying with regret / no sort of employment can they get').

Housing was a particularly virulent issue, since it was in short supply as a result of wartime bombing. While many Jamaicans found themselves scanning accommodation adverts in the news-papers only to read 'Sorry, No Coloureds', other unscrupulous landlords crammed as many immigrants as possible into the city's crumbling tenements. These experiences led to heavy clashes between Caribbean immigrants and white communities in areas like Notting Hill in London and the city of Nottingham (in the Midlands) in 1958, with areas of London like Paddington, Brixton, Shepherd's Bush and Notting Hill eventually becoming ghettoized.[4]

In 1962 the Commonwealth Immigrants Act finally restricted the entry of immigrants to Britain, but by then the Caribbean community was part of the fabric of British life. In his book *Bass Culture*, Lloyd Bradley remarks that

given that the majority of West Indians were Jamaican, that island's ways were bound to emerge as the dominant force in Caribbean Britain. And among the Jamaican communities, sound system culture had, along with oversized suits and broad brimmed hats, been imported virtually preserved in aspic.[5]

It has been estimated that by the late 1950s there were already around 50 basement clubs in south London managed and/or owned by West Indians. These venues – particularly the illegal blues dances – were of inestimable value as sites of cultural expression, social cohesion and autonomy for the Afro-Caribbean community, as well as for the preservation and dissemination of Jamaican music in the UK. Two of the first imported soundmen in the UK were Duke Vin (Vincent Forbes) and Count Suckle (Wilbert Campbell), both of whom had come to Britain as stowaways on a banana boat in 1954. Formerly a selector on Tom the Great Sebastian's system, Duke Vin settled in Ladbroke Grove (Notting Hill) and found employment as an engine cleaner for British Rail.

'I couldn't find nowhere to go for a dance', recalls Vin in Gus Berger's mini-documentary *Duke Vin and the Birth of Ska* (2008).

The country was dead. So I started my own system. People started using basements in houses that were packed til morning. They'd move the bed and chairs out, and use the kitchen for curried goat and beer. People used to use 'grams [radiograms] but they didn't have the power to keep the crowd going.[6]

Vin built the UK's first large-scale set in 1955, naming it 'Duke Vin "The Tickler"'. His first play out was Brixton Town Hall in 1955 – the very first time for a UK system – where he spun the R&B sounds that were then still ruling the Jamaican dances. According to Vin, the first UK soundclashes took place from 1956 onwards, and by 1959 central London had at least five main Caribbean-music clubs, including the Contemporanean in Mayfair, and 59, Flamingo, 77 and Sunset Club in Soho.[7]

Meanwhile, Vin's friend Count Suckle started deejaying at (and running) the Roaring Twenties night club in Carnaby Street, which initially played a mix of R&B, soul and bluebeat/ska. The club became famous, drawing in stars like The Beatles and The Rolling Stones, and was significant in introducing white British youths to Jamaican music – including regular attendee Georgie Fame, a famous British R&B and jazz musician, who wound up collaborating with Prince Buster on hits like 'Wash Wash' (1962). Duke Vin also played weekly sessions at West End clubs such as The Marquee and The Flamingo, the latter run by Melodisc and Blue Beat Records founder Emile Shalit, one of the key figures in bringing early Jamaican releases into the UK – and the man responsible for breaking Prince Buster in Britain. Suckle, meanwhile, also set up Paddington's Q Club in 1962, which drew in luminaries like Marvin Gaye and Elton John right up to its closure in 1986.

By the mid-1960s, sound system culture had spread to most major British cities. The first London sets to follow in Duke Vin's footsteps were the likes of Count Busty the Black Prince in Brixton and King Ossie in Lewisham. Sounds were very much based on the ruling systems in Jamaica, exploiting any connections that existed between the UK's and Jamaica's systems/soundmen, and adopting the names of famous sounds if they did not. Hence the UK's Coxsone International Sound, run by Lloyd Blackford, did have some kind of connection (through friends) with the 'real' Coxsone Dodd in Kingston. Duke Reid Trojan Sound had nothing to do with the Jamaican Duke Reid and, though a respected sound, was mostly referred to as 'UK Duke Reid' to avoid confusion.

Some of the more interesting Kingston–London links of the time included Cecil Rennie, who split off from the UK Duke Reid sound to form UK King Tubby's (Rennie counted King Tubby as a friend). In addition, there was Count Shelly, who, along with noted selector Tuts, became one of the ruling sounds in northeast London and enjoyed a lengthy residency at the notorious Four Aces Club in

Dalston Lane, Hackney, and had direct links with Bunny Lee, Duke Reid and others, which allowed him to begin releasing products in the UK. Jah Observer similarly enjoyed one-off acetates from Kingston's Mikey Dread, while Joey Jay's Great Tribulation sound (later known as 'Good Times' and taken over by Joey's better known brother Norman) had a direct connection with Joe Gibbs.

Initially, these sounds emulated the music policies of their Kingston counterparts by playing American R&B, much of it sourced directly from Jamaica rather than London for reasons of both access and kudos. In fact, so intent were British sounds on possessing the latest Jamaican releases that they grew snooty about homegrown product, forcing exasperated British producers such as Dennis Bovell to buy a 'dinking' machine to knock out the centre of his records and pretend they were Jamaican imports.[8]

The subsequent niche market in Kingston meant record dealers and operators could often command higher prices from the bigger sound systems working in the UK than from locals. Lloyd Bradley asserts that these connections to the homeland played a role in giving British systems a unique character.

It meant a system could play all new tunes each month if it wanted to. British crowds got used to being surprised and selectors cut their teeth not by relying on standards and perennials but by presenting new music. In turn this evolved into an adventurousness that became an integral part of the UK sound systems scene, which continues to enjoy a reputation for experimentation that can make its Kingston peer group look staid.[9]

During the late 1960s and early 1970s, more significant venues emerged in London: 007 in east London, Upper Cut in Forest Gate, Club Rock Steady in north London, Four Aces in Dalston and Ram Jam in Brixton. But parties and 'shebeens' also continued to take place at people's homes and in basements, gradually scaling up to community halls like Gray's Hall on Seven Sisters Road in north London, the Tollington Park Ballroom (also in north London) and the Brixton Recreation Centre, just as they had done in Kingston.

COXSONE, FATMAN AND JAH SHAKA

A nationwide network of sounds was soon touring the country and clashing in various cities, with some sounds playing a different city each night, or even multiple dances on the same night. In terms of dub, one of the most successful early operators was Lloyd Blackford, who came from Morant Bay in southeast Jamaica to Brixton in 1962.

Blackford set up his first London set, Lloyd the Matador, in 1964, borrowing the moniker from the Kingston system established by Lloyd Daley. When his amplifier exploded one day after getting wet, he was more or less forced to work on the UK Duke Reid system before changing his name to 'Lloyd Coxsone' and forming Sir Coxsone Outernational in 1969 in an overt nod to Clement 'Coxsone' Dodd, one of Reid's biggest competitors.[10]

While holding down a prominent residency at the Roaring Twenties throughout the 1970s, Blackford also helped break Jamaican acts like Burning Spear, Prince Lincoln, The Royals and Dennis Brown in the UK (as well as helping launch the careers of homegrown performers like Clarendon Parish, aka Levi Roots) through exclusive Kingston dubplates obtained from Roy Cousins, Niney the Observer, Lee Perry and others.

By the 1970s, Coxsone Outernational – by now featuring the legendary Poppa Festus as main selector – became one of the most important sound systems in the UK, with its fame extending back to Kingston via recordings like 'Coxsone Affair' (1973) and 'Coxsone Time' by I-Roy (1973). Even though Coxsone would become known as a lovers rock sound, he was among the first to play dub, as well as setting the pace with regard to equipment and borrowing the tried-and-tested Kingston strategies of echo, reverb and equalizer. Like Tubby, Coxsone put an emphasis on quality rather than wattage:

> People can't dance to wattage. If a man comes to me and he deals with sound he almost always deals with wattage. Listen, the more you step up weight you lose quality, and a man must be able to hear your vocal playing. Too much sound in this country is running down weight, but I don't see sound as is rootin' down like bulldozer as good sound. I am more interested in quality and selection of music.[11]

Central to his sound, as well as the various echo units, percussion boxes and horns, was a specially made pre-amp with a built-in equalizer. 'Back then, the people building the amplifiers were superstars', explains Coxsone deejay Levi Roots in the documentary *Musically Mad* (2008).

> Our system had a preamp that carried Coxsone through from 70s 'til the mid 80s. It didn't matter if we lost everything else, as long as we had the preamp we was OK. It always travelled in the front of the car with us.[12]

A 'Directory of Sounds' compiled by the NME in 1981 lists 102 sound systems in London alone, with many more operating in other English cities. Many of these carried extra effects like digital delay units, small synths or noise boxes to create klaxon or horn sound effects and would battle it out at either cup or clash dances. These would feature anything up to six systems and take place either over one night or during a succession of heats.[13]

Other main sounds were coming through in the 1970s, such as Fatman Hi-Fi in north London and Jah Shaka in south

London. Ken 'Fatman' Gordon was raised by his aunt in Waterhouse, the Kingston ghetto famed for being a hotbed of Jamaican music, and where King Tubby's studio was also located. During his youth, Gordon used to sneak out of his house at night to attend dances and clashes featuring sounds like Coxsone's Downbeat and Duke Reid the Trojan. He followed his aunt to London in 1963 and within weeks became involved with Sir Fanso The Tropical Downbeat, one of the leading sounds in the Finsbury Park and Tottenham areas in north London, which was rocking crowds with the usual mix of ska and rocksteady imports at venues like Gray's Hall on Seven Sisters Road and the Tollington Park Ballroom. Gordon worked the mic for a while, but when Fanso moved back to Jamaica in the early 1970s, he established his own set called 'Wild Bells', after the label established by Prince Buster.

Despite renaming his set 'Imperial Downbeat', his growing popularity and influence prompted the nickname 'Fatman Hi-Fi'. Featuring selectors Robert Fearon (Ribs) and Michael Edwards, with both Fearon and Raymond McCook also on the mic alongside U Brown (Huford Brown) – and numerous other toasters as occasional guests – the sound maintained strong links to the Waterhouse scene, in particular to Tubby, Bunny Lee and Joe Gibbs, and Tubby protégés Jammy and Scientist. U Brown was one of the most prominent guests on the Fatman sound, stepping up during most of his frequent visits to London in the mid- to late 1970s.

'When I came to the UK in the mid-'70s, Fatman was the first person I associated with', reminisces Brown. Fatman

was good friends with Bunny Lee and usually came to Jamaica to get his dubs. Tubby's was one of his fave dub studios, and it was through these connections that Bunny Lee, along with Count Shelly, gave me my first trip to London after recording the *Satta Dread* album (1976). At the time Fatman was one of the leading sounds along with UK Coxsone, Count Shelley, Jah Shaka . . . the UK crowds liked the Kingston connection, we used to bring the fresh street slang straight from Jamaica etc.[14]

While most of the 1970s sets generally played a percentage of dub, two of the most committed were Jah Tubby's and Jah Shaka. North London's Jah Tubby Sound System was, like may others, built by hand and by 1977 was playing dances. In the mid-1980s, it was joined by the Jah Tubby's and Y&D record labels, as well as continuing a side business for the manufacture of amps and pre-amps and other equipment.

But the most distinctive dub sound of the era was undeniably Jah Shaka who, along with Lloyd Coxsone, was one of the first to play dub in London in the early 1970s. Born in the country town of Chapelton in central Jamaica, Shaka migrated to England in 1956 when he was five, settling in southeast London. In 1962 he began playing in a band that was formed at his Samuel Pepys Secondary School, where he was a pupil, and later became associated with local sound systems like Freddie Cloudburst, which played mostly R&B and soul, and Metro, one of the UK's most respected sounds during the late 1960s. It was through Metro that Shaka set up his own eponymous sound system in the early 1970s, which quickly became one of the most important in the country.

Shaka's name, an amalgam of the Rastafarian term for God and that of a Zulu warrior (he never gives out his real name, speaks volumes about his serious dedication to Rastafarianism. He became well known by playing dubplates freshly acquired from artists and producers who travelled regularly between Jamaica and the UK, such as Winston Edwards (the cousin of Joe Gibbs), Bunny Lee, Lee Perry and Al Campbell. Unlike most sound system operators, Shaka never took on a selector, preferring to act as a one-man-band, choosing his own records, controlling the equipment and deejaying when necessary.

He began taking on – and destroying – sound systems one by one. This culminated in a famed championship showdown with Lloyd Coxsone in Croydon in 1976, which Shaka won; he didn't let go of the 'Champion Sound' title for several years. Shaka's brand of dub was (and remains, since he still plays regularly) deeply Afro-centric, tapping into roots reggae's preconceptions with African music and culture.

Old recordings of his sessions reveal a commitment to the original dub ethic of playing a vocal tune followed by the 'version', embellished with the obligatory sirens and other sound effects. Of Shaka's sets, Les Back, sociologist and author of *Coughing Up Fire*, recalls that 'it was the kind of thing that moved you to your bones. It was a music that wasn't being played by a band but it was live . . . a live form using records.'[15]

Shaka played regularly throughout the late 1970s and early 1980s. He carried his spiritual messages around a multitude of London venues like Club Noreik in Tottenham, Studio 200 in Balham, Cubbies in Dalston and a Friday night residency in the basement of Phoebes in Stoke Newington (formerly owned by the Kray Twins), as well as playing the length and breadth of Britain.[16]

His commitment to the broader view of dub is underlined by his establishment of the Jah Shaka Foundation, which assists aid projects in Jamaica, Ethiopia and Ghana. As a sound system, Shaka has mostly paid respect to the traditions of the original Kingston pioneers rather than breaking new ground. But his commitment to the dub lineage has been a major factor in keeping interest in dub alive after the UK systems started playing trendier music (for example, hip hop and soul) in the 1980s, and in helping to inspire generations of new roots sounds to fire up and spread the conscious messages of Rastafari.

UK DIGIDUB

Despite Shaka being regarded as a 'dub purist', in terms of production he is also one of the protagonists of the 'digidub' scene
in the UK. Rather than working with musicians to provide source
material as the original Kingston dub engineers did, he built his
early dubs from the 'ground up' using drum machines and synths
in his early records. On hearing the music of Dread and Fred in
the mid-1980s, he took his sound into a fully digital style.

Dread and Fred, two brothers from Bedford, southeast
England, were avid fans of Shaka. They started playing basslines
with a Boss drum machine and layering percussion on top with a
borrowed Yamaha DX7. In 1988 they pressed four dubplates and
took them to Shaka, who played them for a month, often saving
one of them until last – the mighty 'Warrior Stance' (1989) –
which became a massively influential tune on the dancehall circuit
and led to the release of a Dread and Fred album, *Iron Works*
(1991), on Shaka's label.

Many of Shaka's albums from around this time were produced by The Disciples, who were key figures in the emerging UK
digidub movement. Initially a two-person crew consisting of
brothers Russ D (Disciple) and Lol Bell-Brown (before Lol moved
on to pursue other projects), they produced several early Shaka
albums before focusing on their own releases and setting up the
Boomshackalacka sound system (and magazine). These productions by The Disciples, Shaka and Dread and Fred helped to
establish a new digital roots sound that caught on in the UK
among a network of systems and producers like Alpha and
Omega, Eastern Sher, The Disciples, Iration Steppas, Jah Warrior,
Channel One Sound System, Conscious Sounds, The Rootsman
and Abashanti-I, to name but a few.[17]

Aba from Abashanti-I used to deejay for Jah Tubby's sound
system, where he was known as 'Jasmine Joe'. Embracing the
Rastafarian faith, he adopted a new and more positive attitude and

with his rediscovered faith, he took on a new name. Since the early 2000s Aba has been playing his sound, and the music created by his brother Blood Shanti on that sound. 'I was born in England, with inner city vibes', Blood told Greg Whitfield:

So many artists strive for a Jamaican sound, or an American sound, but I feel that is the wrong road for UK artists to take. We've been born here and we must create our own sound forms, and put our stamp on the world. Actually, when we create music we reflect and echo what we see all around us, from the point at which we wake up every morning and look around us: When I go outside, I see city smoke everywhere, traffic, darkness, no birds, no trees, no nature. I know that some Jamaican musicians see our music here as too hard and harsh, but we're in a concrete jungle, you overstand, and I can only express myself from the way I live . . . but we still come from a powerful Jamaican root and tradition, even though we have diversified to reflect our condition. My influences are still Studio One, Channel One, classic vibes, straight to the heart.[18]

'Digital' just meant 'drum machine' really', Nick Manasseh has claimed:

But it was the new sound then, nothing could test it for making sound system music really drive. It was also about control – it meant that we could do it ourselves. Strictly speaking Sound Iration isn't totally digi dub anyway – it's all real bass, and all the parts played by hand and lots of bouncing tracks down.[19]

As one half of Sound Iration, and with collaborator/bassist Scruff, Manneseh crafted the classic album *In Dub* (1989). He had first appeared on the UK dub scene at the Notting Hill Carnival in 1985 with a sound system that had been finished just a few days before, and featuring gear from veteran amp builder Jah Tubby. Manasseh's sound would soon grow hugely successful, partly because of regular visits to Kingston to pick up fresh dubs, played alongside their digital (or semi-digital) versions.

Many sounds and systems have continued to carry the digidub flame, such as Oxford's Zion Train and Leicester's Vibronics (Steve Vibronics and Richi Rootz), whose early releases on Zion Train's Universal Egg label were popular with the systems. Over the years, they have worked with artists including Big Youth and Fun Lovin' Criminals, whilst their album UK Dub Story (2008) features veteran UK vocalist Macka B (known for his work with Mad Professor) as well as Jah Marnyah and Echo Ranks, and expands the digidub sound into the realms of world music and dubstep while retaining a strict roots core.

MODS, SKINHEADS AND PUNKS

Long before ska became a runaway success in the 1960s, Britain was already on its way to becoming an important site for the development of Caribbean music. Planetone Records, run by Sonny Roberts, was the first black-owned record label (and record shop) in the UK; but Melodisc Records, founded in 1946 by Emil Shalit, was the first major important outlet for jazz and blues imported from the U.S. Having signed calypso artist Lord Kitchener as far back as 1951, Melodisc also gave birth to subsidiary label Blue Beat, which gave ska its original name, and was enormously significant in terms of the music's dissemination throughout the UK.

Another important black distributor of reggae, Daddy (George) Pecking arrived in England in 1960, and set up his Studio One shop in west London. As the name suggests, the shop was set up as a London outlet for Coxsone Dodd's records, supplying everything from ska, rocksteady and reggae to early UK sound system pioneers such as Duke Vin.

By the mid-1960s, Island Records and Beat & Commercial (a subsidiary of Trojan) were set up to promote and distribute Jamaican music through shops specializing in black music. Ska was already hugely popular throughout Britain at this time, thanks to hits like Millie Small's 'My Boy Lollipop' (1964) and Prince Buster's 'Al Capone' (1967), which were storming the UK charts and even getting appearances on mainstream TV music shows like *Ready, Steady, Go*.

In a somewhat unexpected twist, ska (as well as rude boy fashion and attitude) began to attract the attention of white British Mods (Modernists). With their short-cropped haircuts and love of football, fighting and dressing up, Mods usually hailed from work-ing-class backgrounds and enjoyed bands like The Who and Small Faces. But they were also into rhythm and blues and soul, and were seduced by the upbeat, high energy shuffle of ska, attending nights at the A Train and Ska Bar in London. Skinheads, a later version of the Mods, who were not too dissimilar to them in many ways yet became their rivals, caught on to ska in a big way too. This was to the point that ska was referred to at times as 'skinhead music'. Songs like Desmond Dekker's 'Israelites' (1968) and Symarip's 'Skinhead Moonstomp' (1969) became skinhead anthems, as did Lee Perry's 'Return of Django" (1969) and Harry J Allstar's 'The Liquidator' (1969), which was used as a run-out theme tune at football matches.

As ska morphed into rocksteady and reggae, Bob Marley's arrival in London in 1971 helped seal the deal on Britain's love affair with Jamaican music. By the mid-1970s, reggae was main-stream enough that everyone from The Beatles to The Rolling Stones were referencing it in their music, while British reggae bands like Aswad, Steel Pulse, Matumbi and UB40 hit the charts.

Much more interesting from a subcultural, sonic and even political perspective were the collisions between punk and dub that emerged in the second half of the 1970s and continued through the post-punk movement of the early 1980s. The connections between the musical communities in Jamaica and the UK meant that Britain was no stranger to dub, practically right from dub's nascent days. Perry's dubs were well known from the early 1970s, thanks to his Trojan releases, even if the UK version of his *Cloak and Dagger* album from 1973 flopped. Keith Hudson's *Pick a Dub* (1974) proved popular, as did Niney the Observer's *Dubbing With the Observer* (1975).

By the mid-1970s, albums like Joe Gibbs & The Professionals's *African Dub All-Mighty* series were being well received not just among punks but also by psychedelic rock fans who sensed a kindred 'trippy' spirit between the Jamaican experimenters and the 'cosmic' sounds of Tangerine Dream, Can, Amon Düül and Hawkwind.

Natty Locks Dub by Winston Edwards (1974) was one of the first instrumental dub albums to come out of the UK. Self-produced and mixed at King Tubby's, the album was mostly recorded at Lee Perry's Black Ark studio and partly at Joe Gibbs's studio. The cousin and former business associate of Joe Gibbs, Winston Edwards moved to London and became close to Jah Shaka, from whose Alpha Road house in Lewisham he set up his label Fay Music in 1974. In 1975, Edwards opened the Fay Music record shop in New Cross, which is, like Lewisham, in southeast London. Edwards later worked with UK producer/engineer Dennis Bovell on the seminal UK release *Dub Conference: Winston Edwards & Blackbeard* at 10 Downing Street (1980), though the album that made his name, and helped to push dub to a wider crowd in Britain, was the successful *King Tubby Meets Upsetter at the Grass Roots of Dub*, which was mixed at Tubby's and Perry's studios and produced by Edwards.

Also in 1974, the British Coxsone (Lloyd Blackford) released *King of the Dub Rock Part 1*, originally on the Safari label, and later reissued on Coxsone Tribesman, the label he started in 1977 when his older label Ital Coxsone closed down. As with *Natty Locks Dub*, many of the riddims on *King of the Dub Rock Part 1* came directly from Kingston studios (Channel One, King Tubby's, Harry J's) and were mixed there by Lloyd Coxone and Scientist, though some were provided by British reggae band Matumbi.

By the mid-1970s, race relations were becoming a divisive political issue. They had been simmering since the first wave of Caribbean immigrants had arrived in the UK, but 1976 was a major turning point in the situation. The Labour government, under pressure from the International Monetary Fund (IMF), announced welfare spending cuts and Conservative MP Enoch Powell issued racist diatribes about overcrowding and immigration. The National Front's membership also started to grow. In August 1976, Eric Clapton drunkenly ranted on stage in front of an audience of over 2,000 in support of Powell's attempts to control immigration, and to 'stop Britain from becoming a black colony . . . the black wogs and coons and fucking Jamaicans don't belong here'.[20] This was the same Clapton who had topped the U.S. charts with a cover of Marley's 'I Shot the Sheriff'.

The rant led directly to the formation of Rock Against Racism (RAR), an organization set up by Red Saunders and the Socialist Workers Party to help bring Britain's black and white communities closer through music. While acts like The Clash were already touring with the punk bands The Jam and The Buzzcocks, as well as with a roots-reggae sound system featuring I-Roy and The Revolutionaries, RAR provided an essential platform for dub and reggae bands like The Cimarons (who migrated from Kingston to become the first UK-based Jamaican reggae band) and Birmingham's Steel Pulse to play alongside punk and post-punk bands like Generation X and The Slits.[21] In 1978 alone RAR organized 300 local gigs and five carnivals in Britain, including two enormous London events that each drew audiences of nearly 100,000.[22]

While the frantic, amphetamine-fuelled style of punk did not seem to have much in common with reggae's laid-back riddims and spiritual messages, there were in fact many overlaps. In a sense, roots reggae was every bit as revolutionary as punk, in its dedication to turning over the established order and defying all things Babylon. Even some of the titles were similar: the Sex Pistols' 'Anarchy in the UK' (1976) expressed a not dissimilar sentiment to Max Romeo's 'War ina Babylon' (1976). Bob Marley's 'Punky Reggae Party' (1977) only served to underline the common ground between the two groups, and it was not long before west London record stores like Honest Jon's Records (established in 1974) and Rough Trade Records (established in 1978), both situated off Ladbroke Grove, started selling Jamaican reggae and dub alongside their punk selections.

Given its attraction as a deconstructive and psychedelic process, as well as a bass-heavy genre in its own right, dub had a unique cachet that grew popular with the avant-garde bands – normally termed post-punks – that grew out of the short-lived punk scene. Dub's starkness, flexibility and ethereality were a magnet for bands looking to experiment and find new possibilities and directions for music. As Vivien Goldman put it, 'Dub effectively became the code for "progressive" and "cool" and cutting a dub to your punk single was the hip thing to do.'[23]

Mainstream groups like The Clash started exploring dub and reggae, producing their own punk-rock version of Junior Murvin's hit 'Police and Thieves' (1977), working with Lee 'Scratch' Perry on the (disappointingly average) 'Complete Control' (1977) as well as doing shows with him later on. They eventually hired Jamaican radio jock and producer Mikey Dread to work on their single 'Bankrobber' (1980). He also provided 'versions' of some of the tracks on the dub-drenched, and exhausting, *Sandinista!* album (1980).

Possibly the biggest champion of reggae to emerge from the punk scene was John Lydon himself, the swaggering, cocksure lead singer of the Sex Pistols. Raised in London, and the child of Irish Catholic immigrants, he had a natural empathy for other immigrants, underlined by the title of his memoir *No Irish, No Blacks, No Dogs*.[24] Famously playing Dr Alimantado's 'Born for a Purpose' (1981) on the radio shortly after having been beaten up, and generally praising dub and reggae's anti-Babylon tendencies, Lydon had been introduced to dub and sound system culture by Don Letts, a black DJ and filmmaker who played at the legendary punk venue The Roxy and is often credited with exposing the punk scene to dub. As the story goes, Letts ran out of garage punk tunes while deejaying at The Roxy one night, so started playing the other material he had with him that was mostly dub.

> This was MY thing you know, and the punks loved it. And they loved the drugs too! We used to roll spliffs for them. I had my simple DJ set-up, nothing like the superstar DJ you have now. I had just one little turntable, my tunes and a lot of spliffs! Punks could tune in to the righteous and dread rejection of society present in roots rebel rock, and the roaring avant-garde noise which was the sound of the new emerging bass sounds from Jamaica.[25]

Don Letts's *Dread Meets Punk Rockers Uptown* showcased some of the music popular at the time with Letts and his punk aficionados at The Roxy. This included King Tubby, Augustus Pablo, Big Youth, Junior Byles, Tappa Zukie, Jah Stitch, U-Roy, The Congos, Junior Murvin and Lee Perry.

While the Sex Pistols did not specifically explore dub in their music, Lydon was appointed as artists and repertoire consultant for a new Virgin Records roots and dub imprint called Front Line, through which he managed to get into close contact with Big Youth, U-Roy, Burning Spear and Prince Far I, among others. Suitably inspired, and on the heels of a disastrous Sex Pistols tour of the U.S., he formed a new band called 'Public Image Ltd' (PiL). Featuring his friend John Wardle (Jah Wobble) on bass and Keith Levene, who had played guitar in the earliest incarnation of The Clash, PiL were ostensibly part of the experimental post-punk movement, and their mutual love of reggae and dub was displayed prominently in the music. As Levene himself has said, 'The whole reason PiL worked at all was because John, Wobble and myself were just total dub fanatics and were always going to Blues parties.'[26]

'The first form of music that really took me into another world was dub reggae', says Jah Wobble, who devoted himself to learning bass and developing a throbbing, heartbeat-like bass pulse that become central to the PiL sound.

> I was about 15 and heard it . . . at a party we had gatecrashed in Hackney. I was already a fan of ska, bluebeat and early forms of reggae up until this point . . . However, nothing prepared me for the shock of listening to dub, especially through big custom made 22" speaker cabs. There was the bass taking up most of the signal, resonating deep into my solar plexus, the core of my being. All the big plate reverbs and tape echoes, especially the long decaying halftime ones, conveyed a sense of inner space . . . Most of all I was fascinated by the bass lines . . . the sheer physicality of the experience set it apart from any other.[27]

PiL's debut album, *First Issue* (1978), which became slightly messy due to the group running out of money halfway through recording, was nonetheless overt in its debt to dub, specifically through Wobble's cavernous basslines, which dominated the record and propelled it through the more cacophonous moments. The follow-up, *Metal Box* (1979), was even heavier, and more coherent, despite its ardently experimental heart. Basslines were played with a violin bow to produce a droning quality, televisions were allegedly mic-ed and discarded tape from the studio floor was looped to produce eerie backing sounds. On 'Flowers of Romance', Lydon even takes on the role of the deejay, in that much of his lyrical output ('outbursts' may be more accurate) was produced following the recording of the backing track.

'I had heard Miles Davis and that really rocked my world', Wobble told *Clash* magazine ahead of his and Levene's 'Metal Box In Dub' tour in 2012. He explains that

> I realised that my conception of *Metal Box* and what I envisaged PiL to be was continuing to go down a kind of a road where you can develop in certain ways. More modal and more theatrical in a sense, some of it. But I could definitely see the connection with dub, because there's such a big, fat bottom end and not a lot on top or in the middle, so it was influenced – at least sonically – by the dub approach. So there are these two things informing it.[28]

Killing Joke was another industrial/post-punk band dedicated to dub, mostly through Bassist Martin 'Youth' Glover – who named himself after Jamaican artist Big Youth – and who started the WAU! Mr Modo Records label that went on to release material by Bim Sherman and Jah Warrior. Youth was also one of the early pioneers of dub-heavy remix culture in the 1980s, smuggling dub into mainstream rock and pop, alongside Adrian Sherwood and dance producer Andrew Weatherall, for example. Killing Joke's debut EP, *Almost Red* (1979), fused disco, funk, dub and industrial music. It was released on their own label, Malicious Damage Records before the band signed to Island Records' imprint E.G. Records. Killing Joke's eponymous debut was released in 1980 and hit the Top 40, partly due to support from DJ John Peel and PiL's John Lydon. It was produced by Mark Lusardi, who had worked with the Sex Pistols as well as on PiL's *First Issue* (1978) and Linton Kwesi

Johnson's (LKJ's) *Bass Culture* (1980), and who would go on to work with reggae label Greensleeves Records as their engineer.

'You have to understand, most people aren't aware of their musical history, but the second wave of punk wasn't inspired by The New York Dolls or anything like that', Killing Joke frontman vocalist Jaz Coleman told The Quietus. He explains that

> Because that's when Bob Marley came to Ladbroke Grove, and Don Letts introduced Bob Marley to punk music. That's when 'groove' started. That's when reggae music fused with the rhythms, really fused. [We were listening to] *Garvey's Ghost*, the dub version, we really liked Aswad's dub. English reggae had a very different feel to Jamaican reggae. It had some virtues too. Dennis Bovell, Mad Professor. The thing that was very different about the second wave [of punk] was the mystical. That's where the mystical began. Which was anathema to the first wave.[29]

There are many more lesser-known examples of punks and dubheads fusing their sounds and mentalities, some of which have been captured on compilations like *Wild Dub: Dread Meets Punk Rocker* (2003). The collection features plenty of tracks from the usual suspects (The Ruts, The Clash, The Pop Group, PiL and The Slits), but also tracks from Stiff Little Fingers, Basement 5, Generation x and Grace Jones, plus some rarer alternative mixes and extended versions like The Clash's 'Bankrobber Dub', 4 Be 2's 'One of the Lads', and the Brink Style Dub of The Slits' 'Typical Girls'.

The more recent compilation *Spiky Dread* (2012), put together by reggae producer Wrong Tom, delves even deeper, unearthing underground gems from u.s. bands such as The Offs and Bad Brains, plus oddities like Jah Scouse (produced with the help of Young Marble Giants members), Birmingham's Dangerous

Girls and Bristol's Glaxo Babies. Both comps feature liner notes by Vivien Goldman, a British journalist, writer and musician who has produced records with Adrian Sherwood and John Lydon. She is also Adjunct Professor of Punk and Reggae at New York University (NYU) and was a founding member of experimental New Wave band The Flying Lizards. She has written songs for groups, including Massive Attack, and wrote the first biography of Bob Marley. On the compilation she is featured as 'Chantage', a Paris-based duo made up of Goldman and Eve Blouin, who offer a distinctly female take on lovers rock.

'What was it about Jamaican music, dub in particular, that enabled it to so mobilize all sorts of kids?', asks Goldman in the sleeve notes to *Spiky Dread*. She remarks that

The answer offered by the songs gathered here, is mystery. Dub stripped away the known world of existing tracks, and re-invented them with studio sleight of hand. Dub shook up preconceptions and offered a fractured sensibility that, held together by steady bass, made its own scattered sense. Looking back, it's clear that as we were getting to know Britain's rapidly changing face, dub was our mirror.[30]

DENNIS BOVELL, ADRIAN SHERWOOD AND MAD PROFESSOR

One of the first UK dub producers to make a more mainstream name for himself was Dennis Bovell, who had moved to London from Barbados in 1965, and was immediately thrown into sound system culture because of his father's Tropical Soundmaster set. Bovell, also a guitarist, started operating his own Jah Sufferah Hi-Fi sound as early as the late 1960s. In 1972 he formed the roots reggae band Matumbi, which became part of Jah Sufferah, creating a unique fusion of recorded and live music. 'My real fascination for dub', says Bovell, came from listening to sound system dub cuts made for Lloyd Coxone's Sound by Lee Perry, Errol Thompson and King Tubby, and noticing the similarity to sounds made by Ed Kasner, the engineer on Jimi Hendrix's 'Third Stone from the Sun' track on the *Are You Experienced* album, various Western soundtracks in the cinema and on TV at that time that created mood and mystery with the use of tape delay. Being a studio engineer myself and having a few ideas of my own, I gravitated to it.[31]

Matumbi were among the first UK reggae bands to write their own material rather than 'churning out' covers. Just a year after forming, the group was deemed popular enough to open for The Wailers' London debut at an Ethiopian famine relief show. By the mid-1970s, Bovell had his own residency at the Metro in Ladbroke Grove, and Matumbi were on their way to pioneering the hugely influential UK genre of 'lovers rock'. A reaction to the male-dominated and dreadlock-heavy lovers rock matched dance halls of the time. British female vocalists with sweet melodies and reggae rhythms, Matumbi, with Bovell at the helm, helped to lure women back to the dance and even managed to hit the charts with songs like 'Point of View' (1979), which landed them a four-album deal with EMI.

But Bovell was also an avid King Tubby fan. While at school, he had already begun experimenting with dub tunes, which he took to local cutting houses such as the R. G. Jones Studio, where Cliff Richard's, the Average White Band's and Matumbi's first recordings were recorded. Afterwards, he used John Hessel, who was friends with Duke Reid (and apparently instrumental in building the Treasure Isle studio) and a neighbour of UK reggae/dub aficionado David Rodigan. 'I was assisting him on mobile recordings which included the Latvian song festival at the Royal Albert Hall and Jasper Carrott's early recordings for Sweet Folk

All Records', Bovell relates. 'Jah Shaka joined me to cut there once word had spread that he was providing a reasonable mono cut, which was great for sound systems.'[32]

Bovell also used dub techniques in the live Matumbi shows, especially during their Sunday night residency at the Four Aces Club in Dalston, which marked some of the first ever live dub shows in the UK. The band also recorded their first lovers rock records at the Gooseberry Sound Studios, which opened in the early 1970s as an eight-track demo studio and was used by sound system deejays and producers like Lloyd Coxsone as well as punk bands like the Sex Pistols, who recorded the demos for 'Pretty Vacant', 'New York', 'God Save the Queen' and 'EMI' there in 1977.

Bovell's talents were soon noticed by the post-punk movement – The Pop Group's Mark Stewart hired him to record his scintillating debut single 'She is Beyond Good and Evil' (1979), and he was enlisted by Edwyn Collins's Scottish band Orange Juice to produce their 1984 EP 'Texas Fever'. But it was Bovell's work with the all-female band The Slits that best consolidated the possibilities of the two music styles. Inspired by groups such as the Sex Pistols and The New York Dolls, The Slits formed in 1976 with Ari Up (Ariane Daniela Forster, who was then aged fourteen) on vocals, Palmolive (Paloma Romero) on drums, Kate Korus (Kate Corris) on guitar and Suzi Gutsy on bass. When Korus and Gutsy left, Viv Albertine and Tessa Pollitt took over their respective roles.

Albertine had met The Clash's Mick Jones at art school and had shared a (squatted) apartment with Keith Levene, with whom she had played in a band called The Flowers of Romance, along with Sid Vicious. Dennis Morris, the art editor of Island Records, contacted Bovell to say that Chris Blackwell wanted him to produce their debut album, *Cut* (1978).

Bovell obliged, and helped them to explore dub in a number of interesting ways. Matching deep, dubwise basslines to singer Ari Up's shrill vocals, and slowing down the general pace, he also employed musique concrète-style tricks on tracks like 'New Town' (a song about heroin), for which he recorded the sound of an ashtray being tapped with a spoon, a box of matches being rattled and a match being struck.

Bovell also produced a string of seminal UK dub albums under his Blackbeard pseudonym, starting with *Strictly Dub Wize* (1978) – the reissue of which came with a 'step-by-step guide' by Vivien Goldman – *Dub Conference* (1980) and *I Wah Dub* (1980). These albums, and others of the time, illustrated a marked shift from the original methodology of Jamaican dub, in that they were recorded as complete 'songs' rather than 'versions' of other productions. Despite them being more in the vein of traditional songwriting than dub's post-song deconstructions, they remain recognizably dub with their reggae-paced riddims, deep, plangent basslines and liberal use of reverb and echo.

Bovell also collaborated with poet Linton Kwesi Johnson (LKJ) after meeting him at the Four Aces Club. They produced classic albums like *Forces of Victory* (1979), *Bass Culture* (1980), *Tings An' Times* (1991) and *LKJ in Dub: Volumes One and Two* (1981; 1992) which, along with recordings from Kingston's Oku Onuora and the UK's Benjamin Zephaniah, helped form the basis of the dub poetry movement, ostensibly an extension of the deejay tradition.

Bovell maintained a dual career that straddled the commercial and the more underground and esoteric. In the same year as *Cut* was released (1978), Bovell reached number two in the UK charts with Janet Kay's 'Silly Games'. Since the 1990s he has worked with a large number of high-profile artists such as the Thompson Twins, Dexy's Midnight Runners and Bananarama, Marvin Gaye, Wet Wet Wet and the late Fela Anikulapo Kuti.

Over the past couple of years, and following major neck surgery that has prevented him from playing the bass, Bovell has returned not only to his dub adventures but to the genre's original spirit of remixology. For *Ghosts Outside* (2011), he defragmented songs by Steve Mason (Beta Band; King Biscuit Time), while on *Mek It Run* (2012), he collected together some of his own 1970s masters, including two tracks recorded with I-Roy, and gave them the dub treatment. In a neat homage to the original UK dub producer scene, Bovell borrowed the studio of his old friend and fellow protagonist Neil Fraser (Mad Professor) for the project, and released the results on Pressure Sounds, a seminal UK reissue label that has its origins in Adrian Sherwood's mighty On-U-Sound Records.

ADRIAN SHERWOOD

Like Bovell, Adrian Sherwood has been involved in UK reggae and dub since the 1970s, and was also active as a producer in the post-punk scene. Born a few years after Bovell (in 1958), Sherwood's musical vision was incredibly broad right from the start, using dub as a main approach and constant inspiration, but drawing on rock, funk, world and electronic music too.

Sherwood got plugged into dub and reggae at school. He became involved in the nascent UK reggae scene by working in the school holidays for Pama Records, for whom he travelled the UK on trains promoting their music. Later he briefly worked at Pama's Soundville Record Shop in Harlesden, northwest London, and later spent a brief spell working for the Vulcan record label. Sherwood relates that 'When I was 13 I started out as a deejay at a club called Newlands in High Wycombe, which was run by Joe Farquharson.'

> Loads of people played there and I worked with people like Judge Dread, Dave Lee Travis, Johnny Walker, Emperor Rosko. I believe David Rodigan played one of his first ever gigs there. I used to play the Saturday afternoons, a mix of funk and soul, ska for kids, then graduated to evenings when I was 15 or 16. After a while it turned into a reggae club.[33]

Sherwood went to college but left at age seventeen and joined forces with Farquharson, a man he describes as being 'like a father to me', to set up J&A (Joe and Adrian) Records distribution, one of first independent distribution companies for reggae in the UK. By this time he was already involved in the formation of Carib Gems when he just was seventeen years old, which started to attract heavyweight acts like Black Uhuru, Dillinger, Trinity and Prince Far I.

After leaving Carib Gems in 1977, Sherwood founded the Hit Run label with his friend Doctor Pablo when he was nineteen years old, which is when he began to showcase his own take on dub. Sherwood's very first studio experience was with Prince Far I (Michael Williams), working on an album called *Message from the King*, which was pressed on 500 white labels then licensed to Virgin Records. Since they needed more tapes to make up the project, the duo headed to Gooseberry Studios and got Dennis Bovell to engineer some sessions. 'It was albums like *King Tubby Meets Upsetter at the Grass Roots of Dub* and Augustus Pablo's stuff that turned me onto dub first of all', says Sherwood.

> We all loved reggae, but when the dub stuff came along it was just perfect for sitting down and listening to and getting blasted. I remember albums changing hands for big money as white labels on the grass in London's Brockwell Park. People knew what they were, that they were special and rare.[34]

Sherwood's first proper studio experience was with Prince Far I's backing band Creation Rebel, which included drummer Lincoln Valentine Scott, a key member of the Roots Radics. Their first recording together was *Dub From Creation* (1978), made when Sherwood was just nineteen years old (though with mixing support again from Bovell) and sold from the back of his car. It ended up being played by DJ John Peel. At the same time, he worked on *Cry*

Tuff Dub Encounter, Chapter 1, an album he had just finished mixing for Prince Far I, which was engineered by dub producer and Gooseberry Sound Studios stalwart Mark Lusardi. A high-quality, if fairly traditional-sounding dub album, the follow-ups, *Rebel Vibrations* (1979), the classic *Starship Africa* (released in 1980 but recorded in 1977 and unique in the sense that it was mixed backwards, with the effects before the beats) and their penultimate LP *Psychotic Junkanoo* (1981), all grew bolder in terms of using sound collage techniques to weave elements of world music, industrial noise and ambient sounds into the dub blueprint.

In 1980 Sherwood founded the On-U-Sound Records label. It was a collaborative project involving Sherwood working with members of the original Creation Rebel crew plus various musicians from the Jamaican and post-punk scenes, such as The Slits' Ari Up, who helped form New Age Steppers, and Mark Stewart (The Pop Group), Keith Levene and Jah Wobble (after PiL split), Neneh Cherry, Vivien Goldman and Steve Beresford. Sherwood recalls:

I remember having gigs and in the crowd you would have the Sex Pistols, The Slits, The Clash, Billy Idol . . . sometimes all these people at our gigs on the same night. The crowd would be watching the crowd! That's how I met Ari Up – we did The Slits tour with Don Cherry and Happy House. We were guests with Prince Hammer, then the next month we would support The Clash. We had a bit of a ground swell. We knew The Ruts through Misty and Roots. With a lot of this I was in the right place at the right time and a complete fan.[35]

On-U-Sound Records have been a hugely important element in dub's evolution beyond Jamaica, while remaining spiritually connected to it. Sherwood claims that

I just applied the techniques I learned from Prince Far I, who
was the first person to show me around the studio. I was once
described by Edwin Pouncey as a fan who had got his hands
on a mixing desk. It wasn't meant to be a compliment but
I took it as one. Prince Far I showed me the importance
of having your own sound. That was the whole thing with
Jamaican artists, not to sound like everyone else. Keith
Hudson, Lee Perry . . . they all had their own sound. I just
put thousands of hours into it and made sure we had good
players and plenty of maverick ideas too.[36]

Sherwood collaborated with Mark Stewart separately as
'The Maffia' (Charley Fox, Bonjo I, Evar, Fatfingers and Crucial
Tony – the ex Creation Rebel crew – to create dub-heavy, post-punk
recordings *Learning to Cope With Cowardice* (1983) and *As the Veneer of
Democracy Starts to Fade* in 1985. In another interesting connection,
some of the musicians with The Maffia were Keith Leblanc (whom
Sherwood had met in New York in 1984), Skip McDonald and Doug
Wimbish, who as the rhythm section for the Sugar Hill Gang,
appeared on seminal hip hop tracks like 'Rapper's Delight' (1979),
'The Message' (198280) and 'White Lines (Don't Do It)' (1983).

Sherwood went even more tropically psychedelic with his
early '80s African Head Charge (AHC) project, which featured an
ever-changing collective of musicians based around percussionist
Bonjo Iyabinghi Noah. AHC's surrealist masterpiece *My Life in a
Hole in the Ground* (1981) is one of the major On-U-Sound works,
and was directly inspired by Brian Eno and David Byrne's *My
Life in the Bush of Ghosts* (1981). An eerie, unsettling mix of
African chanting, industrial sounds, animal screams, Chinese
harps and samples of Einstein's voice, the album reintroduced
dub's original spirit of avant-garde sound collage in a whole new
way. Sherwood regarded these studio sessions as 'experiments in
active frequencies, out of time noises, rhythms within rhythms,

The Slits and The Pop Group, Scotland tour flyer.

and endless tape edits (edits on edits) resulting in the ultimate cut-up and paste job'.[37]

Subsequent AHC records such as *Environmental Studies* (1982), for which Sherwood stacked speakers with auxiliary microphones into a toilet to obtain a distant drum sound, and the 'schizophrenic' *Drastic Season* (1987) were textbook postmodernist amalgamations. By *Off the Beaten Track* (1986) and their masterpiece *Songs of Praise* (1990), they had tamed their sound into something coherent yet still hugely combinatory, connecting dub to its African past via chants, percussion and mystical 'rootsical' vibrations. As such,

> Those records were all made using massive tape overloading. And then spending ages mic-ing things down corridors with tubes. Nobody would even be bothered doing things like that anymore. Most people just want to listen to tunes on a compressed, overloaded, 'get as much bass out of it as you can' sort of way. People don't look at sonic as a picture quite like we did

then. We were doing things like Conny Plank and that – taking stuff down phones and mic-ing up the phone, recording it down a tube and phasing the tube. We were doing things like taking something, recording it and then putting a mic in this room and then opening that door and playing it through into the other room and then re-recording it and having a phase in between the two things. Now nobody would go to those lengths. Nobody would be bothered doing those sort of things.[38]

Dub Syndicate was yet another outlet for Sherwood's indefatigable energy and zest for dub. Formed with 'Style' Scott and featuring contributions from the Roots Radics, Sherwood and others, the project kicked off in 1982 with *The Pounding System*. This was a mix of analogue and digital sounds that mixed tough, rigid drum sounds with fluttering piano and horn lines and lashings of reverb and space invader effects.

Tunes From the Missing Channel (1985) featured contributions from Jah Wobble and Keith Levine, and was predicated on Sherwood's discovery of The Emulator, a digital sampling keyboard. More reminiscent of Mad Professor's Ariwa sound, the record was in step with the digital revolution being launched in Kingston by King Jammy's 'Sleng Teng' – a riddim also built on a keyboard – in the same year.

It was around this time that Prince Far I was murdered during a robbery at his house in Kingston. Sherwood was so upset he that did not make another reggae record for a while, concentrating on the Tackhead project and working with mainstream clients like Depeche Mode, Ministry and other non-On-U-Sound Records label projects. He returned to Jamaican music with a series of albums featuring Lee 'Scratch' Perry: *Time Boom X De Devil Dead* (1987), *Secret Laboratory* (1990) and *Dub Setter* (2009). These records helped update Perry from the eccentric Kingston legend of the 1970s to a respected contemporary artist. Apart from being responsible for some of the most innovative experiments in dub over the last four decades, Sherwood has also capably balanced creativity with commerciality, working with post-punk/industrial groups such as Cabaret Voltaire and Depeche Mode on the one hand, and Simply Red and Primal Scream on the other. In 2003 he finally struck out on his own with *Never Trust a Hippy*, which featured collaborations with Sly & Robbie, and *Becoming a Cliché* (2007), which featured Lee 'Scratch' Perry, Dennis Bovell, Little Roy and Mark Stewart. In 2012 Sherwood put out *Survival & Resistance* on Warp Records, a largely instrumental album, partly recorded in Brazil, that carries an updated, slightly mellower sound but without softening the producer's uniquely sprawling aesthetic or, as is clear from the title and the moods and sound environments within, shrinking from social critique.

MAD PROFESSOR

Born in Guyana in 1955, Neil Fraser gained his nickname 'Mad Professor' because of his love of electronics and old analogue technology such as reel-to-reel tape decks and effects modules. Starting slightly later than Sherwood and Bovell (and influenced by the latter as well as dub originators like Tubby, Perry and Thompson), he nonetheless made a considerable statement in the 1980s with his *Dub Me Crazy* (1982–93) and *Black Liberation Dub* (1994–99) series, both of which featured recordings by live musicians filtered and mixed through Fraser's digital desk.

'The thing about dub for me was the blank template', Fraser explains.

Coming from an era where all you heard was songs or instrumentals, suddenly the first set of dubs I heard were almost instrumentals but in this framework taken from something performed. You couldn't quite put your finger on it. To me, it was perfect for driving or making love, because it wasn't putting words in your head. Like a blank canvas with a few guidelines for what you could do.[39]

As a soul fan, Fraser was drawn to Jamaica's covers scene – tracks like Ken Boothe's take on Al Green's 'Look What You Done To Me' – but also to roots albums like The Abyssinians' classic *Satta Massagana* (1976). The first inspirational dub album that caught his ear was Prince Buster's *The Message Dubwise* (1972) as well as Pablo's records and Tubby's B-sides.

> I liked the stuff that was just drum and bass, this raw style, which back then had hardly any echos, just a bit of reverb. Stuff by Errol Thompson and Tubby. I would play it over and over again and it made me want to be in the studio. I remember the B-side phenomenon very well. It grew so popular in the mid-70s that when you went to the shop and listened to new record, you'd play the B-side first. At the time we would go to reggae dances at the Bali Hai in Streatham, the Co-op Hall in Tooting, the A Train in Battersea, and the Swan in Stockwell, upstairs from the pub. The main place though was the Roaring Twenties where Coxsone had a residency. Then there were the sound systems of course.[40]

Around 1975, Fraser visited Bovell at his house and saw him editing with a quarter-inch tape machine. Impressed but penniless, he started looking into building his own recording equipment. He recounts that

> Buying a state-of-the-art machine back then was same cost as a house. That's why there weren't many studios like there were in Jamaica, which is why there wasn't much of a home-grown reggae or dub scene in the '70s. Back then there was no such division between analogue or digital either.[41]

Already building various devices and effects boxes to sell to studios
and sound systems, Fraser started to construct his own studio
equipment including his own mixing board and extra hardware like
the Akai 4000-FS reel-to-reel tape deck. He called the studio 'Ariwa',
the Yoruba word for 'communication'. Initially located in his south
London living room, he moved to a larger space and a proper
facility in Peckham in 1982. Over the years it became a home for
both the lovers rock sound as well as roots reggae and dub:

> I started recording in the Jamaican dub style with a four-track,
> separating the channels and then rebuilding the tracks. The
> only difference was that instead of working from someone
> else's masters, we recorded our own musicians. There were
> lots of those around at the time, more than there are these
> days in fact, so we had good singers and players to work with,
> some of whom, like the guys from Aswad, went on to become
> quite famous. It wasn't easy to get our stuff well known on
> the market at first as everyone wanted Jamaican product but
> we had our ways and eventually things worked out.[42]

The first Mad Professor dub project to catch the imagination
of UK enthusiasts was *Dub Me Crazy, Part 1* (1982), which indulged
in the genre's outer-space aura, complete with cosmic bleeps,
spinning echoes, snatches of melody and clangorous reverb.
Slightly reminiscent of the Black Ark or Errol Thompson's layered effects, it had a much 'cleaner' or modern sound, owing to a
combination of two-inch tape and a new sixteen-track mixing
board (the same kind Scientist was using to change Kingston's
Channel One sound in the late-1970s and beyond).

Fraser quickly followed it with more in the series, with titles
like *Beyond the Realms of Dub*, *The African Connection* (often claimed
as one of his best) and *Escape to the Asylum of Dub*. Fraser
produced and played bass, percussion, synthesizer, vocals, steel

drum across the albums, alongside a host of British reggae session musicians including Errol Reid (on organ and synthesizer) and Preacher (drums and bass). 'It was a crazy thing to do, really', says Fraser of the series:

> I pressed 1500 copies of the first album, which cost a fortune in those days, and they sat there for six months doing nothing. I was there thinking it had all been a waste of money and time. I had a young daughter at the time and a wife and a mortgage. Then John Peel started to play it on his Radio 1 show. This introduced me to a whole load of different people. Then we started doing well with the lovers rock and roots stuff, the studio grew in demand from other producers like Jah Shaka and the Twinkle Brothers and before you know it labels like Warners Brothers were calling me up to get dub remixes of their artists.[43]

By the early 1990s, the *Dub Me Crazy* series was growing stale, and Fraser wound it down in favour of the weightier, more politically charged *Black Liberation Dub* series, which maintained his signature sprinklings of 'space dust' but offered a more militant atmosphere. 'I felt that black people somehow weren't trying any more . . . that they had lost their confidence', says Fraser. Moreover, 'I wanted to remind the scene about black liberation, about rediscovering themselves. It's still something that's needed today.'[44]

As was the case with Bovell and Sherwood, Fraser worked with a steady stream of mainstream rock, R&B and electronica acts from Sade and The Orb to the Beastie Boys and Depeche Mode, though Ariwa has always stayed true to its reggae and dub roots. Among others, Fraser has collaborated frequently with Lee 'Scratch' Perry and U-Roy, with whom he produced the classic *True Born African* album (1991). In 1995 he produced more records with Perry, including *Black Ark Experryments* and *Super*

Ape inna Jungle, which also featured the bass-heavy junglist riddims of production team Dougie Digital and Juggler, and in 1996 he enjoyed a belated post-punk moment by applying his dub aesthetic to the catalogue of American rockers *Ruts DC on Ruts DC vs. Mad Professor – Rhythm Collision Dub*.

But by far his best-known project of that era was *No Protection* (1995), a re-imagined version of Massive Attack's second album, *Protection* (1994), that featured Fraser's old friend Horace Andy as well as plenty of decent dubbed out textures and soul rhythms to work with. In 2005, Fraser teamed up with Kingston originator Scientist for *Mad Professor Meets Scientist at the Dub Table* and in the same year he celebrated Ariwa's 25th anniversary with a tour of the UK alongside Lee 'Scratch' Perry, who also joined him on tour for his latest project *The Roots of Dubstep* (2011), which explores dub's influence on the genre's latest British-born manifestation. Fraser maintains that 'There's nothing new about dubstep.'

Everybody loves dub. Dubstep just extends from that love. The new dubstep thing isn't based on any idea other than the bassline, and we all know there is more to dub than the bassline. Every song needs melody. So they have to go back to the original dub that was based on song. This [*The Roots of Dubstep*] is the dubstep bible! I love electronics and I love experimenting. This [the Ariwa studio] is an experimental station. You must take the technology to excite people, you have to run technology . . . to make it do things that nobody else could do.[45]

4 NYC: DUB, RAP, DISCO AND ILLBIENT

DUB IN NYC

It was not just to Britain that Jamaicans emigrated through the latter half of the twentieth century. In fact, the u.s. was generally considered a more obvious choice, given its proximity to Jamaica, its reputation as a 'land of plenty' and existing links forged through the crop-working trade in the south of the country. Although Jamaicans had already started to migrate to the u.s. in the late nineteenth century, immigration was tightened in the 1920s, and again by the Immigration and Nationality Act of 1952 (often referred to as the 'McCarran-Walter Act'), which restricted entry to the United States to 100 Jamaicans annually (that is, 100 Jamaicans per Caribbean colony and 800 Jamaicans in total).[1]

Owing to the pressure from the effects of the civil rights movement and subsequent diplomatic endeavours by the u.s. government, the stranglehold on immigration was finally loosened in 1965. Jamaican immigration increased accordingly, especially during the late 1970s and early 1980s when political violence back home was at a peak. Around this time an estimated fifteen per cent of the population left, including many professionals such as doctors and technicians.[2]

Jamaicans' preferred destinations included Miami, Philadelphia, Atlanta, Washington, DC, LA and particularly New York City. There immigrants settled in boroughs like Brooklyn, Queens and the Bronx. Despite being largely immigrant districts, life often proved tough for the new Jamaican arrivals, since their patois, styles of dress and mannerisms did not quite match those of the dominant African-American and Latino communities. Although integration was a challenge, Jamaicans held their own, forming their own close-knit communities and, as in the UK, establishing their own musical traditions within these new contexts.

Amid the waves of immigrants were, naturally, many Jamaican producers who wished to escape the familiarity and aggression of Kingston. As in London, though to a lesser extent, studios, record shops and labels started to spring up in the city. Clive Chin, of Randy's Studio 17 fame, moved to New York in the mid-1970s, although he quit studio work to focus on setting up VP Records with his parents and opening a Jamaican restaurant. Three of the most prominent sites in NYC for dub were Brad Osborne's Clocktower Records (and his Brad's Record Den store), Everton Da Silva's Hungry Town label and studio, and Lloyd 'Bullwackie' Barnes's Wackie's House of Music.

Brad's Record Audio Den opened in the Bronx in 1969. Originally an electronic repair shop, it quickly became a record shop following demand from the local community, which initially craved R&B, blues and jazz, then the new reggae sound. Importing music from both the UK and Jamaica, the shop soon became the number one stop-off in the Bronx for old, new and hard to find records, drawing in crowds from all over the city (including The Rolling Stones' Keith Richards, when he was in town).

In 1971 Osborne launched the Clocktower Records Inc. label and an imprint called Brad's, along with fellow Jamaican native Glen Adams, a vocalist and musician who had worked at Studio One, Treasure Isle and played organ for Perry's band The Upsetters. Indeed, the label released music from many high-profile Jamaican artists such as Perry, Cornell Campbell, Johnny Clarke, Horace Andy (for example, his *Pure Ranking* album in 1978), Alton Ellis, Scientist (including his album *Scientific Dub* in 1981), Linval Thompson and Bunny Lee (such as his album *King of Dub* in 1978).

Hungry Town in Corona, Queens, was run by producer Everton Da Silva, who had moved to New York City from Jamaica in 1973. Da Silva also had a great contacts book, working with Augustus Pablo, Roman Stewart, George Nooks, Barrington Spence and Jacob Miller, though the main highlight to come out of his studio was the legendary *In the Light* album with Horace Andy (1977), which was released with a whole album of dubs by King Jammy (*In the Light Dub*). Da Silva also released a stream of excellent singles by Andy ('Youths of Today', 'Fever', 'Do You Love My Music', 'Government Land'). Even when Andy set up his own Rhythm label, he continued recording for Da Silva, churning out singles through the mid-1970s from 'Ital Vital' to 'Control Yourself'.

Their partnership was abruptly ended in 1979, however, when Da Silva was murdered; Andy was also old friends with Lloyd 'Bullwackie' Barnes, with whom he recorded several albums, including the seminal *Dance Hall Style* (1982), which featured reworkings of old songs plus a highly rated cover of 'Spying Glass' (retitled 'Love in the City'). Barnes was initially a singer. Born and raised in Kingston, he hung around Studio One and Treasure Isle during the early 1960s ska era, landing some backing vocal gigs and even engineering for a time at Duke Reid's. Realizing he was not going to make a career in Kingston, he moved to New York (where his mother lived) in 1967. He spent his days working on construction sites and worked as a DJ at night, relying on friends to help carry his sound system, including turntables, crates of records, speakers, on the subway, and playing out at house parties in Brooklyn, Queens and the Bronx, along with in-house deejay Jah Batta. After playing a show that required him to repair his equipment because of stray gunshots, Barnes decided to get out of the sound system business, and in 1972 opened a studio instead.[3] Located initially on White Plains Road in the Bronx, Barnes's first record was produced for Ken Boothe on a label called 'SENRAB' (Barnes spelled backwards). A few years later, he moved to 241st Street, changed the label name to 'Bullwackie's', then 'Wackie's', and began to hone his roots-inspired, analogue dub sound, memorably described by fellow producer Ras Menelik as 'the reggae Motown in the Bronx'.[4]

Helmed by engineers Douglas Levy and Junior Delahaye, Wackie's dealt mostly in classic Studio One and Treasure Isle riddims and used phase-shifting and other established 'lo-fi' techniques to create murky, distinctive textures. The sonic spectres of Lee 'Scratch' Perry and Tubby hung in the Wackie's studio right from the start – the Wackie's sound has been compared to the Black Ark's more than once – and Perry actually produced some of his Clocktower releases there.

Barnes formed his band, the Bullwackie All Stars, from a group of studio musicians. Comprising Jerry Harris, Ras Menelik, Jerry Johnson, Clive 'Azul' Hunt and Douglas Levy, they were the backbone of the Wackies sound, producing records such as their debut *Dub Unlimited* in 1976, the excellent *Creation Dub* in 1977, a brilliant, highly melodic collection of heavy-duty dub, and *Natures Dub* in the 1980s. Barnes went on to work with an increasing number of Jamaican stars, from Jackie Mittoo, Horace Andy, Wayne Jarrett (including his classic *Showcase*, 1982) and Sugar Minott to Leroy Sibbles, and produced local artists such as the female duo the Love Joys and deejay Jah Batta (Tony O'Meally), as well as Barnes's own Chosen Brothers project. Following these high-profile releases Wackie's slid into relative obscurity during the late 1980s, until the reissuing (and remixing) of some of their back catalogue in the noughties by labels like Honest Jon's in the UK and Germany's Basic Channel, owned by Basic Channel/Rhythm & Sound's Mark Ernestus and Moritz von Oswald (see chapter Seven).

One of Wackie's late 1970s releases was especially revealing about what was happening musically in New York City at that time. Titled 'Wack Rap' (1979), the track featured Jamaican singing and 'talk over' from rappers Solid C., Bobby D. and Kool Drop, and is considered one of the earliest hip hop records. Although Wackie's didn't get any more involved in the hip-hop scene, Clocktower made a much more concerted effort.

Aware of the demand for funk and soul breaks that had been developing, Brad Osborne hired a young boy called Tyrone (surname unknown) to start up his burgeoning breakbeat section in the rear of the store. Tyrone – renamed 'T-Ski Valley' – obliged, and asked if he could record some hip hop in return. Osborne booked some time at Bob Blank's Blank Tape Studios, one of the city's most important creative hubs from the mid-1970s to the mid-1980s for early rap and disco artists such as Musique, Salsoul Orchestra, Arthur Russell, Larry Levan, Nicky Siano and Tony Humphries.

Blank was considered one of the founding fathers of the hip hop scene for his remix and production work and Osborne / T-Ski's resulting single, 'Catch the Beat' (1981), was an underground hit. Released on a new rap label that Osborne (and Adams) set up called Grand Groove Records, the track was set around a catchy disco sample borrowed from Taana Gardner's 'Heartbeat' (1981) and caused a minor sensation. Within two years, Osborne and T-Ski Valley had produced no fewer than eight titles on the Grand Groove Records label. He also put out other hip hop acts, including Chapter Three and 'Queen of House Music' Screamin' Rachael, though these early successes were cut short when Osborne was killed.

One of the other Grand Groove acts was Just Four, with a crew that included Imperial J.C. Imperial was a regular visitor to Brad's Record Den and a member of a local sound system called the Herculoids, which T-Ski would also roll with for a while (as the 'Fly Force' MCs). The Herculoids sound system was run by Clive Campbell, better known as DJ Kool Herc, the man who would do more than anyone to expose – and strengthen – the links between Jamaican music and U.S. hip hop.

DJ KOOL HERC AND HIP HOP

Although rap has largely been recognized as an amalgam of many different musical and cultural forms, the overlaps with dub and reggae are too obvious to be of minor importance. Both rely on pre-recorded sounds, both share similar vocal content (lyrics that deal with messages and boasts, insults and party 'raps'), and both grew out of impoverished urban areas as a means of self-expression by their inhabitants.

The Wackie's label and Clocktower Records Inc. were not the only reggae labels to release rap records in the late 1970s. Other labels such as Rota, Express, Love Train, Clappers and 12 Star worked with early hip hop artists. As Dick Hebdige points out, rap was exported back to Jamaica as early as 1979, when Joe Gibbs cut a version of 'Rappers Delight featuring a duo called Xanadu and Sweet Lady, who rapped the song 'New York Fashion' on one side, with 'Rocker's Choice' toasting it on the other.[5] Clive Campbell, or 'DJ Kool Herc', was arguably the first Jamaican to fully get involved in the scene and become a primary influence on its development. A Trenchtown native, Campbell grew up listening to the reggae, jazz and soul collections belonging to his father, as well as to his local sound system, Somerset Lane, and its selector King George.

In *Can't Stop Won't Stop*, Jeff Chang's history of hip hop, Campbell talks about the Somerset Lane sound system, explaining that

> I was too young to go in. All we could do is sneak out and see the preparation of the dance throughout the day. The guys would come with a big old handcart with the boxes in it. And then in the night time, I'm a little itchy headed, loving the vibrations on the zinc top 'cause them sound systems are powerful.[6]

Campbell moved to Manhattan in 1967 (aged eleven years) with his family. He was quickly hooked on the soul and funk records ruling the Bronx then. It was not long before he started playing this music at his own house parties. Campbell's father owned a small Shure PA system, which he lent to a local R&B band. To boost the power of the system, Campbell wired in a preamp to the system, obtained a couple of Girard turntables and two Bogart amps, and began using the channel knobs as a mixer. He also modified the system to be able to handle up to eight microphones, using one for a regular mic, and another for an echo chamber box.

By 1973 the set featured a 300-watt-per-channel Mackintosh amp and a brand new Technics 1100A turntable. Campbell's parties provided a kind of a safe haven from the gang warfare in parts of the Bronx, which may partly explain their popularity. A year later, in 1974, the parties had become block parties, with Campbell, now nicknamed 'Hercules' at school because of his athletic ability and size, but which he further amended to 'Kool Herc', famously using the power from lamp-posts and tool sheds to fuel his sound.

Campbell sometimes dropped reggae and dub tunes into his sets, though soon noted that the response from the dance floor was more dynamic when he played upbeat tracks like 'Bongo Rock' and 'Apache' (by Jamaican disco group the Incredible Bongo Band) or soul tracks like Dennis Coffey's 'Scorpio'. Although Campbell subsequently dropped reggae and dub from his sets, by hooking his mics up to the Space Echo box, and enlisting his friend Coke La Rock to serve as the deejay / crowd hype, he certainly transported something of the Jamaican dance hall to the Bronx.

The dancers – 'B-boys' and 'B-girls', as they became known – responded especially well to the 'breaks' or instrumental solo rhythms in the records, and it was in order to extend these that Campbell developed the technique of using two turntables to alternate between two copies of the same record. Initially, called the 'Merry-Go-Round', this innovation was in essence a form of live dub or 'version', in that it stripped a record of its vocal and melodic elements to focus purely on bass and the drums. In a move reminiscent of Kingston culture, Campbell also soaked the labels off his records to render them incognito and restrict the chances of their being copied.

Interestingly, Campbell has often denied that Jamaican deejay-ing informed his own approach, preferring instead to cite James Brown or the Last Poets as key inspirations. Afrika Bambaataa (fellow hip hop and breakbeat DJ pioneer Kevin Donovan) has even commented that he played more Jamaican music in the hip hop parties than Campbell or Grandmaster Flash, and also remarked that although Campbell grew up in Jamaica, he was focused on playing funky American music.[7] Yet eyewitness accounts describe Campbell toasting in Jamaican style, even when playing soul and R&B records, and when the *Jamaica Observer* asked him about his influences, he named Kingston heavyweights such as Prince Buster, Don Drummond, The Skatalites, Big Youth, U-Roy and 'Coxsone' Dodd.[8] Quoted by Chang, Campbell also states that 'Them said nothing good ever come outta Trenchtown . . . well hip hop came out of Trenchtown!'[9]

Author Garnette Cadogan has claimed that Campbell was not simply responding to his Bronx-based audience, but also channel-ling their interests through a set of priorities and techniques that he had absorbed in Jamaica. There, sound system operators headed from the party to the studio to edit records according to the responses they had just witnessed on the dance floor. Hence,

> We can think of Kool Herc as a one-man sound system-cum-studio, or, if you prefer, a selector-cum-sound system-cum-studio who fused economic expediency with imaginative remixing and improvisation. Like the dub musicians who

re-used existing rhythms to useful and even exhaustive effect, Herc developed a technique that made perfect economic and creative sense, and supplied an aesthetic in which the pleasure of dancers (and a quick, ready responsiveness to them) reigned paramount. Perhaps more than anything else, this is how Jamaican popular music influenced hip hop.[10]

Attendees of Campbell's throwdowns included several other key innovators in the hip hop world, many of whom were Caribbean if not Jamaican. Joseph Saddler, for example, better known as Grandmaster Flash, was of Barbadian origin. Like Campbell, his father owned a large collection of both Caribbean and American records. Flash took Campbell's DJ'ing innovations to the next level, as did the Bronx-born Afrika Bambaataa, whose roots were also in the Caribbean (Jamaica and Barbados) and who promoted peace between blacks and Puerto Ricans via his Universal Zulu Nation organization (an awareness group formed to help stem gang violence), which included the Zulu Nation Sound System. While Herc ruled the West Bronx with his Herculoids Sound System, the South Bronx remained the domain of Bambaataa.[11]

Campbell continued to play shows and maintain residencies throughout the 1970s at early hip hop venues like T-Connection, Sparkle, Audubon, the Godfather's Club and Galaxy 2000, insisting on using his own system even when clubs had their own. In 1977, while attempting to mediate an incident, Campbell was stabbed in his side and hand. While he recovered, the 'baton' was passed to Flash and Bambaataa. Yet, by then, Campbell's influence was deeply ingrained in hip hop's DNA.

DANCEHALL AND RAP

By the late 1970s, Kingston's scene was shifting away from roots reggae and towards the new dancehall style (see chapter Two). New York would prove especially receptive to this new movement, and one of the first to explore it was the Jamaican Hyman 'Jah Life' Wright (also known as Papa Life), a long-time Brooklyn resident. Jah Life had left Kingston before the music scene was properly underway, so when he went 'looking' for Linval Thompson in 1979 (to record him), he was not quite sure where to find him. Instead of Thompson, he met Henry 'Junjo' Lawes, who was also trying to make it into the business. Junjo offered Jah Life some rhythm tracks as well as access to his own vocal artists (deejay Jah Thomas and singer Barrington Levy). As such, they wound up at King Tubby's studio, where the results were mixed by Scientist and released on Wright's Jah Life label.

Junjo stayed in Jamaica to handle the sales and distribution there (and in the UK), while Jah Life headed back to New York, where he joined forces with producer Percy Chin to create new rhythms at Philip Smart's HC&F studio on Long Island. Smart's apprenticeship as an engineer in King Tubby's studio had served him well. After moving to New York in 1976 to open the HC&F Studios, he became involved in many of the 'Sleng Teng' computer-generated riddims recorded in that era, along with many hits that helped to bring dancehall to the mainstream music market in America, including Super Cat's *Don Dada* (1992) and Shabba Ranks's *Mr Loverman* (1992).

By the 1980s, both the dancehall and hip hop scenes had grown more commercial. If anything, Kingston was also becoming more like New York City, with cocaine and business mindsets slowly replacing dreadlocks and weed 'rasta' mentality, and dancehall's lyrics moving accordingly towards materialism, drugs and general 'slackness'. Slowly the perception of Jamaican culture changed. Gone were the days when Kool Herc recalled Jamaicans being thrown into garbage cans by local Puerto Rican and African American gangs. While not many hip hop artists were specifically channelling dub, the scene began to borrow freely from Jamaican patois, its style and its general musical heritage. For example, Yellowman's 'Nobody Move Nobody Get Hurt' (1984) was sampled by Eazy-E for his same-name major hit in 1988, and the riddim from 'Zungguzungguguzungguzeng' (1983) – originally borrowed from Alton Ellis's Studio One hit 'Mad Mad' (1967) – was reused by hip hop heavyweights like KRS-One as well as BDP's Remix for 'P is Free'.

It wasn't long before the scenes achieved parity, with labels like Elektra, East West, Def Jam and Delicious Vinyl working with Jamaican dancehall artists like Cutty Ranks and Capleton, and the major record labels signing up Yellowman, Super Cat and Shabba Ranks. Dub's sonic tropes were all but lost in this mix, but it would not take long to resurface in hip hop's matrix of references. Indeed, in 2010, hip hop and dub were expertly spliced together by New York producer Max Tannone and his Mos Dub project, which mashed together songs by rapper Mos Def with classic dub and reggae samples from King Tubby, Lee Perry, Scientist, The Slickers, Johnny Osborne, Big Youth and Dawn Penn.

DJ SPOOKY AND ILLBIENT

While UK producers and artists were utilizing dubby soundscapes for their own take on hip hop (trip hop, or blunted beats), New York theorist, DJ and producer Paul D. Miller, 'DJ Spooky', created his own genre, 'illbient', a combination of the hip hop slang term 'ill' (meaning good) and 'ambient'. The illbient scene centred around the Williamsburg neighbourhood of Brooklyn and included a community of producers and visual artists like Byzar (Akin Adams), a former engineer at the same New York City studio as Jamaican producer Mikey Dread, dark-dub practitioners Teargas & Plateglass, and shimmering ambient dub creators Sub Dub.

(One half of Sub Dub is Raz Mesinai, who is also a graphic artist; his work was featured in Kode9 & The Space Ape's album *Black Sun* (2011) – see chapter Five.)

DJ Spooky ran the multimedia 'Molecular' event at the Gas Station in the early 1990s, which showcased the illbient genre and associated producers, DJs and artists. It is Spooky who is the leader of the scene and who has the highest profile, thanks in part to his natural media-friendly charisma and way with an intellectual soundbite, as well as his forward-thinking genre blending. His most celebrated albums to date include *Songs of a Dead Dreamer* (1996) and *Riddim Warfare* (1998) that merged electronica, hip hop riddims, reggae and dub to create a dragging, often eerie, low-end sound. 'It was always about dub', he says.

> Beginning, middle and end of my music – dub. The whole Jamaican diaspora is stored in music. You have to look at how other cultures spread around the world to compare. Jewish cultures has [*sic*] the Torah, Chinese cultures has written text, but Jamaica is the loudest island in the world. I'd say dub influenced everything that's going on in NY today – from LCD Soundsystem to Sonic Youth, to Mos Def, Talib Kweli and The Roots. It all goes back to dub.[12]

Spooky was born in Washington, DC, but has been based in New York City for many years. His mother was one of the main art critics for the Kingston *Jamaica Gleaner*, which he describes as 'the *New York Times* of Jamaica'. His maternal uncle is Chester Orr, a retired Chief Justice of the Jamaican Supreme Court. Spooky spent every summer in Jamaica until he was about thirteen.

In 2003 he made his dub connections more explicit with *Dubtometry*, by handing over his Optometry album to Mad Professor, Lee 'Scratch' Perry, Negativland and Twilight Circus Dub Sound System (Canadian multi-instrumentalist Ryan Moore) to remix, dub and generally subvert. The following year Spooky collaborated with Twilight Circus for *Riddim Clash*, an album of dub that incorporated violins, Middle Eastern melodies and xylophone.

Spooky also raided the archives of Trojan Records twice: once for *In Fine Style: 50,000 Volts of Trojan Records* (2006), a 2-CD mix for Trojan Records that was light on mixing and effects but wonderfully heavy on the selection of deejay tracks, and again for *Creation Rebel* (2007), a possible nod to Prince Far I and Adrian Sherwood (see chapter Three). This latter album was a possible look to Adrian Sherwood. Here he mashed together tracks by dub poet Mutabaruka, Augustus Pablo, Wayne Smith, Barrington Levy and others, with added beats, samples, scratching and other sonic manipulations. The fact that his intro features both Mad Professor and scratch DJ Rob Swift arguably says everything about Spooky's meta-cultural tendencies.

I guess it's not one particular artist who has really influenced me, but if I had to pick, I'd say King Tubby. And I had the honour of checking out King Tubby's archive. That was the best experience – he's pretty much the DNA of the idea of using the studio as an instrument, and the equipment he used – stuff that was very inexpensive and crude for its day, but was used with maximum effect.

When you look at any producer today and what tools we have nobody comes close to being as innovative as he was. It's all about bass minimalism. The whole idea of collage that the European artists like Duchamp were doing, in Jamaica came from the roots up – it's truly a post-colonial strategy of putting together your compositions. That's what matters most to me when I hear new or old material – getting people past the psychological implications of colonialism that the likes of Aimé Césaire and Frantz Fanon explored.[13]

DJ Spooky at the Novaro Jazz Festival, 2007.

DISCO AND THE REMIX

The other dominant sound in 1970s New York was disco. Whereas Herc's break-juggling experiments were born largely from a template laid down by James Brown in the 1960s, disco emerged primarily from Gamble and Huff's Philly Sound. This was in addition to its influence from European discotheque culture, particularly from the work of dance music producers such as Italy's 'Giorgio' Moroder and France's Jean-Marc Cerrone.

Although disco does not have the same kind of overt connections to dub as, say, hip hop – which actually 'deconstructed' disco songs via the sampler for early rap tracks such as 'Rapper's Delight' (1979), which borrowed from Chic's 'Good Times', and in addition cleared the original vocals to make way for raps, just like dub had done – it sometimes still possesses certain sonic traits familiar to dub.

One such example can be found in the work of Chic, or more specially in that of their producer Nile Rodgers, who was well known for his emphasis on 'space' in the sonic construct of his songs. In an interview with BBC Radio 4's daily arts programme *Front Row* in 2005, Rodgers explains that Chic lived for 'the break-down'. He describes this as 'the stripping down of the tracks so that people could see how we built them up'.[14] According to recording industry expert Mike Alleyne,

> In relation to 'Good Times', Rodgers notes that the dance crowd's enthusiasm would be ignited by the song's decon-struction and gradual reconstruction. The transparency of this production approach is extended by the direct transfer-ence of the distinctive Chic sound, shaped with co-producer and bassist, the late Bernard Edwards, to records by other artists, practically as a commercial brand expanding its own marketplace space on records with Sister Sledge and Diana Ross. It's a percussive mechanical realisation achieved through technology which Rodgers harnesses and successfully integrates into the fabric of the song. In this sense, his sonic sensibility might be broadly compared to the mixers of dub reggae pro-duction, arguably the masters of postmodern ultra-futuristic spatial reconfiguration in popular music.[15]

Writer Dennis Howard has also noted how the

> dub aesthetic began to emerge in the work of songwriter/ producers/musicians, Nile Rodgers and Bernard Edwards

in the work of disco groups such as Chic, Sister Sledge and
Diana Ross. The emphasis of drum, bass and guitar reminiscent of reggae is clearly evident in their work. Edwards's
bass-lines were thumping and prominent in the mix and had
a thunderous low frequency resonance. Tony Thompson's
drum licks although classic 4/4 had an energy similar to
reggae because of his abundant use of his tom toms. While
Rodgers' guitar riffs were prominent, every one of their
productions possess the same energy of the ubiquitous ska
lick of reggae.[16]

A further parallel between dub and disco is the invention of
the twelve-inch remix, which occurred – like dub – by accident.
The concept of the remix is of course generally linked, and often
conflated with, the concept of 'version'. However, the two developments appear to have happened in isolation.

The disco remix coincided with the creation of the twelve-inch
single. Both were the 'inventions' of disco producer Tom Moulton.
Although he was not a DJ, Moulton saw, in the same way as DJ
Kool Herc, that people danced more wildly to certain elements of
a track. Also like Campbell (or 'DJ Kool Herc'), Moulton realized
that if he could somehow extend these elements, then people
would stay on the dance floor for longer. Rather than loop breaks
using turntables, Moulton looked to the studio for inspiration.
According to Tim Lawrence, in *Love Saves the Day*, it was while
preparing his remix of Al Downing's 'I'll Be Holding On', which
took a three-minute soul song and extended it to almost seven
minutes, that José Rodriguez, the mastering engineer working for
Moulton, happened to cut for him on a twelve-inch blank acetate
disc, purely because he had run out of seven-inch discs. Moulton
was astonished to hear the increased dynamic of the music when
spread out over the larger disc. Moulton told *DJ History* that

A couple of people gave me some tracks and I was able to make them longer and I did them in such a way that they thought wow it's like a long version of this particular song. Then someone asked me to try and do the same in a studio. So I went in there, despite not knowing anything about studios, and told 'em what I wanted and went over to Bell Sound and they said oh, it's too long to make into a 45. I said, what's wrong, what's the problem? There's too much low-end in it. Is that all? So we went back to the studio and re-EQ'd everything so it apparently had a lot of low-end, but it didn't. And that was 'Do It Till Your Satisfied' on Scepter. That was 1973.[17]

As Peter Shapiro also notes in his book on disco, *Turn the Beat Around*,

Moulton wasn't just elongating records to meet the demands of the dance floor . . . [He] was toying and playing with these records, using his equalizer to boost the bottom end and adding breaks to create disco extravaganzas out of three-minute pop songs.[18]

In other words, Moulton was applying both Kingston-style dub techniques as well as the rhythmic extensions that Kool Herc was performing on turntables in the Bronx. Yet, as he pointed out in a recent interview (December 2012), he was blithely unaware of either phenomenon. He recounts that

I wish there was a connection because I am such a lover of reggae music. When I was in Jamaica in 1974 working with Coxsone Dodd and going through all his tapes. I was going to work on these albums back in the States for the *Birth of a Legend* and the *This is Reggae* series. I really went down there because I was such a big Heptones fan. When I went back in

1975 to get more tapes I noticed they were starting the extended dub versions. I thought they were very interesting and I wish there was someway I could have used the spring echo like they used it. We had to keep everything in time or we would lose the dance floor. Because reggae is danced in double time, it would have been very difficult to try to use that in a disco and when they do the dub version the repeats are not in time. Here it was much simpler. We kept everything to a 4/4 time signature. I believe they starting using those mixes here with the dancehall craze started. You would only hear those mixes in a Jamaican club.[19]

The success of Moulton's technique led to the first commercially released remix: Double Exposure's 'Ten Percent' (1976), which was mixed by Walter Gibbons. More than any other figure on the disco scene, which by then featured legendary names including David Mancuso, Nicky Siano and Larry Levan, it was Gibbons who drew on a specific dub aesthetic to push the art of the disco remix into more creative territory.

Where Moulton had used the studio to extend the breaks, Gibbons used a similar technique as DJ Kool Herc, mixing and cutting the breaks on records such as Freddie Perren's '2 Pigs and a Hog', Rare Earth's 'Happy Song' and Jermaine Jackson's 'Erucu'. Unlike Herc, whose mixes were famously sloppy, Gibbons focused intently on precision beat matching. He was also one of the first DJs to start putting his beat mixes on tape (reel-to-reel), make his own edits and restructure tracks specifically for the dance floor. His uncompromising style became known as 'jungle music', a term loaded with dub references, from Perry and Tubby's *Blackboard Jungle Dub* album to the post-rave genre that emerged in 1990s Britain. In fact, the term originated because Gibbons's tracks were often extended by a full ten minutes and featured wild, tribal percussion and unexpected production touches.

In *Modulations*, Peter Shapiro notes how Gibbons 'used dub as a dislocating device, preventing disco's simple groove from developing under the dancers' feet'.[20] His remixes of 'Moon Maiden' by Luv You Madly Orchestra (1978) and Cellophane's 'Super Queen'/'Dance With Me (Let's Believe)' (1978) were arguably even more outré. They were forays into disassociation and strangeness, with contorted voices and stabbing strings. His Bettye LaVette remix ('Doin' the Best that I Can') was a further highlight: a stirring, eleven-minute epic that segued from an instrumental build to the vocals before setting off on a disorienting roller-coaster ride of bongos, handclaps, tambourines and shimmering instrumental interludes.

However, it was Gibbons's other wild deconstructive experiments, such as the Salsoul compilation of his remixes 'Disco Madness', which had greater play from DJs, as well as his astonishing remix of Loleatta Holloway's 'Hit and Run'. Gibbons removed the strings and horns to emphasize the rhythm track, but in true dub spirit, he went further and changed the entire sequence of the song by cutting the first two minutes and all of the verses of Holloway's vocal. According to fellow NYC DJ François Kevorkian, this was 'the real game-changer smash hit that put everyone else on notice'.

If there was anyone else who could be said to have taken the dub baton during disco's ascendance, it would be Larry Levan. Levan was the original resident DJ at legendary nightclub the Paradise Garage, a role he would keep for the entire ten years that it was open. He experimented with drum machines and synthesizers in his productions and live sets, and became a prolific producer and remixer in the late 1970s and early 1980s. Many of Levan's efforts crossed over into the national dance music charts, for example with Instant Funk's significant hit 'I Got my Mind Made Up' (1979). He added dubby effects to a number of tracks, including The Peech Boys' 'Don't Make Me Wait' (1982) and on the album *Life is Something Special* (1983).

Levan came into direct contact with the world of Jamaican dub when he met and worked for the Peech Boys on some of the remixes of songs Sly & Robbie had produced for the Island Records album *Life is Something Special* (1983). This included the landmark Gwen Guthrie 'Padlock' remix EP. He was also known for playing a great deal of reggae-influenced tracks at the Paradise Garage, and used delay processing as well as overlaying sound effects to dramatize records and to create live mixes in much the same way that Jamaican sound system DJs had done. Sly and Robbie, as well as engineer Steven Stanley, exercised an important influence on Levan's tastes during their tenure at Island Records.

Arthur Russell, a good friend of Gibbons and Levan, was overtly influenced by dub (along with just about everything else), especially its more ethereal 'ambient' side. A composer and multi-instrumentalist who lived and worked in New York during the disco era, Russell was a notoriously eccentric character with a penchant for using multitrack tape technology to achieve beguiling compositions that mixed up new wave, disco, hip hop, pop, folk and his own voice and cello.

Following in Gibbons's footsteps, Russell released a number of dub-tinged mutant disco tracks, including Dinosaur's 'Kiss Me Again' (1978), Loose Joints and his remix of 'Is it all over my Face?' (1980). Russell loved Gibbons's mix of 'Set It Off' and the pair frequently worked together. One of their earlier collaborations was a Gibbons remix of a version of Russell's seminal 'Go Bang' (unreleased/unofficial 2004 twelve-inch white label). Russell later asked Gibbons to mix 'School Bell/ Treehouse' (1986), provoking a cosmic, slightly angular splurge of bongos, cello and horns. 'School Bell/Treehouse' would later re-emerge as a voice-cello solo on Russell's groundbreaking *World of Echo*, an album that explores the meditative environment of dub space through his insouciant vocals, cello and electronics, all treated with echo, distortion and reverb.

After working as a drummer alongside Gibbons, French-born François Kevorkian soon moved into deejaying at many New York discos. He played occasional guest spots at legendary discos such as Studio 54, The Loft, Better Days and the Paradise Garage, learning the art of mixing from his peers, including Gibbons, Jellybean and Levan. He also began producing early reel-to-reel cut-ups, many patterned on dub techniques, that incorporated experimentalism into disco. He recalls that 'Being a drummer in New York at that time was tough'.

> There was a lot of competition from people who were way more experienced than I was. It was working with Gibbons around 1976 that exposed me to club music, as I suddenly had to drum along to Donna Summer and Diana Ross. That music was relatively easy to keep up with, but in the end it seemed like less hassle, and less competition, to become a DJ. I started by buying a few records, then started to also edit my own specials with scissors and scotch tape then I would get them cut onto dubplates. It was these 'special edits' that often times got me the job, and it got even better when I was offered a little money by the mastering place each time they would sell a copy of it to other DJs.[21]

Of all the disco producers of that era, it is Kevorkian who has most prominently adopted the dub aesthetic as a modus operandi. Nevertheless, he is keen to point out that dub, or even Jamaican music, were for the most part neither on his, nor on the New York underground disco scene's, radar until at least the early 1980s.

> The only Jamaican record I really heard for many years was [The Mighty Two's] *African Dub: Chapter 3*, which David Mancuso played at his Loft parties. I don't think I even consciously heard a King Tubby record until much later like 1988.

But I was always drawn to music that had a slightly superficial feel, deeper textural production touches, a certain kind of ear candy. Even as a teenager living in France there were certain songs by the Beatles or Led Zeppelin that had a different quality and they always stood out for me in a positive way. Later on I got into Hendrix, Miles Davis, Krautrock bands like Can and Kraftwerk and of course soul, free jazz, jazz-funk . . . but again it was always the slightly trippy, psychedelic stuff that hooked me in.[22]

Kevorkian had still not heard much dub when he was offered a position working to scout artists and build the repertoire for upcoming indie dance label Prelude Records, which allowed him to go into the studio (Bob Blank's was one of them) and make remixes. His initial remix of 'In the Bush' by Musique (1978) became a success in clubs and on the radio, and was the first of many that helped Prelude Records to define that era of New York's dance music. Others remixes included 'You're the One for Me' (1981) and 'Keep On' (1982) by D.Train, and 'Beat the Street' by Sharon Redd (1982). Kevorkian recounts that

> They just locked me in the studio and kept throwing these tracks at me . . . Sharon Redd, D Train. This was early '79. I didn't know about compression and these kinds of techniques. I was so starved for knowledge but it wasn't long before I picked up the tricks of the engineers, who would often just leave me to my own devices instead of watching over me all the time.
>
> Little by little I started twiddling with effects, initially to create transitions or overcome a boring drum break or something. But then around 1981 I heard a remix of Love Money by Tony Williams of TW Funk Masters fame which changed everything – gigantic reverbs, crazy processing . . . that got

me researching and at about the same time I landed a DJ job at a club called AM/PM that played reggae as well as punk and new wave and I had to learn fast; this did a great deal to quickly broaden my outlook.[23]

Kevorkian's work with Prelude Records ended in 1982. This was the same year he had the most number one singles in Billboard's dance music chart, including his mixes of now-classic songs such as 'Situation' by Yazoo and 'Go Bang' by Dinosaur L. The success of his remixes led Kevorkian to producing records for Island Records' Chris Blackwell. His first work for them was the *Snake Charmer* EP (1983), for which he collaborated with noted dub engineer Paul 'Groucho' Smykle, and pulled together an all-star cast comprising Jah Wobble, U2's The Edge and Holger Czukay and Jaki Liebezeit from German Krautrockers Can.

From this point on, dub became a permanent touchstone in Kevorkian's productions. He has applied the dub aesthetic to many of his remixes for Jimmy Cliff, Black Uhuru and Bunny Wailer, U2, Kraftwerk, The Cure, Jean Michel Jarre, Cabaret Voltaire and Depeche Mode's biggest-selling album, *Violator* (as well as many of their twelve-inch club remixes). Dub has continued to inspire Kevorkian. This is notable not only in his remix work, but in his weekly Deep Space NYC party in Manhattan. His weekly Deep Space night party in Manhattan has also brought together many of the key participants in the dub diaspora. These include the dub poet Mutabaruka and U-Roy, as well as dubstep DJs such as Mala and Kode9, and Berlin-based Rhythm & Sound, who played their first NYC DJ set there, featuring a live showcase of Wackie's vocalists.

Started in 2003, a year after the legendary Body and Soul party that he had helped found stopped running weekly, Deep Space NYC has consistently championed a range of eclectic music from funk and disco to dubstep and techno, all of which is unified by the concept of dub. Kevorkian comments that

For me it has never been so much about dub as a strict
musical genre in itself, but rather about taking the aesthetic
and applying it to anything while I am playing, whether it's
disco or rock or whatever. For that purpose I use a mixing
board that allows me to create a very versatile live dub
effect-processing situation.

For me, Deep Space NYC is a place where there has never
been musical boundaries. 40 years on from my initial involve-
ment with music, I've never stop being excited about dub, it
feels as if I've only seen it get progressively more into the
primary focus of what I do because it's like the art form
I truly feel and love. It's such an integral part of the fabric
of who I am. Its spirit is about exploring, improvisation and
experimentation, taking everyday things and making them
otherworldly, abstract and interesting. It takes music out of
our ordinary lives and allows us to build on it and fantasize.
It is indeed an unsung, yet-to-be fully acknowledged art form
whose DNA has permeated and forever altered the very fabric
of much of today's popular electronic music.[24]

5 LONDON II: UK RAP AND THE DUBCORE CONTINUUM

UK FAST STYLE

One of the influential sound systems to emerge in the London scene during the mid- to late 1970s was Lewisham's Saxon Studio International. As Blacker Dread, sometime selector for Coxsone Outernational between 1976 and 1991, noted, while Coxsone was more like a Jamaican yard sound, 'Saxon had a different English vibe'.[1] Owned by selector Lloyd Francis ('Musclehead') and managed by Dennis Rowe (D-Rowe), with Henry Prento and Mickey Boops taking care of the sound engineering, Saxon was set up in 1976. Saxon dominated reggae dancehall throughout the 1980s and into the mid-1990s. The sound started out playing the lovers rock style pioneered by Bovell, but also moved into playing heavy dub and other styles.

One of the key inspirations for Rowe was Jah Shaka. In an interview with DJ Senior P, Rowe claimed that 'Shaka is the only sound that has played from then 'til now and hasn't changed his style. That's my foundation. We were influenced by the way Shaka moved the crowd. Everyone had their style but Shaka was the king.'[2]

By the early 1980s, Saxon's deejays had started to innovate 'fast style', which took the more rapid style of Kingston deejays like U Brown and Ranking Joe and gave it a British edge and an even faster spin. The style is said to originate with Peter King, who was part of the original Saxon line-up, and popularized by his fellow Saxon deejays Papa Levi, Tippa Irie, Asher Senator and

Smiley Culture. Asher Senator's 'Fast Style Origination' (1984), released by Fashion Records, provided a quick-fire overview of the fast style scene, acknowledging King's early experiments with the style in the UK (the tune also came with its own dub mix). Saxon's style and sound was neatly captured on their *Coughing Up Fire* (1984) release, which was the very first release of a live sound system album.

Fast style's relative lack of machismo and upbeat nature made it appealing for females as well as for a younger, more stylish set of reggae fans who liked to wear clothes by Sergio Tacchini, Lacoste and Fred Perry. The lyrical content and unpretentiousness of the fast talk brigade also put practitioners on a more equal level with the audience. In the *Two Big Sound* documentary, Irie recounts that the style came about when the Saxon deejays began to write their lyrics down because they were becoming longer and longer.[3] 'We used to pride ourselves on fullin' up the riddim. While I was on sounds like Tubby's before, we just made lyrics up . . . they were more repetitive in them days, not so much lyrical content, more on the hook.'[4]

Fast style helped Saxon break many UK artists both nationally and internationally. The two main UK labels for dub and reggae at the time were Greensleeves Records and Fashion Records. Alongside the early dancehall releases coming out of Kingston (for example, *The Biggest Dancehall Anthems, 1979–1982*, which featured contributions from Yellowman, Barrington Levy, Wailing Souls and Johnny Osbourne), Greensleeves also put out fast style, released on the specially created UK Bubblers sub-label.

However, it was Fashion Records that worked more closely with the Saxon deejays and other MCs (such as Pato Banton and Macka B) from the UK scene. Fashion was started in 1980 by producer Chris Lane and John MacGillivray, who also ran the popular Dub Vendor record shop and its basement A Class Studio in Battersea, south London. The label's first release, Dee Sharp's

Asher Senator.

Asher Senator   **Fashion**
RECORDS
01 223 3757
01 223 5117

'Let's Dub it Up', reached number one in the UK reggae charts in the summer of 1980. It was followed by more reggae and lovers rock hits from Alton Ellis and Johnnie Clarke, as well as by dub albums like *Raw Rub A Dub*, *Rubble Dub* and *Burial Dub*. The label then started to put out fast style records by Asher Senator, Papa Face and Smiley Culture.

The label's *Great British M.C.'s* (1985) compilation showcased the early scene, featuring tracks like Asher Senator's 'Fast Style Origination', Papa Levi's 'Mi God Mi King' and Peter King's 'Me Neat Me Sweet', along with other B-sides and rarities. With production, and dubs, directed by Lane and his team of musicians (Drummie and Tony from Aswad, Clifton 'Bigga' Morrison, The Investigators and the Massive Horns), and later by Mafia & Fluxy, the label's *JA to UK MC Clash* series also highlighted how UK MCs and

Jamaican deejays were now on a par when it came to lyrical prowess and performance skills. Chris Lane comments that

> As far as I can recall, JA artists like Papa San and Bunny General were definitely influenced by the 'fast style'. None of them did it before the UK deejays and it was definitely a UK thing to start with. U-Roy had recorded a tune with a sort of 'fast' bit in it back in 1972, but I wouldn't say it was any sort of real influence. As for dub, we always mixed dub versions of our tunes, and put them on our twelve-inch releases and the B-sides of our singles. It wasn't as popular with the punters as it had been during its heyday in the '70s but we still liked it. I used to mix and cut dubs for sound systems everyday in the studio. They were mixed direct from the four-track straight to the cutting lathe just like Tubby's, so that every sound system would get a different mix. And we would often record specials for the sounds that wanted them but the novelty value of dub mixes had worn off for the general public . . . they were more into the vocal tunes, especially with the new breed of MCs coming up.[5]

It wasn't long before Papa Levi and Maxi Priest were signed up by major labels (Island Records and Virgin Records respectively) and fast style was climbing the UK charts via tracks like Smiley Culture's 'Cockney Translation' (1984) and 'Police Officer' (1985), and Tippa Irie's 'Hello Darling' (1986), while Philip Levi's 'Mi God Mi King' and Papa Face's 'Dance Pon De Corner' also became big hits on the Jamaican scene. A couple of years later, Senator's collaborations with Daddy Freddie such as 'Ragamuffin Hip Hop' and 'We are the Champion' capitalized on the raggamuffin craze that had been started by Half Pint's 'Greetings' tune in 1986. The latter's album, also called *Ragamuffin Hip Hop*, was released in 1988 and had an influence on the early ragga jungle scene.

Other important sound systems in the early 1980s included Channel One (an overt recognition of the Scientist and King Jammy tunes they were playing). The system was founded in 1979 by brothers Mikey Dread (UK) and Jah T (MC Ras Kayleb joined later), who had been playing parties and blues dances since 1973 with their father's sound system, 'Admiral Bailey'. In 1975 the brothers joined forces with the King Edwards sound, changed their name to 'Channel One' (owing to Dread's history with the Kingston studio) and became a force to be reckoned with in east London. Dread produced major works including Junior Murvin's 'Badman Posse' (1982) and the Singers & Players album *Leaps and Bounds* (both recorded at Kingston's Channel One studio in 1984). Dread also self-produced his 1979 album *Evolutionary Rockers*, or *Dread at the Controls*, which was again recorded in part at Channel One, as well as at King Tubby's and Joe Gibbs. The album went on to become a hit across Jamaica.

Similar to other systems of the time, Channel One regularly played out nationwide, often sharing the same bill as lovers rock, two-tone and roots bands such as Aswad, Misty in Roots, Selector and Bad Manners. In 1983 they played the Notting Hill Carnival

Flyer for Fashion Records Show, Birmingham, 1986.

for the first time, wowing an audience of just ten people; 23 years later they would play before an audience of 10,000 people.

Along with heavyweight sounds like Channel One (run by Mikey Dread and Jah T), Saxon's main competition came in the shape of Unity sound system and record label. Set up in 1982 by former Fatman affiliate and selector Robert Fearon ('Ribs'), Unity Records enjoyed a special connection with Prince Jammy and Bunny Lee in Kingston. Although Jammy gave dubs to most of the big systems of the day, such as Fatman, Jah Shaka and Coxsone, he reserved his special dubs for Unity. This included the mighty 'Sleng Teng', which Unity was the first to play in the UK. Unity latched onto the new digital sound fast and began putting out their own productions, which quickly positioned them at the vanguard of UK dancehall. Using lo-fi equipment rather than live musicians, their early records followed the vogue for electric drums and glitchy eight-bit Casio keyboards. Early hits included Selah Collins's 'Pick A Sound' (1986) and Kenny Knots's 'Watch How the People Dancing' (1987).

The increasing availability of this new digital technology changed dub and reggae in the mid-1980s. Moreover, it caused a revolution in the broader soundscape of electronic dance music. Two of Unity's best-known MCs, Flinty Badman and Deman Rockers, 'the Ragga Twins' were at the forefront of this new dawn in Britain, along with two other UK sound system veterans, PJ and Smiley (Shut Up And Dance). They wove their famed brand of fast-chat/ragga into a heady new mix of accelerated hip hop and acid house that would become known as 'jungle'. And jungle, many claimed, was the UK's version of hip hop, especially since the British attempt to emulate U.S. rap in many ways had floundered.

UK HIP HOP

The UK had a very active hip hop scene. However, it did not have far-reaching international success. Inevitably, U.S. hip hop found its way into the sound systems. By the late 1980s, sounds tended to be split between DJs who stuck with Jamaican music, such as Jah Shaka or Jah Tubby's, and others who mixed it up, playing some reggae or dancehall, along with the imported material such as soul, disco, funk and R&B.

With the widening of musical referents, audiences subsequently grew more multiracial. Hence musical and cultural hybrids emerged. In 1980, east London soul band Light of the World recorded a funk version of 'I Shot the Sheriff', while soul bands like Cashmere began to wear dreadlocks. Mastermind, one of Britain's leading and emerging MC/DJ hip hop teams (playing mostly British hip hop), from Harlesden, came up through a reggae sound system. Max LX of Mastermind Sound commented that

> With reggae sound system battles, the winner is generally the one who has the most exclusive records, or just the greatest number of versions of the same music. With the soul scene, it is basically the technical skill and imagination on the turntables, with any record, whether its electro, classical, new wave, rock or whatever. It is the way you use it, not the actual record, that is important.[6]

Evidently, this change moved at least some sound systems away from the Jamaican system of exclusives and dubplates. In addition, soul, like disco, had followed the reggae format with the advent of twelve-inch records in the late 1970s. These featured an original cut (with vocals) on one side and a 'dub' version on the other and utilized the same melody and/or rhythm. One of the key sounds to

embrace this emerging, multicultural (and multi-sonic) mix was the
aptly named 'Soul II Soul', run by Jazzie B (Trevor Beresford
Romeo).

Each of Romeo's brothers had been involved in sound systems
and clubs in one way or another. When he was just thirteen years
old, Romeo and his school friend Daddae started the Jah Rico
sound, which played mainly reggae. After a couple of years,
and influenced by sounds from West End clubs like Crackers and
Heaven, they changed the sound and the name of the set to 'Soul
II Soul'. Right from the start the ambition was to transcend a 'local
community' mindset and aim for a more international audience
and vibe. It was after landing a regular gig at the Africa Centre in
Covent Garden, in London, under the inclusive banner of
'A happy face, a thumping bass, for a loving race', that Soul II Soul
became a major phenomenon in UK soul music. In 1986 they
signed to Virgin Records as a band. In 1989 they put UK soul on
the international map with their *Club Classics Vol. 1*, which earned
them two Grammy Awards in 1990, and subsequent deals with
major labels including Motown, Epic and Island Records. In 2008
Romeo was awarded an OBE (Order of the British Empire) for his
services to the music industry, particularly in Britain.

Apart from one-hit wonders like Derek B (Derek Boland),
who raced up the UK charts with 'Goodgroove' and 'Bad Young
Brother' in 1988, and Hijack, who were briefly signed to Ice T's
Rhyme Syndicate records, British hip hop didn't enjoy any similar
major successes, at least in the early years. By the mid-1980s, it
was still American rap that was becoming increasingly widespread
on the systems and in the clubs. One of the first dedicated hip
hop nights in London was the Original Language Lab, started in
1982. In 1984 UK hip hop aficionado Tim Westwood (who had a
radio show on LWR (London Weekend Radio), a radio station that
he helped pioneer, organized a groundbreaking hip hop festival
sponsored by the Greater London Council (GLC) at the South Bank

arts centre. The festival put on a display of dancing, mixing, graffiti and rap that attracted over 30,000 spectators. From 1986 Westwood also had a residency behind the decks at Covent Garden's Spats club (with DJ Fingers), and later organized his UK Fresh event, which drew 16,000 people to Wembley Arena to watch Afrika Bambaataa, Grandmaster Flash, Mantronix Lovebug Starski, Roxanne Shante and other artists.

As in New York City, some of the earliest UK hip hop was released on Jamaican labels. One significant release was the now-legendary *Soul All Dayer of the Century*, which came out on Sir Lloyd's Raiders Music label in 1987 with artwork by Greensleeves Records' Tony McDermott. Along with the label's *Live at DSYC* (Dick Shepherd Youth Club) series, the component records of which were recorded live in Tulse Hill, south London, in 1983, and were notable for including some of the first fast chat on vinyl, and featuring the biggest London systems of the time from Saxon to Tubby's, SADOTC also documents the genesis of recorded UK fast chat and rap.

The UK equivalent of Bambaataa's *Death Mix* (1983), which had been recorded at James Monroe High School in the Bronx, the *Soul All Dayer of the Century*, featured a sound-system clash between the Beat Freak (run by Mike West, aka 'Rebel MC', aka 'Congo Natty'), Main Attraction and TNT. (The latter was run by DJ Ron, who would also go on to become a star of the jungle scene.) Recorded at Hammersmith and Acton Town Halls in west London over two days, the record is arguably a wonderful snapshot of a key moment in British sound system and urban music culture. The three systems take it in turns to drop their best tunes – a mix of acid house, old school electro, street soul and reggae. British roots artist Pablo Gad gets spliced with Bambaattaa's seminal 'Planet Rock'; a Beastie Boys instrumental is blended with Joseph Cotton (Jah Walton) and the theme from *Singin' in the Rain*. The mixes are loose but thrilling and interspersed with air

horns, whistles and cheers from the crowd. Although British rap
acts didn't have much luck, at least UK DJs kicked some ass when it
came to scratching. The winner of the inaugural DMC DJ Champion-
ships in 1984 was Roger Johnson from the UK. In 1985 and 1986 the
title was retained by Britons Chad Jackson and C. J. Mackintosh,
respectively. DJ Cash Money took the belts back to the U.S. in 1987,
but the year after, east London's DJ Pogo triumphed, followed by
his friend Cutmaster Swift in 1990.

The problem with British rap was that it was in an English
that sounded 'inauthentic' compared with the American original.
The scene bifurcated early on with artists like Derek B and Monie
Love emulating their American role models a little too closely for
many. On the other hand, acts that had come up through the
sound system and fast style route, such as the London Posse,
Asher D and Black Radical Mk II, developed a more 'homegrown
style', with abrasive cockney accents mixed with West Indian
patois and a barrage of reggae and dancehall samples.

Many of the MCs in this vein had run with reggae sounds. MC
Mell'O, for example, grew up and attended school in Battersea.
He was surrounded by the sound systems of Sir Coxsone Outer-
national and Young Lion respectively. Tim Westwood came up
under legendary radio DJ and Jamaican music aficionado David
Rodigan, while Black Radical MkII has cited Saxon, particularly
Papa Levi and Smiley Culture, as influences.

One of the most successful crews to rhyme in a similar
style to the fast talk MCs were the London Posse, comprising MC
Rodie Rok (later 'Rodney P'), Bionic, Sipho the Human Beatbox
and DJ Biznizz. The band was formed to support The Clash for
their New York show in 1986. For Rodney, who was born and
raised in Battersea, south London, 'Going to New York was a big
lesson for us.'

We realised early on that people didn't want a cheap imitation of [the hip hop] they had. I'm sure a lot of British Jamaicans had the same thing when they went to Kingston – it would have been better to bring something original and authentic to the table than pretend to be Jamaican.

Reggae was how I grew up. It was reggae at home and then around school it was about sound systems, collecting and listening to tapes. Coxsone, Saxon and Unity were the big ones, but I was only a kid so it was more about local ones like Hustler who were down my way in Battersea. It was also part of what we did. My older brother Patrick was a sound-man, still is. We'd steal speakers, chop wood to make boxes, then carry them to the dance.

When we started doing hip hop it was about more than being Jamaican. It was about a black UK thing. Sure we'd listen to dub and lovers rock and all that, but we were into the Tippa Irie's, the people who were more British than Jamaican. That was our whole philosophy with the London Posse. We weren't Jamaican and we weren't American. A lot of rap acts in the UK were mixing the reggae thing but we were the first to chat in the accents so blatantly. We were black kids from the UK and that's how we wanted to sound.[7]

London Posse dropped their self-released debut single 'London Posse / My Beatbox Reggae Style' in 1987. Produced by Tim Westwood, its staggering A-side mixed brash cockney accents and yard slang, while the B-side fused old school beatboxing – the first UK cut to consist solely of a beatboxer providing the backing track – and reggae samples.

The original (nine-minute) mix of their hit single 'Money Mad' came with an intense B-side dub version complete with plangent echoes, reverbs and sirens that were all mixed live. In 1990 they released their one and only album, *Gangster Chronicles*

(Mango Records), which nowadays is considered one of the classics of UK rap (it was rereleased in 2001 by Wordsound). In the early 1990s they released more London-meets-reggae-style hip hop including 'How's Life in London' (1993) and explored the emerging ragga and jungle styles with 'How's Life in London' (Ragga Mix) and 'Pass the Rizla' (1994), produced by rave act Kicks Like a Mule, while 'Style' (1996) was influenced by the drum and bass scene. The group broke up shortly after, with Bionic taking on a role as MC with Hyper D (who also appeared on Tricky's *Juxtapose* album (1999) as 'Mad Dog'), and Rodney teaming up with DJ and fellow reggae/dub fan Skitz, the Dub Pistols and Roni Size, among others.

In the 1990s another British hip hop artist had notable success with the same Britain-via-West-Indies approach. Roots Manuva (Rodney Smith) ambled on the scene with a laid-back style that emphasized, rather than denying, his hybrid British-Jamaican psyche. Owing to his parents' strict Pentecostal faith, Smith's south London home was largely a reggae-free zone. However, his older brother often snuck in imported Jamaican records and copies of the specialist music magazine *Black Echoes*. Although at that point he was too young to immerse himself in London's Jamaican club and party scene, Smith fondly recalls experiencing sound systems at family weddings and christenings, and cassette recordings of leading 'sounds' such as Saxon that were traded at secondary school.

> Before I even knew what a sound system was, I was walking past Stockwell skateboard park and there was this sound being set up. They were probably just trying out their speakers. I was with my mum, holding her hand, and I remember she was quite intimidated by the whole affair. Such a barrage of bass coming from it! And these dodgy-looking blokes standing beside it, just admiring the sound of the bass. It's definitely

a bass thing, a volume thing. I don't know if I rose-tint the memories, but I remember it sounded so good, so rich. It's not like today when we go to clubs and it hurts. It was more of a life-giving bass.[8]

Smith grew up watching artists such as Tippa Irie, Smiley Culture and Maxi Priest climbing the British charts. He was also part of a sound called 'Trojan II' for a while. Although Smith's mellow delivery is spiced with patois and references to London buses and pints of Guinness, his music is defiantly eclectic. His debut album, *Brand New Second Hand* (1999), whose title is a reference to his mother's favourite phrase when presenting him with hand-me-down gifts, joined the dots between trip hop, drum and bass, hip hop and dancehall. It won widespread media acclaim and a 1999 MOBO for Best Hip Hop Act.

Arguably, more than any other UK rap artist, dub has remained a central thread throughout Smith's work. His 'Dub College' is an umbrella concept that includes a club night with established and emerging talent and a podcast tour through the vaults of vintage Jamaican music.

I was drawn initially to production through dub. Its history is cast in stone and anyone trying to deny it is awfully mis-informed. But the meaning of the term has evolved. A kid in Hackney today ain't gonna think of a Studio One instrumental, but a bonus track on a Caspa download or an MJ Cole mix. The dub college is about trying to put all this stuff in context, trace its evolution. I really sometimes wonder to myself: in 100 years time, is someone be able to tell the difference between 2-step and jungle, hip hop and dancehall?[9]

Smith has also released dub versions of his entire albums: *Dub Come Save Me* (2002), a reverb-drenched reworking of *Run Come*

Save Me (2001), and *Alternately Deep* (2006), the dub version to the previous year's studio album *Awfully Deep.* This features alternate mixes, remixes and unreleased material, and remixes from Jammer. For *Duppy Writer* (2010), he handed over his entire back catalogue to reggae DJ/producer Wrongtom, who once produced the seven-inch King Tubby tribute *Wrongtom Meets the Rockers East of Medina* only available with their first LP.

Wrongtom, who also helped put together the dubbed-out post-punk *Spiky Dread* compilation (see chapter Three), was turned onto dub records like *King Tubby Meets Rockers Uptown*, Pablo's *Ital Dub* and Gibbs's *African Dub Chapter 4*, as well as Renegade Soundwave's *In Dub.* His approach on *Duppy Writer* was less dub-based than re-imagining how the songs might have sounded had they been recorded in 1970s Kingston, with warm, vintage-sounding results.

Roots Manuva (Rodney Smith).

I came at music making from a non musical perspective, MCs and lyrics were my main focus, and then gradually I started to pick apart the sounds which made up the tracks I loved. Rather than being interested in one particular instrument, I wanted to know how those sounds were captured and how they worked together, so I guess dub versions were a great way of getting my head around production – that moment everything drops out except the bass, or guitar, or whatever, it's like peering behind the great wizard's curtain and discovering all this magic is being made by a normal guy sitting at his mixing desk. I love the idea that someone who can't necessarily play an instrument or make music in its traditional sense can create something through deconstruction, it's quite empowering.[10]

For his album *Wrongtom Meets Deemas J Album in East London* (2012), the producer/DJ teamed up with MC Deemas J, formerly of Fatman Hi-Fi and a dabbler in the garage and jungle scenes to create a 'modern reggae record'. The album covers all of the main influential Jamaican sounds from dub to rocksteady to dancehall, with Deemas paying verbal tribute to everyone from U-Roy to the Fashion/Saxon crew. Notably, the sleeve artwork is by Tony McDermott, who designed the celebrated Scientist covers in the 1980s.

THE DUBCORE CONTINUUM: JUNGLE 2 DUBSTEP

As UK rap generally maintained a low-key presence compared to its American counterpart, the legacy of fast talk MCs and many of the rituals of the sound system merged into jungle. Along with the Ragga Twins, two of the early pioneers of jungle were PJ and Smiley (later Shut Up And Dance), who in 1986 had set up the Heatwave sound with DJ Daddy and DJ Hype. When they started

Heatwave, PJ and Smiley were still in their teens but were already sound system veterans. They joined a growing number of sets which would mix up hip hop, soul, funk and reggae but retained the sound system tradition of playing in empty houses or warehouses and trading in dubplates and specials. PJ reflected in 2012:

We was young when we started out, like twelve or something, so we didn't really understand sounds like Jah Shaka at first. That came later because it was more for the grown ups. By the time I was sixteen or seventeen we were going to his dances though, as well as Jah Tubby's, who actually came and played one of our school dances in the '80s in Hackney! We were just kids when we started our first sound.[11]

Heatwave was also unique in so far as DJ Hype was one of the first to start cutting and scratching reggae and dancehall tunes in the same way that Herc had done with funk and soul, thereby bringing more of a hip hop feel to the set. Smiley comments 'Not everyone liked it, but we just kept going. We always started off with dub in our sets, Augustus Pablo and that kind of stuff, as a warm up. It was always there, and stayed there when we made our first productions too.'[12]

Those first productions borrowed from house music, pop, dub, reggae and hip hop. For example, 'Lamborghini' (1989) sampled the Eurythmics' 'Sweet Dreams (Are Made of This)'; '£10 to Get In' used bits of Suzanne Vega's 'Tom's Diner' and added some ragga vocals and a throbbing acidic beat; '5.6.7.8' (1989) sampled George Kranz's 'Din Daa Daa'. Around 1990 they drafted in the Ragga Twins to record some of their vocals. Subsequent tracks like 'Illegal Gunshot' (1990) melded the latter duo's notorious fast-ragga to an upbeat, dancehall-inflected riddim. The B-side, 'Spliffhead', with its sampled ragga vocal, atmospheric synth build, sirens and mash-up feel, laid the foundations for the jungle/rave phenomenon that would take the British underground by storm (aided by DJ Hype, who was by now co-producing jungle by The Scientist).

Although submerged in a maelstrom of influences, the influence of dub, reggae and the sound system scene can be heard explicitly, from the heavy dub sample in '18″ Speaker' to song titles like 'Hooligan 69' (1991), named after a dubplate special that Jah Tubby used to play.

Jungle took off in a way that British rap never did. It was unstoppable in the late 1980s and early 1990s. The Ragga Twins and Shut Up And Dance were joined by Lenny De Ice ('We Are i.e', 1991), Bodysnatch's 'Euphony' (or 'Just 4 U London', 1992) and more commercial fare such as The Prodigy's Max Romeo-sampling 'Out of Space' (1992).

In *Last Night a DJ Saved My Life*, jungle DJ and producer Fabio, who started out as a house DJ on pirate radio along with his long-term music partner Grooverider, recounts how early rave clubs were very similar to Jamaican blues parties, which he subsequently claims were the 'original club scene'.

On Saturday nights you could have five or six parties going on. They were in people's houses, or they'd rig up a sound system in old squats. They'd charge like £2 on the door, they'd have a little bar set up; the whole thing was about going in and buying drinks. You'd have the guy who hosted the night – the MC – and the guy who used the play music; there was this narration and it was brilliant.[13]

Greensleeves Records, which had championed Jamaican and UK-based Jamaican music throughout the 1980s, also supported young UK jungle producers, especially those who were sampling their catalogue (including Bounty Killer, Beenie Man, Barrington Levy). The scene reached its peak in the mid-1990s, defined by tracks such as Code Red's 'Conquering Lion' (1994), which

combined elements from Reggie Stepper's 'Drum Pan Sound',
Supercat's 'Oh It's You' and Barrington Levy's 'Murderer', Rat
Pack's number one hit 'Searching For My Rizla' (1994) and M Beat
and General Levy's 'Incredible' (1994), which made it onto the
BBC's chart show *Top of the Pops* and also got Levy ostracized from
the jungle scene for 'selling out'.

Music writer Simon Reynolds once described jungle as 'postmodern dub on steroids'.[14] Especially around the mid-'90s, it was
difficult not to see the overlaps between the half-time basslines,
double-time percussion (presaged in echo-drenched dub tracks)
as well as the foregrounding of tracks with deejaying and/or
fragmented texts. It was no coincidence that one of jungle's
main cutting houses, Music House, had posters of King Tubby
and Jah Shaka on the walls.

While dub's specific 'versioning' strategies have by now been
replaced by the sampler-fuelled mash-up, its influence on jungle is
still evident. Indeed, jungle's programmed beats and layered
samples proved a perfect match for dubwise basslines that sounded
huge at the outdoor raves and underground venues then taking
over from the sound systems in the UK. However, associated rituals
such as dubplates, specials, rewinds and live MCs (as well as those
sampled on the records) were preserved wholesale.

Jungle even had its own recyclable riddim in the shape of The
Winstons' 'Amen, Brother' break. The record's funk-heavy drum
solo performed by Greg Coleman entered the hip hop scene when
it was then sped up for the *Ultimate Breaks and Beats* album (1986).
It was sped up and sampled interminably for a never-ending flow
of classic tunes, from Lennie de Ice's 'We are i.e.' to LTJ Bukem's
'Demon's Theme' (1992) and Shy FX featuring UK Apachi's
'Original Nuttah' (1994).

Congo Natty (Mike West) was one of the first producers to
properly bring reggae artists into jungle, working with artists
including Dennis Brown, Tenor Fly and Barrington Levy. His

album *Black Meaning Good* (1991) is one of the proto-jungle classics, and led to cult tracks like 'Tribal Bass' and 'The Wickedest Sound' (featuring Tenor Fly). At the time of writing, he is working with Lee 'Scratch' Perry on the *21st Century Dubwise* project. This is in addition to a collaborative project with Mala that has a mysterious King Tubby connection. As such, West sees no difference between the cultures of dub and jungle:

> Dub music is the foundation of what I do. I grew up on dub. I would work as a youth to save money to buy the last dub LPS from the year. Lee Perry, King Tubby, Prince Jammy. Dub and reggae was my first teacher. Dub is inside me, sub basslines run through my veins. I would stand in front of the double eighteen-inch bass speakers and not move till I left the dance as a thirteen year old. Jungle music is the son of dub reggae and so is grime, dubstep, hip hop, all sub bass music comes down from the [Black] Ark. Dub is the building block – the stone the builder refused is now the cornerstone of music and culture. It's the heartbeat of mankind.[15]

As the sound system scene started shifting back to a roots-driven 'digidub' sound, jungle played an important role in the survival of the MC. The Ragga Twins, 5ive'O, Navigator, Moose, Det, GQ and Stevie Hyper D were some of the names chatting over the hyperkinetic breaks and hyping the crowds, along with the occasional live appearance from sound system stars such as Tippa Irie. MCs were also prevalent on pirate radio stations, which were essential to making the sound known nationwide. (In recognition of this airplay, Kool FM, one of the main junglist stations, was memorialized in Krome & Mr Times's 'The Licence', which features a sample of Saxon's Papa Levi.)

While jungle had been all the rage at UK clubs like AWOL (A Way of Life), Jungle Rush, Jungle Fever, Roast and Thrust, by

1995 the scene had reached its peak and ragga-tinged songs were starting to sound gimmicky. DJs such as Fabio and LTJ Bukem made a conscious effort to drive the music into new, mellower directions at a new club night called Speed. In the meantime Goldie was forging his own unique Metalheadz sound (and brand) at the Blue Note Club.

In 1995 the ragga jungle scene was all but over. After all the adrenalin-fuelled 'jump up' activity, it was time for a more thoughtful refinement of the genre, which arrived in the form of drum and bass. Despite borrowing its name from the alternative Jamaican term for 'version', British D&B moved slightly away from the dance hall, switching testosterone-fuelled riddims and hip hop/ragga chants for more subtle drum patterns and soul and jazz-influenced musical elements. Nevertheless, the emphasis on the bassline remained, as did sound system rituals such as rewinds and dubplates.

The same rituals were maintained by the next development in the so-called hardcore continuum: 2-step garage. Also known as 'UK Garage' (UKG), 2-step grew out of the house and garage scene. From 1995, this began to merge jungle with imported U.S. house (known as 'garage') by beefing up the rhythm and the bottom end and throwing in the occasional cut-up or time-stretched ragga vocal for kicks. A good example is 187 Lockdown's 'Gunman' or Double 99's 'Rip Groove' (1997).

One of the early leading UKG protagonists was Karl 'Tuff Enuff' Brown, who along with Congo Natty had been part of chart-toppers Double Trouble and the Rebel MC in the late 1980s. After starting out on a sound system called Knight Rider that played dub, reggae, lovers rock and rare grooves, Brown joined forces with DJ Matt 'Jam' Lamont to form the Tuff Jam production team. Their singles and remixes, which ranged from mixes of garage anthems such as 'Rip Groove' to high-profile artists including Usher, Coolio, Boys II Men and En Vogue, had an influence on the emerging sound. Their work was also helped along by a peak-time radio show on Kiss FM. Furthermore, their compilation *Tuff Jam Presents: Underground Frequencies Volume 1* (1997) featured many of the seminal 'speed garage' tunes of the time, mixing up British and American tracks such as Roy Davis Jr's 'Gabrielle', Armand Van Helden's 'dark garage' mix of the Sneaker Pimps' 'Spin Spin Sugar' and more tracks by Double 99, Tine Moore and Tuff Jam themselves.

It was 'Gabrielle' (1996) by Chicago producer Roy Davis Jr that helped kickstart a move towards the syncopated, more insouciant sound that would become known as '2-step'. While speed garage and 2-step coexisted for a year or two, by the end of 1998 it was the latter that ruled the airwaves – both the commercial dance stations and pirates like Freak FM, Kool FM, Deja Vu and Rinse FM. Adding to the fresh, mainstream appeal of the 2-step sound was its openness to vocals and MCs, which took it into both more mainstream and more underground directions. DJ Luck & MC Neat's *A Little Bit of Luck* (2001) was a highly commercial example, while producer Sticky produced a number of rawer, more underground hits featuring MCs mixing up Jamaican and London sounds, including Ms Dynamite's 'Booo!' (2001) and Stush's 'Dollar Sign' (2002).

One of the main protagonists of the cleaner, 'skippier' sound was MJ Cole (Matthew James Firth Coleman), a classically trained musician who worked as a sound engineer for seminal jungle label SOUR (Sound of the Underground Records). His silky, saccharine hits such as 'Sincere' (1998) and 'Crazy Love' (2000) were joined by similarly insouciant fare including Ramsey and Fen's 'Lovebug' (1998), DJ Luck & MC Neat's 'A Little Bit Of Luck' (2001) and 'Masterblaster 2000' (a Stevie Wonder cover), and Craig David and Artful Dodger's chart-topping hit 'Re-Rewind' (2000).

But even as UKG was embracing a summery, feel-good vibe, it was starting to darken at the edges. Oxide & Neutrino's 'Bound 4

Da Reload' (2000) sported aggressive gunshots and sirens (sampled from the theme tune of BBC hospital drama *Casualty* and the British film *Lock, Stock and Two Smoking Barrels*), and MC-led 'posses' started to appear, such as the So Solid Crew and their rivals, the Hit Squad. Members of the Hit Squad joined with another crew, Pay As U Go, who in turn were rivalled by Ghana-heavy grime collective Ruff Sqwad from the Bow area of east London, where grime was officially born. Pay As U Go emphasized their Jamaican influence with club hits like 'Know We' (2006) and 'Champagne Dance' (2007), and one of the Posse's key members, Wiley (Richard Kylea Cowie, a former jungle MC), went on to form the Roll Deep collective with former Ruff Sqwad members Dizzee Rascal and Tinchy Stryder.

Seminal grime compilations *Run the Road* (2005) offered a snapshot of the scene's main players. These included Roll Deep, Dizzee Rascal, Jammer, Kano and Wiley, and female MCs Shystie, No Lay and Lady Sovereign. By this point the scene had developed some specific characteristics: a combative, anti-mainstream attitude, a deliberately DIY infrastructure (with homemade CDs and DVDs, basement battles, dedicated pirate radio stations such as Rinse FM and Freeze FM) and legions of 'rudebwoys' spitting uncompromising lyrics about life in London.

Grime's raw production sound, built on Sony PlayStations, is reminiscent of the lo-fi sound of the 1980s digidub scene. The bedroom experimentation is also reminiscent of Kingston's own restricted environments. Indeed, it is sometimes just as innovative, with tracks such as Tinchy Strider's 'Underground' (2006) using the sound of barking dogs as percussion. The scene even has its own labyrinthine riddim culture, with producers building rhythms and several different versions, freestyles or radio sets recorded over them.

Grime carries specific links to the dance hall. One example is producer/MC Jammer (Jahmek Power), formerly of the Boy Better Know and NASTY Crews, the man behind the formative *Lord*

of the Mics DVD series. Power's father had a sound system (and
a ten-piece roots reggae band), and Power was 'rockin' the mic'
at dances before he was a teenager. At the age of eleven, Power
put together a recording studio from equipment his father had
brought home. In relation to Jammer, Lloyd Bradley describes
how grime

> follows the Jamaican sound-system model from the 1950s,
> whereby producers recorded tunes to play at their dances
> and whatever got a good reception from the crowd got
> released, on their own labels. It allowed the music to develop
> organically, rather than be forced to conform to established
> commercial guidelines or playlist pressure.[16]

Jammer's debut album *Jahmanji* (2010) is a potent mix of fragmented riddims, intensely rapid vocals and experimental twists.
On 'Back to the '90s', it acknowledges proto-jungle / rave as an
influence. Jammer also explains how grime is starting to cater to
broader and changing tastes, and how more musical and lyrical
aspects will come through:

> Like the lover's rock thing with reggae, the more melodic
> thing will come back. Now the mainstream is catching up with
> us, we've got more opportunities to make different styles of
> grime. Like with hip-hop, where the artists have become the
> people who run the business, so will we.[17]

Over the years, the grime scene has indeed enjoyed commercial
success. Dizzee Rascal's *Boy in da Corner* (2003), a heavy and
occasionally aggressive album by anyone's standards, won the
Mercury Prize. Wiley's debut album, the even rawer *Treddin' on
Thin Ice* (2004), similarly garnered many accolades. Both artists have
since hit the charts with more commercial offerings, opening the

way for hip hop/grime crossover acts such as Ms Dynamite, Sway, Tinchy Stryder and Magnetic Man. Yet even the genre's godfathers, Wiley and Dizzee, still create potent songs packed with a rebellious, street-smart energy. Wiley has proved especially unpredictable, regularly sacking his manager and giving away entire .zip files on Twitter packed with recordings .

The thread of British MC culture is charted back to the Jamaican deejays on *An England Story: The Culture of the MC in the UK, 1994–2008*. The album is compiled by Gervase de Wilde and Gabriel Myddelton, founder of the bashment/dancehall Heatwave sound system in London and associated Hot Wuk nights. The compilation aims to show how dancehall is the root of jungle, garage, grime, dubstep and funky. It covers 25 years of recorded MC-led music, including tracks by Roots Manuva, Tippa Irie, General Levy, Estelle and Papa Levi, as well as grime MCs including Doctor (the son of Saxon owner Dennis Rowe). In the sleeve notes, de Wilde and Myddelton write that

> The global preeminence of American hip hop means that music like grime and UK hip hop is often seen as a form of rap, whereas it owes as much to reggae music and culture as it does to any American influence. Black music in Britain has fashioned its own identity in contrast to that of America, Africa, or elsewhere, by drawing on the unique relationship that the UK has with the Caribbean.[18]

Or as Rodney P puts it in the same sleeve notes, 'This is a UK thing, it's hip hop and it's reggae and we do reggae – and those Americans don't know about that.'

While grime's emphasis on verbal prowess provided a fresh angle for British MCs, one that ultimately references Kingston's original deejay culture, another genre evolved from 2-step that focused more on the sonic side of dub. Known at the time of its emergence as 'dark garage', this sound stripped 2-step back to an often menacing skeleton of heavy bass and stark, rattling rhythms. The style would become known, aptly enough, as 'dubstep'.

Although there were proto-dubstep experiments even before the millennium, dubstep really came on the radar around 2003. Whereas grime was born in east London, dubstep was a south London movement, which grew initially out of the Big Apple record shop in Croydon. In contrast to the cocaine / champagne lifestyle of 2-step (and associated clubs such as Twice As Nice), dubstep nights attracted the kind of people who liked to keep their heads down and zone out to the music's alienating, spaced-out feel.

One of the first club nights to embrace the sound was Forward (FWD»), held first at the Velvet Rooms in Soho, London, in 2001, before moving to the Plastic People venue in Shoreditch. Run by Ammunition Promotions, the company also responsible for various early dubstep labels like Tempa, Soulja, Road, Texture, Lifestyle and Bingo, the original FWD» line-ups included many regular and guest DJs – Hatcha, Youngsta, Kode9, Skream, Benga, for example, who would become the first luminaries of the dubstep scene.

While much of dubstep is so far removed from its original Jamaican namesake that it cannot be compared to it, certain of the scene's protagonists display a respectful appreciation for the Kingston originators and the rituals of the dance hall. Although they are ostensibly two separate music forms, there are some obvious overlaps. Dubstep tracks often, but not always, use spatial atmospherics, low-end frequencies and dark, psychedelic moods, and they are mostly produced at 140 bpm (beats per minute). This makes them rhythmically compatible with much original, and new school, dub, as well as drum and bass.

Many producers and DJs in the dubstep scene used to cut their recordings as one-off ten-inch dubplates. Some, like south

London collective Digital Mystikz (Mala and Coki), the owners of the DMZ record label along with old friends and collaborators Loefah and MC Sgt Pokes, still work closely with sound system culture in their ethos and sound.

Their hugely influential nightclub DMZ, held at Mass in Brixton, carried the slogan 'Come and meditate on bass weight'. And over the years, Mala (Mark Lawrence) has put out a consistent flow of dubstep tunes notable for their stripped down, minimal drum programming and deep, meditative bass. This includes his twelve-inch split-collaborations with Loefah for his 2004 A-side 'Da Wrath' and Four Tet for the B-side track, as well as solo releases on DMZ such as 'Left Leg Out / Blue Notez' (2006). In 2007 he remixed Johnny Clark's 'Sinner', and teamed up with On-U-Sound to remix Lee Perry's 'Like The Way You Should' and 'Obeah Room' (as 'Digital Mystikz'). 'New Life Baby Paris' from 2008 samples the introduction to the Misty in Roots debut from 1978. His collection of tracks (he doesn't like to refer to it as an album) called *Return to Space* (2010) was also notable for its intensely brooding dubwise style. Mala pinpoints his influences and musical direction as follows:

> We just produced our music based on whatever we were listening to. Which happened to be music with heavy, sub-low frequencies like jungle, dub and reggae. In that sense dubstep was a reflection of what we were into. I wasn't a dub fanatic or trying to recreate it or anything, but it was definitely in the mix. My father is Jamaican and so are Coki's parents . . . Growing up in South Norwood in south London, we heard Jah Shaka, Iration Steppas, Aba Shanti-I, Channel One, Jah Tubbys, though mostly it was jungle raves. But even there I remember the people setting up the sound systems at raves like Metalheadz, and that definitely had an influence on how I wanted my sound. That weight and frequency. I also just feel lucky growing up in London, with its multicultural community

Mala and Mikey Dread (left), February 2012.

and concrete. My sound couldn't have developed the way
it has anywhere else in the world. Britain isn't Jamaica but
it's still an island, with an island mentality.[19]

Mala is one of the few producers left on the dubstep scene who
cuts dubplates. His preferred cutting house is Transition in south
London. He laments the fact that many of his peers have given up
because the technical requirements for playing vinyl are not met
by promoters and music venues.

> I don't think there's anything intrinsically wrong with other
> formats, but I just prefer analogue. Cutting your own plates
> means you learn a lot about your own productions. You
> hear them differently. Doing this made me very objective
> and critical, because in the end you're paying £30 or £40 for
> two sides of a dubplate so it has to be right or you waste

your money. It definitely raised my game as a producer.
There's also the community angle. You get to work with
an engineer who will often end up mastering your records.
They're community centres too; I met Kode9 for the first
time at Transition. It's a bit like record shops. It's a shame
these things are disappearing as they're removing the human
side of things. What does this mean for future generations?[20]

His latest project (2012) took him to the Caribbean – not Jamaica
but Cuba. There, in collaboration with Havana Cultura and Gilles
Peterson, he worked with local musicians to create a strange but
unique amalgam of dubstep tempos and live Cuban rhythms, all of
which are played at 140 bpm, digitally mixed and processed
through Mala's desk.

It was a pleasure to work with them and the rhythms and
percussions they play. It felt completely natural, although to
have musicians of the calibre of Roberto Fonseca, who used
to play with the Buena Vista Social Club, making music just
for me, at my requested tempo in a beautiful studio in Havana
was, well, mind-blowing.[21]

It was DJ Mary Anne Hobbs's *Dubstep Warz* (2006) special on BBC
Radio 1 that helped tip dubstep towards the mainstream, and ulti-
mately towards its most clichéd 'brostep' phase (see, for example,
Rusko's smasher 'Cockney Thug', 2009). By the end of the noughties,
the music was being adopted by artists including La Roux (notably,
Skream's version of 'In For the Kill', 2008, and artists such as Sonny
Moore, aka Skrillex, who stripped away all the interesting subtleties
of the sound and reduced it to its lowest common denominators).
But not everyone has followed the genre into its 'dumbed down'
phase. As seen in Wiley's hit 'Wot Do U Call It?' (2004), the divisions
between house, garage, dancehall, grime and dubstep have not

always been clear cut, and many producers have continued to deliberately dissolve the boundaries entirely; 'Switching Songs' (2008), by
grime MC Durrty Goodz, referenced this trend by stringing together
dozens of well-known 2-step, grime and dubstep riddims.

Labels such as Night Slugs (Jam City, Girl Unit) in London,
run by former grime DJ Bok Bok, have captured some of this
in-between music. One of the best-known labels, however, is
Hyperdub, which scored an unexpectedly huge hit with secretive
producer Burial and his second album, *Untrue* (2007). The record's
singular blend of rattling garage and dubstep beats, sombre late-
night melodies and melancholic soul samples felt like an update
of the uniquely British Massive Attack sound. The Hyperdub
label, whose roster also includes artists like Darkstar, Ikonika,
Joker and Flying Lotus, was formed by DJ, producer, writer and
academic Steve Goodman (Kode9) in 2004. Originally from
Glasgow, Goodman moved to London at the end of the 1990s
to be closer to the jungle scene that he loved. He attended nights
like Metalheadz before starting Hyperdub as an online magazine,
with the 'main editorial remit [as] the Jamaican influence on
London electronic music'. In 2004 he turned Hyperdub into a
label to release his own 'Sine of Dub' single (as Kode9), which
reduced Prince's 'Sign o' the Times' to a minimal dub pulse.

> I came up with [Hyperdub] as a concept for a website. It
> was a way of trying to have a word that would just describe
> a lineage of Black Atlantic music particularly coming out of
> dub and funk. Early '70s Jamaican and Afro American music
> in particular, right through to jungle and garage. It was just
> an attempt to . . . [there's] not an exact word that captures
> that, but just have a loose sense of the feeling of those musics
> for about the last 40 or 50 years, and the skeleton of what it
> was that held them together . . . just rhythm and bass.[22]

As a producer, Goodman has collaborated with Lee 'Scratch' Perry ('Yellow Tongue', 2009) for a limited edition vinyl release, as well as with Digital Mystikz. However, his two main musical statements are his collaborations with MC Spaceape – *Memories of the Future* (2006) and *Black Sun* (2011). On these records, Goodman strips songs down to a translucent, sometimes unnerving core, fusing them with the 'dread poetry' of Spaceape (Daddi Gee).

One of the newer Hyperdub artists is King Midas Sound, formed by Kevin Martin, poet Roger Robinson and Japanese artist and singer Kiki Hitomi. Martin prompted Goodman to start the Hyperdub label. With a background in rockabilly, punk and post-punk, It was Martin who allegedly has an impressive CV that includes working with MCs such as Warrior Queen, Flowdan and Tippa Irie, while merging various genres including dancehall, noise, grime, hip hop and dub. His highly acclaimed two-disc compilation *Macro Dub Infection* (1995) collected together some of dub's less obvious collisions with other music by Tricky, Two Badcard, Skull vs. Ice and Mad Professor, amongst others. Martin's own musical personas and hybrids have included the 'jazzcore' outfit God and industrial hip-hop troupe Techno Animal, plus collaborations with post-punk legends Keith Levene (The Clash and PiL) and Mark Stewart. For his project The Bug, Martin also worked with Stewart on a remake of T-Rex's 'Children of the Revolution' in 2011.

> I feel scarred for life by my first experience with sound systems. I can still remember vividly the first one I went to, which was in the east end of London. It was in a horrible old warehouse and it was The Disciples and Iration Steppas having a face off. There was no light apart from a bulb over each sound system, there were about 50 people there, no-one clapped . . . all of which was completely new to me. I was coming from a noise cum punk cum free jazz background

and this was pretty radical – no stage show, no audience par-
ticipation other than almost a complete homage or faith in
the sound, and a total absorption in the frequencies. For me
it was incredible.[23]

The Bug, one of his longest-running projects, started in 1997 as a
collaboration with DJ Vadim. For later Bug releases, he teamed up
with UK dub veteran The Rootsman for a series of singles under
the name Razor X Productions. This led to the album *Pressure*
(2003). The apocalyptic dancehall production continued along with
rootsier collaborations with MC Daddy Freddy, New Flesh's Toastie
Taylor, Roger Robinson and Paul St Hilaire ('Tikiman'). After
discussing further ideas for collaboration with Goodman, Martin
began working with dubstep luminaries such as Digital Mystikz,
Skream and Loefah, with whom he launched a monthly reggae
club night entitled BASH in 2006 at Plastic People that ran until early
2007. For The Bug's *London Zoo* (2008) album, he brought in the
British reggae legend Tippa Irie, Warrior Queen and Flowdan. He
formed King Midas Sound shortly afterwards – the first KMS
single, the ghostly 'Cool Out' (2008), was followed by a debut
album in 2009 called *Waiting for You*, which combined faintly
glowing basslines with Robinson's ghostly, reverb-drenched vocals.

Without You (2011) is a dub version of *Waiting for You*, created
by artists like Kuedo, Hype Williams (another interesting contemporary dub-practitioner), Mala, Gang Gang Dance, DeepChord
Presents Echospace, Nite Jewel and Cooly G. In a constant attempt
to seek new dub 'percolations', Martin's project in 2012–13 has
been a sub-label called Acid Ragga, which has released a series of
seven-inch tracks that explore the relationship between acid house
and ragga dancehall, and leads up to the subsequent Bug album
Angels and Devils (2013).

6 THE BRISTOL SOUND

CITY CONTEXT

The fact that Bristol, in southwest England, played a vital role in the transatlantic slave trade during the eighteenth century is evident in some of the city's street names – Blackboy Hill, Jamaica Street – as well in the name of as its largest concert venue, Colston Hall. This venue, a former sugar warehouse, is named after Edward Colston (*d.* 1721), a wealthy merchant intimately involved with the Royal African Company. Colston enabled Bristol to get a foothold in Britain's profitable slave trade. In 1709, some 57 Bristol ships were engaged in it. By the 1750s, the city even came close to surpassing London as a leading slave port (though it was eventually overtaken by Liverpool). Through the eighteenth century and just beyond, the local population was snared in the trade and its associated industries in some way. The subsequent African-Caribbean influx gave – and still gives – Bristol a distinctly multicultural demographic that sets it apart from other cities in the southwest of Britain, and indeed from many other British cities.

Colston Hall has become a 'sticking point' for local bands like Massive Attack, who have not only refused to play there, but have – unsuccessfully so far – campaigned to have it renamed. In the past, racial tensions have surfaced in the city in many other ways. In the early 1960s, the Bristol Omnibus Company went on strike after the majority of white workers voted to protest against non-white people being employed there. Although the situation ended without violence, in the 1980s, police and youths clashed during the St Paul's area riots, after a 'stop and search' at the Black and White Café.

Much of the city's racial mix, as well as its conflicts, have been centred on St Paul's, a relatively small area that has long represented Bristol's African-Caribbean community, as well as its white working class. The area was immortalized in Ken Pryce's *Endless Pressure*. Pryce notes that in 1979, Bristol's West Indian community was almost entirely made up of working-class Jamaicans, 'predominantly country people and a high proportion from St Thomas' Parish in Jamaica.'[1] His book also traces the growing influence of Rastafarianism and reggae, and the rise of blues parties and after-hours venues such as the Plantation Club, in the area. In the 1970s, the city – and especially St Paul's – had its own 'special brew' of reggae, funk and punk. DJs such as Dennis Richard, Martin Star and Superfly played funk and disco in clubs like The Granary, Le Carno and Top Cat. Bob Marley and The Wailers visited the city in 1973 and Gregory Issacs and Dennis Brown played the 'Top Rank' club on their UK tours in the late 1970s.[2]

Local reggae bands soon emerged, such as Talisman, who formed in 1977 and consisted of three black and two white members. Talisman were all but ignored outside Bristol until UB40 took them under their wing. After their 'adoption', they toured with groups like Burning Spear, The Clash and The Rolling Stones, and went on to release their key album *Takin' the Strain* in 1984. Black Roots (from the St Paul's area) formed a couple of years after Talisman, and released a string of albums in the 1980s and into the 1990s. These included several dub albums, some of them mixed by Mad Professor. The band found an early champion in DJ John Peel, who claimed: 'if anyone tells you there is no such thing as good British reggae, first tell them they are a herbert and then listen to Black Roots.'[3]

In the 1980s, St Pauls was full of 'shebeens' such as Sam's Blues and Green Street. Alongside reggae and dub was, inevitably, a punk scene, in which most of the members of well-known 1980s and 1990s 'posses', like the Wild Bunch, Smith & Mighty and Massive Attack, were involved in some way. Bristol's punk bands, with names like Lunatic Fringe, Vice Squad and Chaos UK, thrashed it out at venues like the Berkeley Rooms, Trinity Hall, the Tropic Club and the squat/café/ bookshop Demolition Diner, mostly in emulation of bigger bands like the Sex Pistols and Crass (who played Trinity Hall in 1980). But the venue where punks most often hung out with reggae fans – and later with the hip hop crowd – was The Dug Out. 'The Dug Out was a meeting spot for the ghetto and Poshville where black and white would hang out', states photographer BEEZER, who chronicled the city's trip hop scene during the mid-1990s:

We were there almost every night, playing disco, funk and punk. It was our Studio 54, and it put Bristol on the map. We were totally into dub and reggae; it was an amalgamation of cultures with no barriers. We didn't know we were part of something that would be influential later, but even at the time it felt like something special was going on, although it was still just, like, going out on a regular Wednesday night.[4]

MARK STEWART AND THE POP GROUP

'After the last war I remember the Bristol Omnibus Company and other firms set up recruiting stations due to labour shortages', says The Pop Group's Mark Stewart.

And as the first Jamaican guys arrived in their immaculate suits, I remember my grandad telling me how he welcomed his new neighbours with open arms, calling them gentlemen. He was very impressed at how they polished their shoes, and cared more about their appearances than some of the local riff raff.[5]

The Pop Group, comprising Jon Waddington (guitar), Gareth Sager (guitar), Simon Underwood (bass) and Bruce Smith (drums), along with Mark Stewart (lyrics, and vocals), was formed in 1977. It was led by the eccentric (and often 'incendiary') front-man Stewart, whose political rants were delivered over the band's abrasive mix of funk, dub, jazz and punk. He adds:

> My connection with dub and reggae in general comes from the street cinema I witnessed growing up within Bristol's bass culture. It was always totally mixed. The original mods listened to bluebeat, and the later suedeheads love of ska and reggae for the smoothies nurtured me together with the general raggamuffin culture of my mother's home turf, St Paul's, where blues clubs like Ajax were a home from home. It was *Presenting I Roy by I Roy* (1973) that pulled the [reggae / dub] trigger, as well as gigs like The Revolutionaries at the legendary Bamboo Club and sound systems clashes like Metromedia and Stereograph where I witnessed dub basslines sounding like power lines being strummed across huge electric pylons. Also, my father is a Hermeticist and maybe through him I was drawn to the parallel mystic revelation of Rastafari. Later on, I also have amazing memories of hanging out with Niney the Observer and Keith Hudson in the Bronx.[6]

The Pop Group's first album, *Y* (1979), was produced by reggae and dub veteran Dennis Bovell. Its radical, avant-garde and deeply politicized sound caught the attention of the national music press and the group ended up playing alongside a broad array of acts from dub-poet Linton Kwesi Johnson to This Heat, Pere Ubu and Patti Smith. Stewart relates that

> We actually tried to get King Tubby to work on the album, but Dennis's dub mix of Elizabeth Archer and The Equators' 'Feel

Adrian Sherwood and Mark Stewart, London 1985.

Like Making Love' [1977] dub blew my mind. As a band we were, and I always am, totally hands on. I just have visions of 3D supersonics and try and crash together things to create sparks. Nothing is sacred and dub's deconstruction of the so-called real is how my mind works anyway, with filters, delayed gratification, multiple dimensions, weird science and para or hypernormal shit. I see dub as a kind of skeleton key to reality.[7]

Stewart remembers knocking off school on Fridays and heading to Bristol's Revolver Records to listen to the new reggae pre-releases. These would be delivered in a van driven by a young Adrian Sherwood. When The Pop Group split, following their second album in 1980 (*For How Much Longer Do We Tolerate Mass Murder?*, which included a contribution from U.S. proto-rappers The Last Poets), Stewart headed to London to collaborate with Sherwood's On-U-Sound collective. There he recorded as Mark Stewart and The Maffia, New Age Steppers (with Cherry and Ari

Mark Stewart.

Up from The Slits), industrial strength hip hop crew Tackhead and
as a solo artist.

Despite leaving Bristol for a time, Stewart had a formative,
if largely unacknowledged, influence on the first generation of
electronic musicians to emerge from the city. He played a role
in the so-called trip hop movement by working with pioneering
groups like Smith & Mighty, Tricky and Massive Attack. His song,
'This is Stranger than Love' (1987), which merged a sample of Erik
Satie with his own distinctive vocals, presaged the tempo and vibe
of the trip hop sound that was to come. Stewart also helped to
organize the now famous battle at London's Titanic Club between

the Language Lab and the Wild Bunch sound systems, which inadvertently introduced producer Nellee Hooper to Jazzie B from Soul II Soul. Stewart wound up sharing a flat with Tricky, and was responsible for literally shoving the reluctant performer on stage the first time, as well as working on the track 'Aftermath' for Tricky's influential debut, *Maxinquaye*. He explains that 'The Wild Bunch was really our posse. DJ Milo, Nellee Hooper, Willie Wee, Delge, Mushroom and some of the unseen backroom crew were the makers of the scene, and Daddy G was always a very trustworthy hand on the rudder of our pirate ship.'[8]

Stewart has continued his multi-genre experiments on records such as *Edit* (2008) and *The Politics of Envy* (2012), which features production by Killing Joke's Martin Glover and a string of dub and punk aficionados like Massive Attack's Daddy G, The Clash guitarist Keith Levene, Tessa Pollitt of The Slits, Douglas Hart of The Jesus and Mary Chain and Lee 'Scratch' Perry. As such,

> Politics of Envy is me finally coming full circle by working with so many of my absolute idols, like Kenneth Anger, whose cut and paste and slash juxtaposition techniques in film are very dub, and Lee 'Scratch' Perry, who from an early age has been a massive influence on my worldview. His work at the Black Ark on tracks like the cataclysmic Vampire Dub by Devon Irons is absolutely classic. It was also a complete pleasure for me to finally get something released with Daddy G.[9]

Stewart also fulfilled something of a lifelong ambition by releasing a dub/remix version of the album. The clue to Stewart's remixing modus operandi lies in the title, *Exorcism of Envy*.

> The method to the madness of dubbing [for me] is to ghost and spook out the original work, somewhat in the nature of an exorcism, with me as the puppet master, so the mad cast of

the original album, like Kenneth Anger, Lee Perry, Gina Birch of The Raincoats would wake up on another planet where they could then breed and hybridise. It's like a strange mutation or what I call a funkenstein, slashing frequencies, mashing up the bassline till it sounds volcanic. Someone I would have loved to have got in for this was Ari Up from The Slits as I fondly remember our nights out at the Bali Hai in Streatham skanking at the bass bins to the Jah Shaka sound system.[10]

BRISTOL SOUND SYSTEMS AND THE BRISTOL SOUND

Bristol's large West Indian community made it ripe for the vibrant sound system scene that had been developing in the UK since the 1950s. Visiting systems such as Jah Shaka and Saxon were not only made welcome, but were supported by local sets like Roots Spot Crew, The Wild Bunch, City Rockers, UD4 (run by the brother of drum and bass producer Roni Size), Red Eye Hi Power and the Three Stripe Posse. Three Stripe was a soul, funk and reggae sound run by Rob Smith and Ray Mighty, who would also help to lay the foundations of what became known as 'trip hop' – a term that, like many, they utterly abhor – or the not-much-more-enlightening 'Bristol Sound'. Smith was originally part of a reggae band called 'Restriction', which released a four-track twelve-inch in 1983 that was mixed and engineered by Mad Professor. The other member of Restriction was Dave McDonald, who would become Portishead's soundman. It was at the Gwyn St Blues Club that Smith first met Ray Mighty and the other members of Three Stripe. Apart from playing blues clubs and St Paul's carnival, the sound used to unofficially 'string up' at Glastonbury Festival and events like the Elephant Fair in Cornwall. Smith remembers that

My first taste of a sound system was probably at Gwyn Street Blues in St Paul's. I was living just across the road and from

there the dull thud of bass could be heard every night. Inside
the packed smoky basement, chest-shaking bass would roll
out of the boxes. I always thought that it sounded better
when the wooden panels were slightly loose so you could
hear a kind of 'hum' or 'buzz' mixed in with the bass.[11]

Smith clearly remembers Jah Shaka visiting Bristol to play at
Trinity Hall.

The ambience of his sessions still uplifts as well as excites.
I remember one session in the early 80s when the bass was so
heavy I thought the hall was shaking but later realized it was
actually my eyeballs vibrating. One poor lad was quivering in
the corner, so freaked out and stoned that he was convinced
that the 'Lion' was waiting for him outside.[12]

Around the same time that Stewart released 'This is Stranger
than Love' (which featured production from Smith & Mighty with
Stewart's overdubbed vocals), the duo were dabbling with their
own proto-'Bristol Sound' tunes. The first two were Bacharach
and David covers: 'Anyone Who Had a Heart' (1988) had a looping
hip hop riddim, a funked up bassline and vocals by local reggae
singer Jackie Jackson sporadically interspersed with scratch stabs
and sirens. 'Walk on By' followed the same formula: it took a
classic song and added a huge bassline, Jackson's vocals, plus
programmed hip hop rhythms. In 1989, they produced a cover
of Rose Royce's 'Wishing on a Star' for Bristol crew Fresh Four,
which featured a young DJ Krust and Suv, who would later form
part of the Full Cycle jungle crew and Roni Size's Reprazent, plus
fellow drum and bass artist Flynn, of Flynn & Flora fame. More
pertinently, Smith & Mighty also co-produced Massive Attack's
debut single 'Any Love' (1989), yet another hip-hop-meets-soul
amalgam.

Rob Smith DJ, Tokyo 2010.

After signing to London records, the duo spent an acrimonious four years fighting to release an album they had produced before being unceremoniously dropped from the label. Undeterred, they continued to perform remix and production work for artists such as Beats International, Neneh Cherry and The Ragga Twins. In the 1990s, Smith started a drum and bass crew (and record label) called 'More Rockers' with Peter D Rose, another collaborator from Bristol and sometime member of Smith & Mighty. More Rockers unleashed three celebrated volumes of Dubplate Selection (1995–2001), which rubbed blistering ragga jungle against deep dub basslines and blissed out ambience. Smith & Mighty finally released their long-awaited debut album, *Bass is Maternal*, in 1995. The record took a fairly experimental approach, massaging dub, rock, hip hop, reggae and electronic music into various shapes that mostly aimed at the dance floor.

Another notable Bristol sound was Henry & Louis, run by
Andy Scholes and Jack Lundis. As producers and DJs, the pair have
moved through the dubcore continuum pretty much in parallel
with their old friends Smith & Mighty. They have explored drum
and bass, trip hop and dubstep. Scholes started working with the
Red Eye Hi Power sound around 1981 alongside Saul Hooper
(King Solomon) and Kev Rogers (Farmer G). In 1988 he met
Lundis, who had a background in studio production, and they
began producing roots music. Their first album, *Rudiments* (1995),
was released on Smith & Mighty's More Rockers label, and they
went on to work with Horace Andy, Prince Green and Donette
Forte (as well as contributing to *Bass is Maternal*).

In 1996 Louis went to Kingston with some of Smith's already
mixed dubs, recording vocals on top to create the album *Time
will Tell* (which was mixed at Bob Marley's house). Ali Campbell
of UB40 chose Henry & Louis as the support for their global tour,
and Louis got to meet his hero Augustus Pablo in 1998. Pablo had
heard *Time will Tell* and wanted to tell them that it was a joy to
hear that the old methods of roots production were still alive.
Scholes recounted to Adam Burrows that

> There I was, on Tangerine Hill, looking at him with that thing
> in his mouth . . . the big smoking chalice. He had cancer, but
> like Bob Marley, he wouldn't take the treatment. He couldn't
> eat. He just sat there drinking this thing called bitters, and
> smoking. When I left, he gave me these boxes with 'Rockers 1'
> written on them – ninety 7″ singles, all his own productions.
> They're probably worth thousands.[13]

Like the Three Stripe Posse, the Wild Bunch mixed soul, funk,
hip hop and reggae on their sound. Their preferred hangout was
the Dug Out, where Wild Bunch member and reggae DJ Daddy G
(Grant Marshall), later of Massive Attack, was resident at the club

from 1982 until 1986. The first incarnation of the Wild Bunch crew featured Marshall, Nellee Hooper and Miles 'Milo' Johnson, Claude Williams (aka Wille Wee), with graffiti artist and rapper Robert Del Naja (3D) and Andrew Vowles (Mushroom) joining later.[14] As well as playing the Dug Out every Wednesday, the Wild Bunch played illegal parties on The Downs (parkland northwest of the city centre), in abandoned warehouses and at private parties, as well as official gigs at venues like The Granary. At St Paul's Carnival they often played right through until dawn. Daddy G says that

> The Wild Bunch was all about being on the road rather than in the recording studio, we were basically DJs who occasion- ally introduced live instruments like drums and bass into the show. There were loads of reggae sound systems around at the time but we were the main jamming system with a bit of everything thrown in, there was always a very mixed and wide range of people coming to our jams. We've never aspired to please little sections like a pure soul or reggae or hip hop crowd, we've always done our own thing, mixing in punk or rock n roll or anything, people just get into what's happening.[15]

Indeed, Del Naja remarks that in those early hip hop days 'you had Saxone and Coxsone and all those sound systems and Tippa Irie and Philip Levy, and all those people and it was totally poetically on the mic [sic] in that way'.[16]

The Wild Bunch released two singles for the Fourth & Broadway label – 'Friends and Countrymen' and 'The Look of Love' (1988) – yet another Bacharach song – both of which failed to sell. After DJ Milo quit the country and The Wild Bunch imploded, some of the remaining members, Marshall, Del Naja and Vowles (Mushroom), became a studio band called Massive

Attack, bolstered by contributions from a rotating cast of friends and vocalists like Tricky Kid (soon shortened to 'Tricky') and producer Nellee Hooper. Released on their own Massive Attack Records label in 1987, their first single 'Any Love' (co-produced by Smith & Mighty) featured Daddy G and Carlton on vocals and was more uplifting in feel and tempo than later Massive Attack tracks. It took a while for them to really get anything together ('We were lazy Bristol twats', in the words of Daddy G to *The Guardian* newspaper), but pushed along by their friend Neneh Cherry, they finally recorded and released their debut album, *Blue Lines*, in 1991.

Blue Lines managed to define Massive Attack's musical vision. In addition, it was also the first major manifestation of a uniquely British hip hop sound. Featuring R&B singer Shara Nelson and Jamaican dancehall star Horace Andy (whom they blagged into recording with them, despite having only released a couple of singles, and who has since remained one of the band's most consistent guest vocalists), the record shimmered with all the influences that had been echoing around Britain's sound systems for the last decade: feel-good soul, bass-heavy dub reggae and a smattering of electronica and jazz.

Who did what on the record remains a mystery. Production is credited to Massive Attack, Cameron McVey (Neneh Cherry's partner) and the late Jonny Dollar, who had recorded Neneh Cherry's debut *Raw Like Sushi* in 1989. Dollar's invented surname allegedly came from being the only person to be paid for studio work on *Blue Lines*, and he is generally regarded as responsible for shaping the group's disparate ideas into something musically groundbreaking.

The term 'trip hop' was coined by music journalist Andy Pemberton the year *Blue Lines* was released. However, it was not used to describe Massive Attack's sound but that of DJ Shadow's 'In/Flux' (1994) whose varying beats per minute, spoken word

samples, bizarre noises, prominent bass and slow beats, gave the
listener the impression they were on a musical trip, according to
Pemberton.[17] 'In/Flux' was released on James Lavelle's Mo' Wax
label, which was also dragged into the trip hop category, and
became very influential throughout much of the 1990s. In 2001,
Mo' Wax put out the 'dub-dancehall' compilation *Now Thing*,
underlining the label's fascination with the quirkier and often
darker side of Jamaican music.

Another band to be tarred with the trip hop brush was
Portishead, named after the small town they came from just
outside Bristol. Made up of Beth Gibbons, Geoff Barrow and
Adrian Utley, Portishead released their debut album, *Dummy*,
in 1994, and to similar acclaim as *Blue Lines*. Portishead's sound
was less tied to reggae and Bristol's sound system culture than
to torch-song jazz and the film soundtracks of John Barry and
Ennio Morricone. Yet it shared Massive Attack's and The Bristol
Sounds' obsession with slow, torpid grooves and moody atmospherics. (There were some personal links too, namely, Barrow,
who had been a former tape operator in Massive Attack's studio,
and *Dummy*'s engineer Dave Mcdonald, who used to play with
Rob Smith in the reggae band Restriction.)

Yet another musical milestone was put out in 1995 by Bristol
rapper and friend of Massive Attack, Tricky. The masterful
Maxinquaye, which felt much like a continuation of Massive
Attack's abstract stream-of-consciousness murmurings but even
more jagged and cerebral, featured duets with Tricky's then-lover
Martina Topley-Bird, and Mark Stewart ('Aftermath'), as well as a
cover of Public Enemy's 'Black Steel in the Hour of Chaos'.
A devout follower of 2-Tone, and The Specials in particular,
Tricky drafted in Terry Hall to feature on his album *Nearly God*
in 1996. Although he went to Jamaica (also in 1996) to record his
third album, *Pre-Millennium Tension*, at Grove Studios, Ocho Rios,
which has a Rastafarian influence throughout, it is *Maxinquaye*

that perhaps most represents Tricky's love of dub. In an essay
for *The Wire* magazine in March 1995, Ian Penman wrote that
on the album

> Tricky sounds like ghosts from another solar system. Not so
> much fear of a black planet as fear of a planet left behind – fear
> of the space and silence out there, which is internalised into this
> odd, liminal, multi-layered music. Tricky whispers, he doesn't
> scream, and it's all the more unsettling (politically as well as
> aesthetically) for that. He has adroitly staged his inaugural
> ceremony as a disappearance, a mutation, a street-political
> sideswipe and a polysexual put-on . . . even the name is double
> or triple (it's his name – except when it isn't – as well as the
> group's) and no matter what the track, there is always some
> Other voice (Martina, Mark Stewart) floating about as ballast.[18]

While Tricky's entire 'feint and suggestion' methodology
(his 'tricknology') could be seen as a massive 'big up' to Jamaican
dub culture, Massive Attack went even further with their second
album, *Protection* (1994), by hiring Mad Professor to work his
cosmic dub magic on the entire record. Titled *No Protection* (1995),
the idea came about after Frazer had remixed a single from the
album. The band asked for more of the record to be remixed and
the project eventually turned into a track-by-track retake, with all
the original material stripped back and slowed down to emphasize
the riddims and the vocals splayed through the mix.

BRISTOL DUB AND BASS

The next big thing to emerge from Bristol was drum and bass,
perhaps best exemplified by Roni Size (Ryan Owen Granville
Williams). Born to immigrant Jamaican parents, Williams grew
up in St Andrews, the same Bristol suburb as Tricky, Massive

Attack and Smith & Mighty, where he got hooked on hip hop
through the usual network of sound systems, house parties and
underground clubs. After being expelled from school, Williams
began dabbling with house and reggae production in the late
1980s. He met fellow Bristol DJ Krust (a former member of
the Fresh Four), and the pair formed v Records with London
producer Jumpin' Jack Frost, who had previously played at
several Massive Attack parties in Bristol. Williams also set up
a sister label, Full Cycle, with Krust and fellow DJ/producers
Die and Suv, who would also form the core of the Reprazent
project, along with several musicians, vocalist Onallee and
rapper Dynamite MC, who began MC-ing on Gloucestershire
pirate radio station Crush FM. The Bristol scene in the early
1990s, says Roni Size,

> was absolutely wicked. I'm a lucky guy to have been there.
> Nowadays I drive through St Paul's and I can look back in
> time at all the people and the parties [Wild Bunch]. Those
> days were phenomenal. I carry that history with me! There
> were a lot of people who used to travel down from the
> outskirts like Goldie, who were involved too. But Bristol
> was kicking, man![19]

Reprazent's debut album, *New Forms* (1997), brought a jazzy,
funky vibe as well as a live sound to drum and bass. 'We [Reprazent]
are coming from the funk era, like Parliament Funkadelic, George
Benson, and Motown. That's what we grew up listening to.
People saw a double bass, and to them it was jazz. But it was
more than that.' Although Size states reggae as an early influence,
amaican music was less prominent than other styles on *New
Forms*. This was deliberate. Thompson says that 'All our parents
and the parents of our friends were from Jamaica. You sort of
rebelled against that upbringing, because they were still stuck in

that Jamaican mentality. We weren't exactly Jamaican. We were Jamaican/English.' The record won the 1997 Mercury Music Prize and Reprazent were inevitably hailed by the media as a continuation of the Bristol Sound. The group's second album, *In the Mode* (2000), was more hip hop influenced and gave Dynamite a larger role as the group's MC/ rapper.

Following the decline of drum and bass in the late 1990s, the Bristol scene followed the same bass-heavy 'continuum' as London, and wound up with an especially adroit dubstep scene. In 2008 Radio 1 DJ Mary Anne Hobbs profiled twelve of the city's main protagonists on a show called *Bristol: Rise Up*.

Producers like Appleblim, Peverelist, Pinch and Rob Smith (under the RSD moniker he uses for dubstep productions) were featured on the show. Most of RSD's best tracks were collected together on the *Good Energy* album (2009), which was released on Punch Drunk, the label set up by Peverelist (Tom Ford) to put out music by Bristol-based dubstep artists. Through Punch Drunk, Ford, who also runs Rooted Records, Bristol's answer to Croydon's Big Apple shop, has released grime-influenced material (Gemmy and Guido) as well as the influential *Worth the Weight* compilation (2010), which profiled the the past half-decade of the local dubstep scene.

I'm into dance music culture, rhythm and the dynamic between bass and drums. I think of my music as drum & bass – that's still the basis. Reggae, jungle and dubstep – it's drum & bass music. That's what the emphasis is on. So it is dance music. I'm not interested in loudness wars or who can make the nastiest bassline or the hypest moment in the dance. My music is a bit more subtle. I'm interested on building vibrations on a longer time scale rather than the 'big drop' culture that is so dominant. It's not 'deep' though, or 'chilled' – I'm still trying to take your chest out with bass.[20]

Another key Bristol dubstep authority, and a long-term pal of Ford's, is Rob Ellis (aka Pinch). Turned on to the sound by a Kode9 set at London's FWD club in 2003, he was inspired to start his own night in Bristol called Context (and then Subloaded and Dubloaded). The dubstep scene in Bristol was so small when Context started that the 'dubstep' section in the shop had to be book-ended by dub at the beginning and drum and bass at the end. Ellis was too young for the Dug Out/Wild Bunch days, but was a big fan of Massive Attack, Tricky, Portishead, Roni Size and Smith & Mighty. Briefly a drum and bass DJ, Ellis lost interest in that scene and started getting hooked on grime, garage and Basic Channel techno, and trying to mix them all together. A turning point for Ellis as a producer was his 'anthemic' track 'Qawaali' (2006), named after the Sufi Muslim form of devotional singing. Its popularity transcended the dubstep scene, and it became a dance floor favourite with a wide range of house and techno DJs.

A year later, he dropped his debut album *Underwater Dancehall*, which featured guest vocalists like MC Juakali, singer with dub band Babylon Station and MC at New York's Dub War, the first dubstep night in the U.S., Rudey Lee, a key figure in Bristol's reggae scene and a former collaborator with Smith & Mighty, and local talent Yolanda Quartey, who has toured with Massive Attack and Dizzee Rascal, among others. The album came with a second disc of instrumentals, some of which, like 'Angels in the Rain', had been subjected to delays, fragmentation and other post-processing effects. 'I listened to dub from a young age via my older brother', says Ellis.

> I had tapes of On-U Sound and Sly & Robbie's *A Dub Experience* (1985) from around ten to eleven years old but I didn't get into the '70s stuff until I was older, around twenty. I followed jungle and UK garage and spacious techno

directly before I became involved in the dubstep scene.
I don't see dubstep as a Bristol thing or a London thing
anymore. It started in London and I believe that Bristol
has had its own take on things. But I don't see that as one
particular sound either. The likes of Headhunter, Peverelist
and Appleblim stand quite apart from, say Joker, Gemmy or
Guido and someone like Jakes has a totally different energy
again. The shared aspect is the community here as much as
an appreciation of sound system culture.[21]

In 2010, Ellis was one of the first to bring Jamaican dub and
dubstep together with the *Scientist Launches Dubstep into Outer
Space* project. This involved Kingston originator Scientist
versioning twelve exclusive and unreleased dubstep rhythms
from producers including himself, Kode9, Shackleton and Mala.

I liked the idea of him taking dubstep music into the world
of dub and seeing what he would do with it. He wasn't
very aware of dubstep music initially but he did embrace
it wholeheartedly. I think dubstep was a term coined to
reference the origin of the meaning of 'dub' rather than
a direct reference to the music genre itself. It was used to
refer to dark stripped down garage beats that didn't use
a full vocal – much like dub was to roots. There was very
little overtly 'dub' in the early music of dubstep outside of
a few Horsepower tracks like 'Gorgon Sound' that used
some dub flavoured samples. The spirit of dubstep was
quite true, in my opinion, to the original dub mentality:
experimenting with rhythm and space. Now most dubstep
has very little in common with dub – the likes of Skrillex
and so forth have filled every available space with micro
wobbles and trancey riffs.[22]

Adrian Sherwood and Pinch.

In 2012, Ellis remixed Mark Stewart's 'Autonomia' (from his *Politics of Envy* album). His latest project is with Adrian Sherwood. The pair have been collaborating since 2011 and were, at the time of writing, preparing to release an album in 2014.

I've long been a fan of Adrian, since a kid really. I was lucky enough to be able to invite him to play at a Tectonic label night at Fabric in October 2012. We got on and he invited me to play a Paris On-U Sound night where we decided to get into the studio a few weeks later. Initially we were just going to combine forces to make some dubplates for each of us to play but things were going really well and it quickly turned into a bigger project. I really do very much enjoy working with Adrian and I'm really happy the project has grown the way it has.[23]

7 BERLIN: GLITCH AND TECHNO

REGGAE IN GERMANY

Of all the countries to succumb to the dub 'virus', Germany may
seem an unlikely candidate. Historically, Caribbean immigration
to Germany has been low. The post-war influx of *Gastarbeiter*
('guest workers') to West Germany came from Italy, Greece,
Turkey and Yugoslavia, and flowed into the East from Vietnam,
North Korea, Angola and Cuba.

Reggae was given virtually no media attention in the country
until the Bob Marley 'explosion' meant it could no longer be
ignored. Indeed, Marley provided inspiration for the few German
reggae bands to emerge in the late 1970s. Apart from Papa
Curvin, one of the first Jamaicans to form a roots reggae band
(Malcolm's Locks) in Germany, reggae has tended to be dominated by white singers, and bands such as the Herbsman Band,
fronted by Jamaican singer/deejay Sista Gracy. In addition, there
is Munich's Dub Invaders (a sound that is more reggae than dub,
despite the name) a group that has supported Dennis Brown and
Burning Spear, and Hannover's Felix 'Fe' Wolter, who works as
'Dubvisionist' as well as 'The Vision', with Natalie Deseke (Sista
Natty) and Jens Müller.

While these artists have worked diligently enough in their
own realms, it was mostly the second wave of activists and reggae
fans in the 1990s who formed Germany's current infrastructure
of record shops, studios and sound systems. Today, it is one of
the most extensive in Europe, and boasts around 40 major sets,

including the massive Pow Wow in Cologne and Conquering
Sound in Hannover, who were one of the first sets to adopt the
original JA style. In more recent years, labels like Germaican
Records and Best Seven, and artists like Seeed and Gentleman,
have helped to bring dancehall to Germany. But one of dub's
most unique manifestations occurred in the country's capital,
when the Berlin Wall fell in November 1989.

A vibrant and liberal underground party scene quickly
developed in the city, comparable to the one simultaneously
mushrooming in the UK. However, the difference between the
two scenes was that Berlin's municipal infrastructure had been
thrown into chaos and many of the vacant apartments and
buildings abandoned by East Berliners, especially along the
route where the wall had run, could be squatted and transformed into temporary clubs and bars. One of the first acid
house clubs in the city, UFO, was opened in a Kreuzberg cellar in
1988. Set up by Interfisch label owners Achim Kohlberger and
Dimitri Hegemann, who had been involved in the arts since the
early 1980s, UFO moved to the Schöeneberg district before
closing in 1990 because of financial problems. Hegemann then
opened Tresor with Johnnie Stieler in East Berlin in 1991, in the
vaults of the former Wertheim department store next to Pots-
damer Platz. The Tresor Records label began soon after.

As the 1990s progressed, Berlin became a haven for Detroit
producers, with Jeff Mills and Blake Baxter taking up residencies in
the city. Tresor was heavily involved in this formative Berlin–
Detroit connection, releasing Underground Resistance's *x-101* /
x-102 / *x-103* album series and – in 1993 – *Tresor II: Berlin Detroit –
A Techno Alliance*.

BASIC CHANNEL AND DUB TECHNO

In addtion to Tresor, one of the key meeting points for Berlin's early techno scene was the Hard Wax record store. Opened in 1989 by Mark Ernestus. Hard Wax imported records from Chicago as well as from Detroit, though it had a stronger connection with the latter city for perhaps obvious reasons. Like Berlin, Detroit's scene was built around one-person labels with no official distribution. The scene had a similarly fierce underground feel, whilst the city was similarly strewn with abandoned spaces where illegal parties were held. The huge influence of Kraftwerk on Detroit techno was almost certainly a help.

'It was an amazing coincidence that the Wall had fallen with that whole generation from the East becoming able to participate in the scene', remembers Ernestus.

All these abandoned buildings, the confused and overwhelmed authorities, and the record supply through Hard Wax and the Detroit connection. It was mental, week by week it was too much to handle . . . I also remember how we laughed at the established music media embarrassing themselves with statements like 'It's not music, it'll all be over in six months. We couldn't have cared less about their recognition.'[1]

Sometime in the early 1990s, Ernestus met Moritz von Oswald, a classically trained percussionist, the great-great-grandson of Otto von Bismarck and a former member of Thomas Fehlmann's 'no-wave' band Palais Schaumburg. Their collaborative partnership led initially to the Maurizio M-series, whose first release, the *Ploy* EP (1992), featured a remix by Underground Resistance on the B-side, and the words 'UR – Thank You' engraved in the run-out grooves. Around the same period, they began producing as Basic Channel, and set up a record label of the same name. Although it

only operated for two years (1993–5), the label released nine
records that defined the dub-techno blueprint and had an
immeasurable influence on what today is known as 'minimal
techno'. Mastered by Detroit's National Sound Corporation,
the main mastering house for the Detroit dance scene, tracks like
'Lyot RMX' (1993), 'Phylyps Trak' (1993) and 'Quadrant Dub' (1994)
came with cavernous basslines, a wicked sense of disorientation
and lashings of crackle and delay – a clear consequence of the
duo's interest in dub.

Following the winding down of the Basic Channel project in
1995, the duo, who like their friends UR in Detroit are notoriously
reticent about giving interviews, set about consolidating their own
self-contained production/distribution line to include a recording
studio (which they moved to around 2000), Dubplates Mastering
studio (which they later sold), Ernestus's Hard Wax shop (which
is still in operation) and several labels. Their Chain Reaction label
became an important imprint for the duo's friends, Monolake,
Vladislav Delay and Porter Ricks. In a rare interview at the Red
Bull Music Academy in Barcelona in 2008, Oswald discussed his
love of dub. He explained that he listened to reggae

> while working in [the] record shop. We got Channel One
> stuff and Lee Perry from Britain, and these import 12″
> rarities. Whenever a record came in it was something we
> listened to and discussed, as they were so hard to get. At the
> beginning of the '90s I started to get into it again with Mark,
> who was even more into the hard core 7″ culture than me.[2]

In the interview, Oswald expressed the idea that dub was a chance
to develop something new:

> Version and dub and these things are something I feel a bit
> bad categorizing or describing too much. There are many

examples of how people are doing it. For example, you hear a
breakdown and you hear things come back in, you play
around with effects but leave some room for the six or eight
elements that work together really well. It's a matter of listening to how the original is put together. If it's put together very
well you don't have so many elements. If you have doubt
about the original elements it will be different.

By 1996 Oswald and Ernestus were teamed up with
Dominican vocalist Paul St Hilaire (formerly 'Tikiman'), who
had come to Berlin in 1992 to replace a singer in the band Livin'
Spirit. Tikiman met Ernestus and Oswald in 1995 and together
they recorded a club track called 'Acting Crazy' under the project
name 'Round Three'. The track sent Tikiman's vocals echoing
across deep, minimal house beats. Ernestus relates that

> We were so excited about this collaboration that we straight
> away formed the Burial Mix label to take it a step further
> into more dub and reggae oriented productions. By that time
> I had gotten a bit disappointed with club techno. That raw,
> revolutionary spirit had faded a bit. I had been heavily into
> dub and reggae before techno but it was pushed to the side
> for a while when house and techno were exploding in Berlin,
> but then it started to creep back up on me.[3]

Rather than their former approach of applying dub's spatial
aesthetics to techno, the duo reversed the process and applied
techno's digital production values to dub, creating a spaced-out,
'hauntological' sound for 'Never Tell You' (1996), released through
Burial Mix. 'Music A Fe Rule' (1997), produced under their
Rhythm & Sound moniker, was tougher and sounded even more
narcotic. It plied a stepper's riddim and Tubby-esque clangs with
filtered vocals, again supplied by Tikiman. And although the

Rhythm & Sound label stopped releasing records in 2002, Oswald and Ernestus continued recording under the Rhythm & Sound artist name, releasing their music via Burial Mix. The *Rhythm & Sound* album (2001) collected their first slew of singles, and was followed by *Rhythm & Sound w/ The Artists* (2003), which featured eight more Rhythm & Sound tunes voiced in Berlin, New York and Jamaica by seven artists, including Cornel Campbell, Paul St Hilaire, Shalom, The Chosen Brothers, Love Joy, Jennifer Lara and Jah Batta. Released simultaneously, *The Versions* contained the corresponding instrumentals rendered denser and more minimal by Ernestus and Oswald. In 2005 the duo released *See Mi Yah*, a classic 'one rhythm' album, featuring ten vocal tracks over one instrumental 'version' of the 'See Mi Yah' rhythm, which was pre-released as a series of seven-inch singles (and three alternative instrumental versions).

In 1997 the duo remixed a Chosen Brothers cut called 'Mango Walk', which was released as a double A-side with the original 1979 track (which had been produced and mixed at Wackie's) on one side and the Rhythm & Sound version on the other. In the Red Bull interview video, Oswald plays the Rhythm Sound mix of 'Mango Walk' and explains how it was achieved.

It was done completely live in the mix. It's not a short process. It's more weeks than days, to decide what to leave and take, what works and doesn't, what you can create that's new and to retain the affection for the old record also, and keep the feeling, transport it. For me it's very important. The bass is modified and simplified. The vibes of the guitar-sounding synth cards or patterns also appear again in the new track. But the rhythm and speed are changed. We only had two tracks, not the multi tracks, if they even existed, and we didn't sample anything. We made a whole new track. I like this about remixes, if they're done as a new track.

We also change the context, as it is played in a completely different environment.[4]

'The Wackie's remix came about via Honest Jon's and Rae Cheddie', says Ernestus.

Rae had been running Wackie's UK in the eighties and had a lot of master tapes, one of them containing Mango Walk, an unreleased old favorite of his. The Honest Jon's guys were putting together an interactive CD Rom, and asked us about the remix as a part of that project. I had known Rae for a while and right around that time met Lloyd [Barnes] for the first time in a record store basement in the north Bronx on a trip digging for old vinyl.[5]

In 2001, the duo began reissuing the best of Wackie's back catalogue, including Horace Andy's 1982 *Dance Hall Style* album. In 2003, in collaboration with Mark Ainley from Honest Jon's, they set up a new label, Basic Replay to re-release classic albums from U.S. labels, including Keith Hudson's *Playing it Cool* (originally put out in 1981 on Joint International, the label cooperation between Hudson and Wackie's Lloyd 'Bullwackie' Barnes) and White Mice (self-titled and Versions albums out originally in the late 1980s on the Intellitec Muzik label), and singles, including Jackie Mittoo's 'Ayatollah'(which originally came out on Nefertiti, 1979). In 2010, Ernestus and Ainley set up the Dug Out imprint, dedicated to reissuing obscure reggae and dub records. The imprint focuses on the 1980s digital era and includes singles from King Kong, Willie Williams, Naphtali and Anthony Red Rose.

More recently, Oswald has returned to live performance with the Moritz von Oswald Trio (featuring Vladislav Delay and Max Loderbauer). This is a left-field hybrid of live improvisation and precision electronics that still draws on both dub and techno.

Meanwhile, Mark Ernestus has turned his attention (and dub appreciation) to Africa, and exploring the Senegalese artist Mbalax via his Jeri-Jeri project.

In 2009 Ernestus also set up Wax Treatment with DJ Pete from Hard Wax. Featuring a monolithic sound system (Killasan), a selection of 'bass-heavy sounds' ranging from dub to dubstep, occasional MCs like Koki and an authentic Caribbean food shack, Wax Treatment brings the spirit of the dance hall to Berlin. Tikiman, meanwhile, has gone on to work with Modeselektor and The Bug, among many others.

POLE

The Basic Channel empire, in particular the Dubplates Mastering facility, became a breeding ground for other artists, many of whom carried the flame for dub-techno productions as well as push these experiments into new terrain. Vainqueur, Substance, Porter Ricks and Monolake (Robert Henke and Gerhard Behles), all released dub-influenced music throughout the 1990s.

Another former engineer at Dubplates and Mastering, Stefan Betke, formed his own unique take on dub, helping create the so-called glitch or clicks and cuts genre. Betke's *nom-de-disque*, 'Pole', is based on a Waldorf 4-Pole filter he received as a gift from Thomas Fehlmann and the Ocean Club, and accidentally dropped and broke in 1996.

[Thomas] was staying in my flat together with the Ocean Club members for Popkomm 1996 and gave me this filter. It had fallen down the night before and so it was broken. I said don't worry I'll repair it, but then left it in the studio. I plugged it in and it started to make all these noises, I thought fuck, it's broken and left it in the corner, still connected to the mixing board. I muted it and forgot it was there. Then one day I worked on something and un-muted the channel and it was working well over the track with drums as background noise. Then I muted the drums. The whole thing is based on a mistake; without that I would not be Pole.[6]

Initially based in Cologne, Betke moved to Berlin in the early 1996. His first trilogy, 1, 2, 3, and R, a collection of remixes and new interpretations of his 1998 debut EP *Raum*, are mostly electronica comprised of dub basslines and itchy, clicky rhythms provided by the eponymous filter that were exercises in minimalism. *1* (1998) was his chief manifesto, a blend of slow-motion aquatic dub waves with static and jazzy inflections, and dashes of 1970s prog-rock and Latin music. On *2*, he shifted the emphasis away from random crackles to concentrate more on basslines and pure dubs. On *3*, he veered more towards electronic dub techno.

When I started making these albums, I was more into the electronic jazz and hip hop thing. I was interested in heavy bass sounds but didn't make the connection until I moved to Berlin and Christoph [Grote-Beverborg] from Dubplates Mastering asked if I listened to a lot of reggae and dub. I said not really, but he told me I had a lot of influence from it. Hard Wax was right next door so I went and bought my first dub record by Barrington Levy, a version of an original reggae album. 1 and 2 were composed when I moved here to Berlin. On 1, there was already a big dub influence, it just wasn't so obvious, hidden behind this film soundtrack-like music. But there were already all these heavy basslines and strange echoes and reverbs and all that, which is the method of dub. I made the track called 'Berlin' when I had a small apartment here and was travelling back and forth. I remember being inspired at Love Parade to make this track.[7]

Although he felt drawn to the work of Lee Perry ('especially tracks like "Bucky Skank", the weirdo sound, the snares and animal noises'), Pole says he never wanted to become a dub artist, and was influenced only by the method of dub to create a new atmosphere or space.

That's maybe the reason I liked the seven-inches with noises better. Dub is a bit like old Chinese sword movies, where they jump and fly up to the trees and walk on top of the trees – this is dub as well. It's the same idea, you take something that's existing and over-do it as much as possible, but then you need a grounding. Since my approach to dub was never to be a musician with the religious idea behind, etc. I just picked out the method of dub to create the space I needed.[8]

Pole moved into more experimental slightly dance floor territory on *Steingarten* (2007), an album that draws on dub for its looping rhythms and occasional use of delay. He also enlisted British dub-step luminaries Shackleton and Peverelist for remixes, and went even further into dubstep territory with the release of *Round Black Ghosts* (2008). Put together by Betke, Tim Tetzner from Dense and his ~scape label partner and sometime collaborator Barbara Preisinger, the compilation features tracks from Pole (the supine 'Alles Klar') as well as dubstep/garage stalwarts like Pinch, Peverelist, 2562, Untold, Elemental and Dutch producers Syncom Data. Most recently, Pole teamed up with Swedish noise/ electronic producers Roll the Dice (whose *Live in Gothenburg* album, 2011, he mastered) for an EP titled *In Dubs* (2012). The EP carries titles such as 'Calling Dub Workers', 'Echo Hands' and 'The Skull Is Built Into the Version' and, as such, highlights the dub connection. At the same time, Betke released his new twelve-inch trilogy 'Waldgeschichten' on his new artist-run label, Pole.

JAHTARI

Betke's work proved to be a key influence on Jahtari, a label based in Leipzig in the former GDR. Run by German producer Jan Gleichmar and techno DJ Christoph Rootah, the label was set up in 2005 specifically to explore the spirit of King Tubby through a 'battered old laptop'. At the time of writing, the label has signed over twenty artists, including London's Mikey Murka and the American-based Burning Spear collaborator Ras Amerlock. However, Gleichmar, who produces as Disrupt, remains the lead artist on the label. Since releasing his *Foundation Bit* album (2007), which matches heavy bass frequencies to eight-bit melodies and samples of everything from the film soundtrack to *Alien* to LFO's 'We are Back', Gleichmar's reputation has developed internationally, even receiving airplay from the BBC DJ Mary Anne Hobbs.

Neither Disrupt nor Rootah have reggae backgrounds, says Gleichmar: 'Christoph comes from Detroit and Chicago stuff, as well as Berlin, Cologne and Frankfurt, like the early Gigolo releases'.

The years after the Wall came down were the exciting ones – lots of empty spaces, the police didn't care much, new drugs, exciting times. I was more into Atari Teenage Riot and pretty much everything Digital Hardcore Recordings did, punk and breakcore produced with home computers. Also Aphex Twin and lots of early Warp records plus all the early jungle were very interesting. And finally Mille Plateaux and the Clicks Cuts movement – what you'd now call electronica – was a major input, especially the idea of creating music using the mistakes your computer makes.[9]

One of their early transitions into reggae and dub was the work of Berlin's Basic Channel (and later, Rhythm & Sound). It was through Ernestus's Hard Wax store that the pair were able to explore techno as well as dub and reggae artists.

> Basic Channel were crucial for us, even more so than Rhythm & Sound. Some of the first dub LPs we ever bought I'd still rate as all time faves, absolutely timeless. Particularly Lee Perry's *Super Ape* and the first Wackies LPs by Bullwackie Barnes, as well as Horace Andy's *Dancehall Style*, Wayne Jarret's *Bubble Up* and the Love Joys *Lovers Rock*. The dubs on those are incredible. At the same time, Bernd Friedmann's album *Just Landed* triggered something back then for us and Pole was a massive influence, not only the sub-bass of his records, but the classic reggae he used to DJ before his live sets.[10]

Rather than emulate the 'Old Masters', Gleichmar and Rootah blend their love of dub with their passion for the classic video

Disrupt Studio.

and computer games that they also grew up with, as well as throwing in the occasional vocalist or film sample. The bleeps and wobbles that skim across the recordings are reminiscent of the digital dancehall records of the 'Sleng Teng' era – but with a thoroughly modern twist. Gleichmar adds that

> You couldn't beat the records from the golden era even if you had exactly the same gear. But what we can do is learn from them and try to update it or adapt it to our place. Reggae has to be roots music, but our roots aren't a Kingston ghetto, we come from a different place and time.[11]

Their *Jahtarian Dubbers* releases, currently up to No. 3, have proved especially popular, featuring selections of tracks that range from relaxed ambient dubs to classic-sounding digital dancehall, and others that sound very close to dubstep. Other signifcant hits have included Soom T's 'Dirty Money' EP, Jahtari and Soom T's 'Ode 2 A Carrot', Solo Banton's 'Talk To Me' and 'No', Pupajim's 'Double Lock / Trouble Again' and Solo's 'Music Addict' EP. Although they once termed their sound 'digital laptop reggae', both Gleichmar and Rootah have tired of the limitations and recently started to revert to analogue studio equipment.

> When I first heard digital reggae, funnily enough I didn't like it at all. But one day Christoph played me King Tubby's *Soundclash Dubplate Style* compilation [1988] over his sound system and it clicked. For many years I was strictly limited to a laptop, pretty much the cheapest instrument you can get, but we switched to hardware-only in the last year or two and I'd say we're way more imaginative – basically doing it just like Perry and Tubby again, but using newer synths they didn't have.[12]

BERND FRIEDMANN

Dedicated to blurring the boundaries between analogue and digital, the live and the programmed, former Cologne-based artist Bernd Friedmann moved to Berlin in 2009. Friedmann began making music in 1978, continuing all the way through his fine art studies in the 1980s. In aiming – among other things – to subvert prejudices about the authenticity of programmed music, and creating compositions that refuse to adhere to conventional (media-invented) genres, he came up with his Burnt Friedman pseudonym. He has gone on to release a stream of albums in different styles and under several other names: Drome, Nonplace Urban Field, The Nu-Dub Players. He has also released collaborations with various musicians, vocalists and producers such as Uwe Schmidt (as Flanger), drummer Jaki Liebezeit, saxophonist Hayden Chisholm, London-based singer and producer Steve Spacek and David Sylvian.

Friedmann's approach to music, perhaps best summed up in the non-committal name of his long-running Nonplace label, has led him to explore a variety of music styles in often enigmatic, playful and ironic ways – *Difficult Easy Listening* (2004), as his compilation had it. His Nu-Dub Players was conceived in 1996 during a vacation in New Zealand. Their debut album *Just Landed* (2000) featured dub-influenced songs built on an Atari and a sampler, along with an eight-track tape recorder, but were structured to give the impression they had been created by a live band.[13] To further this impression, Friedmann's friend Pete Antonio invented elaborate sleeve notes that detailed the sessions and gave information about the band members, who bore deliberately outlandish names like Bernie The Bolt, The Cousin of the Sausage Smearer, DJ Booth and Crucial Guenther.

Since it's the case that with studio productions you create an artificial world that has nothing in common with a 'live on stage' situation, it's almost logical to play about with the realities you've constructed. I used that method for the first recording of the imaginary band. I was trying to simulate a dub band on 'Just Landed', and I was sure I'd installed enough attributes . . . extravagant liner notes, unplayable breaks . . . to make it clear it was my own fabrication. But in fact, few listeners appreciated my attempt at irony. Those who weren't in the know thought the project was based on music produced by a real band. Maybe it was because dub techniques *per se* confuse our understanding of the reality of played music . . . As far as my dub-related tracks are concerned, I could handle the instrumental versions of Scientist, for instance, more easily than other original vocal tunes. It took some time until I grew fond of rocksteady and roots music and I believe it required a dislocation to open up to it. Around 1996 I started travelling around the world for longer periods so that fortunately the dead weight of my cultural identity was at stake. The idea to create the Nu-Dub Players occurred while travelling New Zealand, staying with [producer, radio DJ and writer] Stinky Jim and constantly listening to all kinds of reggae tracks. On the other hand, on a global level, the acceptance and success of reggae and dub is not purely down to happenstance, but to the universal qualities of the musical elements, because – when subtracting lyrics – 'reggae' becomes 'regular'.[14]

The Flanger albums – *Templates* (1999), *Midnight Sound* (2000) and *Outer Space / Inner Space* (2001) – similarly employed intricate programming (as well as some live recordings) to give the impression of live jazz instrumentation. All of the albums were built from an audio sample archive of jazz instrumentation, composed mostly of drums, vibes and keyboards. 'A producer only really comes into his own at the mixing desk', states Bernd.

Bernd Friedmann, 1988.

The place where all the sounds converge. When I first started programming completely – in other words, when I started using samplers, keyboards and computers – then the desk became the sole musical source in the sense that it was the only place where improvisation was possible. All the other studio equipment required logistical and administrative efforts, but the desk was the place for immediate, spontaneous action. 'Dub' is what I call this method, since I use it on existing signals and rhythms, and it allows me to obtain constantly different results on the basis of the same material. The more pronounced the level of improvisation during the mix, the more the raw material, the original, is forced into

the background and sometimes even maltreated to the point
of being unrecognizable. The dub procedure allows you to
highlight certain musical features of a song while wholly
ignoring other ingredients – most likely foreground
components such as vocals or instrumental solos. The
resultant 'numbers' come closer to my own perspective:
they're de-cored, to put it figuratively, no longer have a centre.[15]

In recent years, Friedmann has continued to explore the musical
peripheries on his *Secret Rhythms* recordings with Jaki Liebezeit,
who was a jazz drummer in the 1960s and went on to form the
influential avant-rock band Can in 1969. Their five albums to date
have attempted to unlock staid Westernized concepts of rhythm,
fusing hypnotic, uneven grooves with musical accompaniment
from collaborators like Joseph Suchy and Hayden Chisholm.

SHACKLETON

The last few years have seen much talk of a 'Berlin–London' axis,
a Utopian (or perhaps Dystopian) matching of dub-techno and
London dubstep. While there have been some collaborations, and
even a dubstep night, Sub:Stance by DJ/producer Scuba (Paul
Rose) and DJ Paul 'Spymania' Fowler, has been launched at the
city's most famous techno club, Berghain, the idea is mostly a
media fabrication.

Perhaps one of the most exciting moments, though, was Shackleton's gloomily poignant 'Blood On My Hands' anthem (2006).
With 9/11-themed lyrics written (and sung) by Shackleton, the song
not only found its way into the record boxes of techno DJs, but was
remixed by techno veteran (and long-time Berlin resident) Ricardo
Villalobos into a stunning nineteen-minute minimal classic.

Born in the north of England, Sam Shackleton moved to
London, where he discovered proto-dubstep (then just called

Flanger flyer.

'garage' or 'dark garage') at FWD. He set up his Skull Disco label
in 2005 with Laurie 'Appleblim' Osborne while becoming a regular
at DMZ, where the dubstep sound became more defined. Skull
Disco stopped trading in 2009 after releasing several singles –
mostly double A-sides consisting of a track from each producer
– that were notable for their sparse, claustrophobic sound as well
as their unique 'punk-dread' artwork (created by Zeke Clough).
The label also released two compilations, *Soundboy Punishments*
(2007) and *Soundboy's Gravestone Gets Desecrated by Vandals* (2009).
In terms of dub, Shackleton recalls being influenced initially by
PIL's *Metal Box* as well as by a copy of King Tubby's *Unleashed Dub*
(1991) that he bought for a friend as a birthday present.

> We used to listen to that loads when it was early morning/late
> evening, after listening to more hectic stuff. I suppose since
> then I have heard most of the well-known releases but the

King Tubby stuff has always been to my taste as he tended to go with the more minimal aesthetic. It's hard to overestimate the influences of the original pioneers. I think that there are a lot of techniques that were used by the early dub producers that are now staples in music generally, but I think it is more the synergy of using advanced production techniques with people moving on a dancefloor that is the important thing. Things like tape delays and reverbs had already been in use for decades before the golden years of dub, I suppose the point is making a sub-genre that put these at the forefront.[16]

In 2009, Shackleton recorded his debut solo album for Berlin-based techno label Perlon. With the functional title 'Three EPs', it takes his skeletal sound into even more far-reaching places, veering fairly close at times to PIL's *Metal Box*. In 2011 he also put an album together with Bristol's Pinch (*Pinch & Shackleton*), which managed to pair their respective sounds into nine tracks of mostly compelling darkness. Its clear from these releases that Shackleton is not the type of producer to be overly restrained by genre, preferring to explore his own rhythmic and sonic influences in his own way, and at his own pace. Underlining this is his most recent release at the time of writing, *Music For the Quiet Hour/The Drawbar Organ*, which steps further away from prescribed structures to transport listeners into a subterranean world of dark, dubby and often unnerving aural cinema. At 137 minutes long, the album – released on his own Woe To The Septic Heart label – has a twenty-minute centrepiece, 'Music for the Quiet Hour Part 4' that features the voice of a grandfather (Vengeance Tenfold) dictating a letter to his grandson.

I tend to look at it more as experiments in psychedelic music techniques. Lots of artists try to find ways to dismantle the time narrative and spatial perception I suppose, whether that be with filtering techniques that reduce sounds that should normally be loud to whisper levels, or delays that keep a word 'hanging in the air' . . . or reverbs that play with our sense of scale or our perception of our surroundings. On one level, I just make the music that I want to make but when I have to think about it, I suppose that this explanation would lend an element of reason to the madness.

It is hard for me to have any real perspective on the dub-step thing as I feel that I have been defined by it and have been afforded a great opportunity by its existence, which I am really grateful for. But, by the same token, I feel totally alien from it due to the evolution of the music and genre name and the conjecture that surrounds it. I always liked the producers who were most minimal and had the raw edge of the original dub aesthetic without relying on easy signifiers.

All music has a time and context though and I am not really so interested in referencing a particular, often overly romanticised, past or a sound in this way. The thing is that you can copy a sound but it is what is being communicated through that sound that is important or the music will seem like an empty pastiche. Yes, I suppose there are parallels in sensibilities but London 2004 had a different dialectic to Kingston 1974, and the best stuff felt particular to that era or time in my humble opinion.[17]

8 CANADA'S DUB POETRY AND DANCEHALL

REGGAE AND DUB IN CANADA

The first Jamaicans to arrive in Canada were around 600 Maroons (descendants of slaves) in 1796 who had been exiled by the colonial government. Canada was also involved in the slave trade. By 1800, Jamaicans were working as labourers in the Cape Breton mines. However, all migration to Canada from the West Indies was halted after 1920 when the Canadian government announced that non-white people were no longer welcome. Nevertheless, just as in the UK, the Second World War created a demand for unskilled workers.

Post-war lifting of restrictions enabled some 200,000 West Indians to settle in Canada between 1946 and 1980 (a figure equivalent to 2 per cent of the country's population in that era). The labour drive was restricted for a period in the 1950s but then relaxed again in the 1960s, owing in part to the enforcement of the Family Reunification programme in 1962, and the implementation of a points system in 1967. In 1976 the system became more flexible, with a revised points system (essentially a watered-down version of the U.S. amendments eleven years earlier), and therefore made it easier for the Jamaican families of people who were now Canadian citizens to migrate to Canada.[1] Finally, between 2002 and 2012, 21,000 Jamaicans migrated to Canada.

As was the case in Britain, Jamaicans came to Canada in search of a better life, settling in cities like Ottawa, Hamilton, Montreal and Toronto, with the latter two cities absorbing the majority of the migrants. Inevitably, plenty of musicians arrived too. Among the more high-profile were rocksteady singers such as Leroy Sibbles (of The Heptones), singer Alton Ellis, and guitarist Lynn Taitt; Tony Gits and Ernie Smith of Roots Revival fame; gospel singer Carlene Davis; Ken 'Mr Rock Steady' Boothe and his former singing partner Winston 'Stranger' Cole; reggae/dub producer Willie Williams; Faybiene Miranda and Joe Cooper, who moved together and formed the band Tropical Energy; singer Johnny Osbourne, and keyboard legend Jackie Mittoo.

Unlike the UK, which had labels like Trojan Records and Island Records and a long history of two-way musical traffic, Canada had no 'infrastructure' for reggae in the 1970s. The musicians therefore set about creating one. Cole opened the first Caribbean record shop in Toronto and released several albums; Sibbles made albums for new local independents labels like Attic, and formed the band Truths and Rights. Smith began to write songs for Ishan People, an influential band formed by Johnny Osbourne and several other Jamaican musicians.

Ishan People were one of the first bands to really make a splash locally in Toronto. In 1976, they recorded their first album, *Roots*, for GRT Records, and their eponymous follow-up a year later. They also became part of the local reggae/punk crossover, performing on the same bills as local punk groups like Dead Boys, Sophisto Joe Mendelson and The Government. Ishan People split in 1979 and Osbourne returned to Jamaica to record classic albums like *Truths and Rights* (1980) and dancehall hits like 'Buddy Bye' (1985), which was based on King Jammy's Sleng Teng riddim. But by then, the band had already influenced a whole new wave of reggae acts.

Musician-producer Williams and keyboard player Mittoo made a living at the clubs that cropped up along Toronto's Yonge Street, and released songs and albums. Mittoo recorded *Wishbone* in 1971 for the Summus label, and *Reggae Magic* for CTL in 1972, while Williams's 'Messenger Man' (1977) and 'Slave' (1980) were

Toronto's Truths and Rights

partly recorded in Channel One and Joe Gibbs in Kingston, and partly at Summer Studios, one of the leading Canadian reggae studios.

Summer Records was set up in 1974 by Jerry Brown, a former singer with ska-reggae group The Jamaicans, in Molton, Ontario, with his business partner at the time, Oswald Creary. The label's first single was the reverb-drenched reggae/rocksteady hybrid 'Love Makes the World Go Round' by Johnny Osbourne (1974). Since the scene was so young, there was no airplay, no media attention and no sales. In 1976, another migrant from Jamaica, King Jammy, who had helped Brown wire his studio, joined Summer Records, but his arrival caused friction between Brown and Creary, and the latter left to found his own label, Half Moon Records.

Undeterred, Brown began selling his records to other markets, including Jamaica, aided by the cunning use of 'Made In Jamaica' stickers on the records. In 1977 the label's first full-length album, *Innocent Youths*, by the in-house band Earth, Roots & Water was released. In 1979, Mittoo and Williams created a new version of the song 'Real Rock', which was released on the Summer label as 'Armagideon Time'; The Clash covered the song and it became a hit in Jamaica. The second, and last, full length released by Brown was Noel Ellis's *Noel Ellis* (1983).

Summer's release schedule was somewhat irregular as Brown was not well financed (he was mostly working full time as a mechanic). In 1985, Jammy moved back to Jamaica and changed reggae forever with 'Sleng Teng'; Brown also flirted with the digital trend with hits like 'Call Me Nobody Else' by Unique Madoo 'Ska Doo' and 'Run Them A Run' by Willie Williams, but eventually reverted to analogue style. By 1988, Brown could no longer afford to keep Summer Records going. He sold the house in Malton, as well as the equipment, and in 1992 moved back to Jamaica. In 2007, Seattle-based reissue label Light in the Attic Records rounded up most of the best Summer releases on *Summer Records Anthology (1974–1988)*.

Half Moon Records, set up by Creary, began releasing music in 1975 by the same band of ex-pat artists – Stranger Cole, Johnny Osbourne, Leroy Sibbles – but also by Kingston heavyweights, including Augustus Pablo and 'Godfather of Reggae' Joe Higgs, and homegrown acts like Dill Smith and Pat Satchmo. Along with his in-house band, Super 8 Corporation, Creary also made a series of heavy Tubbyesque dubs, such as their take on Stranger Cole's 'Freedom, Justice & Equality' (1975), and Higgs's Augustus Pablo-helmed classic 'Creation' (1975).

Another producer from the early days was King Culture (Everett Cooper). Cooper had managed a pressing plant and ran the sound system Emperor Lion in Kingston before moving to Toronto in 1976. In 1979 he launched King Culture Records and Videos, a retail record / video outlet on Eglington Avenue, in which he also built a studio to record a mix of local and Jamaican singers such as The Uplifters, Rod Taylor, Derrick Harriott and Barry Brown, often putting a homegrown and JA act on separate sides of a seven-inch. His album *King Culture in Cultural Mood* (1981), partly mixed at Kingston's Channel One, won Best Dub Album that year at the third Canadian Black Music Awards. In the same year, he also received an award for Reggae Producer of the Year / Top Reggae Distributor.

Cooper also produced *We Are Moving* (1983), the debut album from The Uplifters (Egbert Dennis and Marcel Williams), who worked as backing singers for Leroy Sibbles, and two albums (*Funky In A Rub-a-dub Style* and *Round the World*) for the Jamaican deejay Stamma Rank, who worked on Sibbles's Papa Melody sound system when he arrived in Toronto in 1969. In terms of sound systems, Cooper's album *A Special Tribute to Some of the Stop Sound Systems* (1993), features 14 dubbed out dancehall tracks dedicated to some of Jamaica's top sets (King Tubby, Tippa Tone, Jack Ruby, Duke Reid).

All of this early reggae activity engendered a second wave of acts, including Nana McLean, Messenjah, Mojah, Fujahtive, Sattalites, 20th Century Rebels and Sonia Collymore, who were more proactive in defining a different sound that related to their mixed cultural influences. Messenjah, an influential group recognized as one of Canada's leading roots-reggae bands, was formed in Kitchener, Ontario, in 1981. They were produced and eventually led by guitarist-producer Carl Harvey, who had gone to Toronto from Jamaica at a young age, and joined successful Toronto funk and soul band The Crack of Dawn.

In the mid-1970s, Harvey visited Jamaica regularly, recording as a member of Bunny Lee's Aggrovators and working with Jackie Mittoo and Willie Williams along the way. In the 1980s, he became the lead guitarist of Toots and the Maytals and toured with Mittoo.

Of the four albums Harvey produced for Messenjah, two were nominated for Juno Awards (Canada's annual music awards). The band toured heavily, with a notable appearance at the Reggae Sunsplash festival in Montego Bay, Jamaica, in 1985. Following the second album, *Jam Session*, Errol Blackwood left to pursue a solo career with Harvey taking full control for the third record, *Cool Operator*, in 1987. After several more albums the band disbanded in 1997.[2]

LILLIAN ALLEN DUB POETRY

Arguably one of Canada's most interesting – or at least long-lasting – connections to dub has come about through its poetry scene. Dub poetry can be viewed as at the same time an extension of and deviation from Kingston's deejay culture. If the former is spontaneous, evolving from the urge to 'nice up the dance', the latter tends to be pre-written and intellectual (often political), and is often performed outside the dance hall.

Performance approaches vary. Some dub poets prefer to publish their work; others prefer to perform on a stage; others still record their poetry, sometimes with musical backing and sometimes not. Some artists, of course, do all of these things. Whichever way it is presented or performed, dub poetry is undeniably part of the rich culture of African-Caribbean oral traditions (which includes proverbs, riddles, hymns and folk tales).

The 'father of Jamaican dub poetry', and the person to coin the term 'dub poetry', is Jamaica's Oku Nagba Ozala Onuora (Orlando Wong). He has said the term refers to

a poem that has a built-in reggae rhythm, hence, when the poem is read without any reggae rhythm 'backing' so to speak, one can distinctly hear the reggae rhythm coming out of the poem.[3]

After serving a spell in prison for a failed bank robbery, then being shot for trying to escape and placed in a hard-core institution, Onuora began writing poetry in 1971. By 1976 he had won prizes at the Jamaica Literary Festival and had his work published in the national media. *Reflections in Red* (1979) was his first musical release. It was also the first Jamaican dub poetry recording, and featured backing from Aston and Carlton Barrett at Tuff Gong studios and released on Bob Marley's 56 Hope Road label. Fellow dub poet Michael Smith would only release one album, *Mi Cyaan Believe It* (1982), before he was murdered in 1983, allegedly by political opponents associated with the right-wing JLP (Jamaican Labour Party).

While the formal practice of dub poetry took a little longer to arrive in Canada, the scene that formed around poets such as Lillian Allen, Clifton Joseph, Ahdri Zhina Mandiela and Ishaka, among others, has proved ultimately to be more coherent and more extensive from a community perspective. Allen, who helped to develop the reggae band Truths & Rights and collaborated on some of their lyrics, is one of the first Canadian dub poets to release her work.

A book of poems, *Rhythm an' Hardtimes* (1982) came first, followed by the cassette release of *Dub Poet: The Poetry of Lillian Allen* (1983). Next came the EP *De Dub Poets* (1985), in combination with fellow Toronto poets Clifton Joseph and Devon Haughton, and backed by Truth & Rights. It was in 1978 at the eleventh World Festival of Youth and Students in Cuba that Allen met Onuara. Allen recounts that

We were doing our own thing in Toronto without really calling it dub poetry or connecting it with dub. I actually started out writing poetry and performing at festivals, churches and school events in Jamaica even before I was a teenager. The legendary [Jamaican poet, folklorist, writer, and educator] Louise Bennett was our beacon. When I moved to North

America I became engaged in exploring and developing my poetic expression with other young West Indians and we explored reggae and other rhythms we knew and the ideas and stylings of deejays like U-Roy as well as Augustus Pablo, Peter Tosh and Bob Marley. When I met Oku in Cuba he stood on this broken wall at the José Marti school and did an entire performance. For an hour. Just for me! I loved his personality and what he did, and he told me it was called dub poetry.[4]

Although dub as a music form was not a specific influence on Allen, she did regularly use music for her performances and jam sessions, and collaborated with local musicians like Billy Bryans, Dave Grey and Terry Lewis. These artists contributed to Allen's albums, including *Revolutionary Tea Party* (1986) and *Conditions Critical* (1987), with the former carrying notable songs such as 'I Fight Back', 'Riddim an' Hardtimes', and 'Birth Poem'. Both records were released and distributed by Allen's label, Verse to Vinyl, and received Juno awards for the Best Reggae/Calypso Album in 1987 and 1988 respectively.

Allen also formed De Dub Poets with award-winning poet, journalist and broadcaster Clifton Joseph and Devon Haughton. This was alongside her work with the Truths & Rights Band.

We always had music around even if it was a mishmash. We had congos, steel drums, reggae, soca . . . whatever worked, although reggae was always the music of choice for its political stance. I grew up near two dancehalls in Jamaica and some of my relatives in NYC have record stores, so I definitely heard the likes of U-Roy and Studio One in the overall mix; and you could even consider some of Bob Marley's work as recitations . . . even without musicians, the riddim or pulse is the music and an exaggerated cadence serves as chords. The poetry recited by itself is much closer to music than dry speech.[5]

Lillian Allen Live In Concert flyer.

Throughout the 1980s and 1990s Allen wrote and published books of poetry, short fiction and plays. She was featured in the National Film Board of Canada (NFB) film *Unnatural Causes* (1989), co-produced and co-directed the documentary *Blak Wi Blakk* (1994), and released her third album, *Freedom and Dance*, in 1999. In 2003 Allen was a driving force – along with Afua Cooper, another female star of the Canadian dub poetry scene – in the founding of the Dub Poets Collective, a creative organization totally dedicated to promoting dub poetry as a vital cultural practice.[6] Allen continues to be active on the Toronto scene. At the time of writing, her latest work is called *ANXIETY*, and creatively combines and extends the vocal and poetic elements in the musicality of dub to engage and create the listening experience.

Right now I'm actually returning to the idea of dub as a
concept. It's one of those things, like jazz, that becomes rele-
vant to whatever situation is at hand, exploring and challenging
its own aesthetics and meaning . . . and just when you think it
might just fizzle or break apart it revives and reminds us that we
survive, that things move and loop back. The aesthetic framework of dub is felt by the heart and I'm perhaps more
conscious of it now than I was. The drum and bass is in my
bones and in the exuberance of the Jamaican language and in
the way I think and speak. Dub is meant for the heart and soul.
It's a science of beauty and balance and when you close your
eyes it channels you, unclogs the clutter. I'm wide open to dub
and dubbing it, so let's see what comes along in the next while.[7]

CANADIAN HIP HOP IN THE DANCE HALL

Allen points out the natural closeness between the Canadian
dub poetry and hip hop scenes. Canadian hip hop, especially that
coming out of Toronto, has often carried a strong reggae/dance-
hall bent, from the breezy-Carib style of the Dream Warriors
in the late 1980s to the yardcore stylings of contemporary urban
artists like Kardinal Offishall and Choclair.

Michie Mee (Michelle McCullock) was one of the the first
female MCs to make any mark on mainstream Canadian culture.
Born in Jamaica, she moved to Toronto as a child and began
performing professionally at the age of fourteen. On a trip to
New York – using fake ID to enter clubs – she met celebrated hip
hop group Boogie Down Productions and convinced them that
she was a rapper.

When BDP came to Toronto in 1985, McCullock ended up
performing on stage with them. In addition, BDP's KRS-One (Kris
Parker) and Scott La Rock produced a compilation of Toronto hip
hop, *Break'n Out* (1987), featuring acts like Rumble & Strong,

Michie Mee & DJ L.A. Luv (Phillip Gayle), plus R&B duo Street Beat. One track, Michie and L.A. Luv's 'Elements of Style', included an intro by KRS-One that bigs up Michie Mee as the 'Cultural Representative of Canada'.[8] The record is said to be the last that Scott La Rock produced before being shot in 1987.

While Rumble & Strong would go on to briefly work with producer/DJ Junior Reid in Kingston (and have their tunes pressed up as dubplates by King Jammy), it was Michie and L.A. Luv's 'Elements of Style' that made an impact in the U.S. It also got the duo signed with Atlantic. Their subsequent debut album, *Jamaican Funk Canadian Style* (1991), incorporated dancehall reggae and led to the single 'Jamaican Funk'. Over 60,000 copies were sold in the U.S., and the record was nominated for a Canadian Juno Award in 1992.

After the duo broke up, L.A. Luv joined the Dream Warriors, while Mee went on to tour with acts such as Public Enemy and Queen Latifah. In the late 1990s, Mee starred in the CBC television series *Drop the Beat*, one of the first shows set in and around hip hop culture.

> I was an aggressive Jamaican. I had to show them I was different from my American counterparts . . . I could do what they did, but they couldn't do what I did – one side hip hop, the other side reggae . . . I was just being myself. I was that reggae chick from Caribana – born in Jamaica, made in Canada.[9]

Another cult hip hop group, the New York-based Main Source, also had a Canadian element in the shape of Toronto's Sir Scratch and K-Cut (Kevin McKenzie), who went on to produce for a range of hip hop artists, including Big Pun, Fu-Schnickens and Queen Latifah.

McKenzie also mentored Watts, another Toronto-based talent, who has gone on to produce for high-profile artists such as Redman,

Method Man and Joe Budden. Watts's father was a drummer in popular reggae band Messenjah; having learned to play the drums as a child, he was playing them professionally by five and opening for international reggae band Third World at the age of seven. At twelve he performed in front of a crowd of over 50,000 at Toronto's Rogers Centre alongside Nelson Mandela.[10]

One of the greatest links today between Jamaica and Canada is Kardinal Offishall, a 6ft 4in. Toronto native and one of the best known hip hop producers and performers in Canada. Well known for blending reggae and dancehall influences into his music, he started rapping at a very early age and was winning competitions before he reached his teens. By the age of twenty he was signed to a publishing deal with Warner / Chappell Music Canada and released his debut album, *Eye & I* in 1997. A year later he joined fellow Circle member Kareem Blake ('Choclair'), also of Jamaican descent, and Rascalz for 'Northern Touch', a song that put the Canadian hip hop scene into the mainstream market.

D'BI YOUNG ANITAFRIKA

'I grew up alongside contemporary hip hop artists such as Jully Black, Kardinal Offishall, J Wyze, Socrates and Motion, who actually mentored many of us', says D'bi, one of the new generation of dub poets in Toronto whose work often overlaps with hip hop.

Many of us were also fortunate enough to be mentored by elder artists such as my mother Anita Stewart, Lillian Allen, Verle Thompson, Star Jacobs, Winsom Winsom, Amah Harris, Ivor Pecou and more through the Fresh Arts training program; a community youth initiative which helped us as emerging artists for five years. If you listen to most of our work you will see that there is a social conscience that runs

through our themes. I feel that this is in part due to the
critical-thinking skills that were imparted on us through
the Fresh Arts programme.[11]

Anitafrika's mother, Anita Stewart, was a pioneering dub
poet and member of the Poets in Unity group. Anitafrika moved
to Canada from Jamaica in 1993 and exploded onto the Canadian
theatre scene in 2001 with *da kink in my hair*, which played at
London's Hackney Empire Theatre in 2006 and has toured
globally. Since then, she has written eight plays – *solitary*, *yagayah*,
androgyne, *she*, *domestic* and *the sankofa trilogy*, as well as the award-
winning monodramas *blood.claat*, *benu* and *word! sound! powah!* –
and published two collections of poetry.[12]

I grew up on all the different kinds of Jamaican music, from
dancehall, to rub-a-dub, to reggae, to dub poetry and so much
more. I have always been desperately in love with dancehall, its
unapologetic sexual adventure and daring. Dub poetry is the
music I respect the most, and for me represents a meeting
place between the rebelliousness of dancehall and the consciousness of reggae. To be a practitioner of dub is a role I
take very seriously. I feel that with it comes an incredible
responsibility and accountability to lead by not causing further harm to the people who listen to my words. In many
ways, I believe that artists are spiritual leaders. People listen to
our words and it affects them on both a conscious and subcon-
scious level. We manipulate the very vibrations of which we
are made. This is spiritual work so I approach it with that kind
of reverence.[13]

As well as a dub poet and playwright, Anitafrika is a Dora-
winning actor, appearing in films, plays and sitcoms. In 2007
she facilitated a summer dub theatre programme for youth in

Toronto, which led her to founding and working in the role of artistic director of the anitafrika dub theatre. She is the originator of the dub poetry-inspired arts-based personal and professional development methodology.

> My work is grounded in dub. Dub poetry is Jamaican-derived reggae-grounded performance storytelling that chants for the upliftment of the peoples using various forms of spoken and written poetic constructs, emerging out of African oral story-telling traditions that accompanied enslaved African peoples to the new world. The eight principles of dub poetry . . . four of which were named out of my mother's theoretical observations of dub poetry in the early '80s, and the other four I named out of my own observations of dub poetry over the last decade . . . ensure the genre's undeniable ability to transform the people who witness it: self-knowledge, oral-ity, rhythm, political content and context, language, urgency, sacredness and integrity foster an ecosystem of accountability and responsibility between the dub poet and the people.[14]

D'bi has also produced two politically fuelled dub poetry albums. The *wombanifesto* (2010) is backed by a wide variety of hip hop beats, Cuban and world rhythms and dubstep. *333* (2011) is a collaboration with Tanzanian producer Jakofire Pro and South African producers Mandiemafu and Baski Njovu, and is dedicated to all dance hall queens, queers and questioners of the status quo.[15]

MOSSMAN

One of Young's live collaborators is Montreal-based Mossman (Moss Raxlen), who began collecting records, writing, producing and deejaying in the mid-1990s. In 1997, Raxlen produced his first album, *Message in the Dub* – although it was not released until

much later – and started a recording studio in downtown
Montreal. There he recorded several more notable dub albums
between 2000 and 2005. Shortly afterwards, in 2001, he started
his Dispensation label and opened the Sketchy Wax record store
for seven-inch reggae, dub and dancehall vinyl records.

> My biggest influences in terms of dub is the stuff put out
> by Lee Perry and Scientist in the 70s, and Half Moon and
> Wackies in terms of north American dub . . . I'm a massive
> Perry fan, and those labels had a similar vibe to the Black Ark,
> a kind of underwater sound. The very first dub album I
> worked on was a band called Jah Children from Montreal.
> Being a musical person that can play bass, piano and percus-
> sion, when I got the opportunity to work with the band's
> masters I just cut loose. A sound engineer called Bunny
> (Bayani C. Esguerra) was my mentor, as well as a good friend.
> Working with him on that record was my apprenticeship. I did

Shemurenga album artwork.

D'bi Young Anitafrica.

a bunch more records, while collecting lots of old equipment like the Soundcraft mixing board, Space Echos, Phasers like Perry used to use. But when the sales started dropping because of the internet, I stopped.[16]

One of the session musicians in Mossman's studio was legendary guitarist Lynn Taitt, who had gone to Toronto in the 1970s and lived with Alton Ellis for a spell before moving to Montreal. Through his connections, Raxlen landed Taitt a show at the Montreal International Jazz Festival, which helped revive Taitt's career. In 2005 Moss finally released his first *Message in the Dub* and in the same year produced *Mossman Meets Vander's Montreal Dub Sound System*.

While Perry's inspiration was obvious on *Mossman vs. The World Bank*, right down to the piano fills and telltale Mutron effects, Raxlen's latest collaboration with the Ark of Infinity band, *Mossman vs. Mr Tsunami at Dub Corner*, has a more modern electronic-oriented sound – one much closer to the Scientist school of radical reverberation.

> For the *Mossman vs. The World Bank* disc I was really going for that multi-layered sound Perry had back in the day. But the new one is definitely a more modern approach. We used drum machines on the whole thing this time, so yes, Scientist was an influence, but as far as engineering techniques, it's always been the big three for us: King Tubby, Lee Perry and the Scientist.[17]

In 2007, Raxlen produced *Rocksteady: The Roots of Reggae*, a film / album project that he co-created and which has received world-wide acclaim. Since then Raxlen has spent a lot of time deejaying and promoting the film. He is currently preparing the release of a new documentary and album project that was made with Taitt in 2007 but was never released because of Taitt's death in 2010. He is also currently managing another veteran reggae ex-pat, Stranger Cole, as well as operating as a part-time DJ and manager for Kingston's original female deejay, Sister Nancy (who is now based in New Jersey).

Another of Raxlen's key contributions to Canada's dub scene was his monthly Dub Lounge event in Montreal. The event featured a host of guest Montrealer MCs and DJs and ran from 1997 to 2010, making it the longest-running dub-themed night in Canada. From 2006 to 2008, one of Raxlen's most regular collaborators was DJ / producer Scott Monteith (Deadbeat).

DEADBEAT

The extent of Monteith's love of Jamaican reggae and dub is obvious in his dub-infused house and techno productions. Since the late 1990s he has crafted productions for labels such as Betke's ~scape, Cynosure, Wagon Repair, Musique Risquée and his own label BLKRTZ.

> I started raving in Toronto in the early 90s and always gravitated towards the chillout rooms. Through that I got into jungle and ambient acts like Bandalu, The Orb, Psychic Warriors, all the dub influenced stuff. Then I started to buy Basic Channel's stuff – 'Radiance' was the first one I got – and then right into the Burial Mix and Rhythm & Sound stuff. I also latched onto the early copycats, like Deepchord from Detroit, Blue Train and Mosaic.[18]

It was when he moved from Toronto to Montreal in 1994 that Monteith got more into Jamaican dub, via a roommate who would point out the original samples in the jungle records he was playing. A little later he met Raxlen and helped him to relaunch the Dub Lounge night, which had been in hiatus.

Until 2002, Monteith's productions and DJ work had been comprised of fairly straightforward techno. It was following a request to play a live show for a Micro_MUTEK show in Montreal in 2002 – scheduled right before Caribbean vocalist Tikiman – that he realized that he needed to create something different. Whilst experimenting with dub and reggae soundscapes, he started to put together what would become his debut album *Wild Life Documentaries* (2002), a series of drifting, ethereal pieces awash with granular noise and microscopic riddims.

Monteith went on to release *Something Borrowed, Something Blue* (2004), which applied a more romantic pop sensibility, but maintained a broadly experimental approach. The track 'Head over Heels' was notable for its use of chirping crickets in place of micro-digital riddims. In 2008 came *Roots and Wire*, a deep and heavy record that drew again on house and techno, and featured Tikiman on 'Babylon Correction'.

> Dub has always been my strongest pull and main focus. I love the delays, the never-ending hypnosis, the real simple but groove-driven melodies. In a way, I think I'm drawn to them in part because my dad is a Protestant minister and in one sense they're like hymns. For me, from a historical perspective, techno is tied to dub/sound system culture, since they both thrive on people wanting to provide special exclusive records for their crew or party or whatever.[19]

After his move to Berlin in 2008, where he still resides, Monteith's studio mix, *Radio Rothko* (2010), pulled together a range of dub techno classics from Various Artists ('No.3'), Basic Channel's 'Quadrant Dub', Monolake's 'Static', Maurizio's 'M6A' and Substance & Vainqueur's 'Reverberation'. *Drawn And Quartered* (2011) comprised five elongated tracks, each one over ten minutes in length, covered in shrouds of digital mist and featuring clanging, unexpected chord changes and delays.

VERSION XCURSION

Founded by Lee Castle ('Sassa'le'), a veteran DJ, producer and radio host originally from Bristol in the UK, Version Xcursion was created to play dub-centric UK underground music, such as work by Massive Attack, Dizzee Rascal, Smith & Mighty, Tricky, Portishead, Craig David, Scientist and Mad Professor, to Toronto audiences. In 1997, Castle co-founded the Flirt Sound System with T-Step and drum and bass deejay Marcus Visionary. Visionary put on a series of underground garage events in Toronto between 1996 and 2002, and even

Mossman Dub flyer.

managed to pull in a high-profile slot from Craig David just before the club closed.

In 2004 Castle joined forces with Aram Lee ('Citizen Sound') to release a Version Xcursion album, *Radio*. This gave rise to the single 'Rock Da Dub', three soundclash EPS (the 'vx meets' series), and their release *Past & Present* (2009), which featured remixes from Rob Smith of Bristol-based Smith & Mighty.

My musical journey started as a kid and teenager listening to hip hop with groups like Public Enemy, De La Soul, A Tribe Called Quest and Boogie Down Productions. I was also getting into reggae at that time, mainly Marley, Gregory and Dennis Brown. From there I found dub music and quickly fell in love with the innovators like Lee Perry and King Tubby. It was through Massive Attack's *Blue Lines*, and a compilation called

Dubmission, that I began to really start exploring dub music and its heavy influence on so many modern genres. This sound got me into DJ'ing, radio and eventually production.[20]

Scaram's 2011 debut outing, *Citizen Sound*, features a host of local musicians and singers (Prince Blanco, Richard Underhill) and takes global sound system culture as an overall influence.

Citizen Sound evolved from everything I was doing musically. It was a chance to create something new outside of what I was doing with vx at the time. I wanted to treat it like a sound system, build my own riddims, work with guest vocalists, record some dubplates and remixes and ultimately rock a dance floor. I've released a full-length album, several singles, remixes and traveled to Europe and played shows in London and Amsterdam. Dub is still the root of my production, it's just more focused now. I've been at it just over a decade, and I'm always learning, still so much to discover. Dub is definitely part of what keeps me going and keeps me inspired.[21]

CONCLUSION

DUB IN THE TWENTY-FIRST CENTURY

According to Adrian Sherwood, 'The dub thing has been hijacked by just about everyone who likes to use reverbs and phasers.'

> The version thing, where you had twenty or thirty cuts and five different versions, is sadly gone of course, but the fact that people are using reverbs and delays and explosions and big fat bottom end shows that the influence of what we were all a part of has been immense.[1]

At the time of publication, in 2014, it is over 40 years since the first dub albums were released in Jamaica. What began as a serendipitous accident in a cutting room in Kingston has had a significant influence around the world, not only sonically but in terms of studio methodology too.

Apart from the genres and styles covered in this book, traces of dub can be found in a multitude of other forms, from most electronic and DJ music (especially in performances that involve live sound effects), to movements like Krautrock, typified by bands Can and Neu!, and post-rock, played by Tortoise and Bark Psychosis, to world music, exemplified in the work of Bill Laswell and Dub Colossus and ambient music (see the work of The Orb and Brian Eno, for example). Dub's influence reaches today's global network of producers, sound systems, MCS and DJS.

Many of dub's original pioneers are sadly no longer with us. King Tubby was shot outside his Kingston home in 1989; Augustus Pablo died of a collapsed lung in 1999; Keith Hudson died of lung cancer in 1984; Errol Thompson died after multiple strokes in 2004; Henry 'Junjo' Lawes was killed in London in 1999. Yet those who are still alive are mostly connected to dub in some way.

Perry, who left Jamaica in the 1980s after torching his Black Ark studio, re-emerged in London and the Netherlands before eventually moving to Switzerland, where he now lives. Of all the original dub masters, he has been most active, working with Sherwood's Dub Syndicate for *Time Boom X De Devil Dead* (1987) and *From the Secret Laboratory* (1990); Lloyd Barnes for *Satan Kicked*

Lee 'Scratch' Perry and Dubblestandart 2010.

Lee 'Scratch' Perry and Dubblestandart 2010 flyer.

the Bucket (1988); Adrian Sherwood on *Dub Setter* (2009). He had also collaborated with Mad Professor on albums in the mid-1990s, such as *Black Art Experryments*; *Experryments at the Grass Roots of Dub*; *Super Ape Inna Jungle*; *Who Put the Voodoo Pon Reggae*; and *Dub Take the Voodoo out of Reggae*.

Along the way, Perry has embraced modern, dub-influenced styles like digidub, jungle and dubstep. In 2008, when Perry was 70, he teamed up with New York-based Subatomic Sound System and Viennese dubsters Dubblestandart (as well as Ari Up from The Slits) for a collaborative remix in a dubstep style called *Return From Planet Dub*. This included new versions of several of Perry's most famous tunes and riddims ('Disco Devil', 'Chase The Devil', 'Croaking Lizard') from Lee's influential *Super Ape* album. Another track, 'Wadada', was originally recorded by Dub Syndicate and features the late Prince Far I. 'Chrome Optimism', meanwhile, is built around David Lynch samples and was released two years later on a twelve-inch format with remixes from RSD (Rob Smith) and Subatomic under the moniker 'Dubblestandart Meets David Lynch & Lee Scratch Perry'.

It is clear from these releases, which range from respectable to excellent, that Perry is still approaching his art from a creative perspective, and not just as a vocalist. Sherwood recounts that he and Perry 'worked very closely on the production of *Time Boom*'.

> He was hands on with that one and you can hear how full of his ideas it is. I feel after that he decided to take something of a back seat. Speaking for myself, each time I've worked with him I've tried to make him contribute more than just vocals, because he is still full of ideas in all areas of the production, just not as hands on.[2]

Hopeton Brown, 'Scientist', has lived in Los Angeles since 1995. He has spent much of the last couple of decades releasing his lesser-known 1980s dubs as well as fighting for royalties from labels such as Greensleeves Records in the UK, as he claims that the label released his records without his knowledge or consent. He took Greensleeves Records to court in 2005 for the use of five tracks on the video game *Grand Theft Auto 3*. Greensleeves Records maintained that since the recordings had been produced at Lawes and King Tubby's studio, neither of whom were alive at the time of the hearing, Brown was neither the owner of the recording nor of the composition copyrights. Brown lost the case, but at the time of writing is still fighting it. In 2012 he began touring with the Roots Radics to perform on the very same project that the video-game tracks had come from the classic dub album *Scientist Rids the World of the Evil Curse of the Vampires* (1981).

While dub was phased out in Kingston in the 1980s, the sound system tradition has continued. One of the deejay legends preserving the sound is U-Roy, whose King Stur-Gav sound, helmed today by Brigadier Jerry, Ranking Joe and General Trees, is still going strong.

Mungo's HiFi, based in Scotland, which runs a night in Glasgow called 'Walk n Skank' and puts out 'forward thinking reggae music', is part of a new generation of sound systems, labels and producers who are operating at an international level. It is not just through cities that the dub 'virus' has travelled either. For example, online record label A Quiet Bump, based in rural Irpinia, Sardinia, releases rich, intricate digidub that spans house, hip hop and techno. Even the infrastructure of Los Angeles' trendiest hip hop scene, which revolves around cutting-edge producers like Flying Lotus, is loaded with dub connotations, from a label called Dublab, a studio called Echo Chamber and a club night named Low End Theory.

In fact dub has even transcended music. In 2010 New York-based artist Sean Dack produced the art show 21st CENTURY DUB DUB, an 'investigation into ideas of the copy and the original, the use of appropriation and notions of physical versus intangible media'. The show consists of *Version/Variation*, a 26-channel audio installation. The piece collects and compiles every commercially available version of Erik Satie's 'Gymnopedie No. 1' (1888) and overlays them to create a slow, sonorous 'version'.

Dub has even infiltrated science, in the shape of the British University of Birmingham's Genomic Dub Collective. It was dreamed up by 'an eclectic mix of individuals, united by a common love of science and music',[3] including a professor of microbial genomics, a Jamaican scientist (who speaks Jamaican Creole), a programmer and a clinical psychologist. Between them they aim to create a brand new musical genre known as 'genomic dub', which 'celebrates recent successes in the field of genomics and evolutionary biology, highlight[s] common threads between current scientific, artistic and social issues with the past and explore[s] the potential for encoding macromolecular (protein and DNA) sequence data into dub music'. In 2005 they created *The Origin of Species in Dub* – a celebration of Darwin's masterpiece realized through the medium of reggae music.[4] The group's objectives are

> to engage the interest of both the scientific and wider public, bringing an appreciation of science to sections of society who usually ignore or devalue it and an appreciation of reggae and of Jamaican culture to a scientific audience. We aim to stimulate interest in science and its impact on society through cover notes for our dub tracks.[5]

TECHNOLOGY AND AUTHENTICITY

As dub's influence continues to reverberate through the music of the twenty-first century, technologies and approaches have changed, and questions have been raised about authenticity. For example, does a dub recording made in a bedroom with free software on a laptop really have anything to do with the experiments of King Tubby, Lee 'Scratch' Perry or Scientist? Can an instrumental or extended mix really be called a 'dub version' (as they sometimes are)?

Dub arose as a creative solution to practical challenges within a specific set of circumstances in 1970s Kingston. By transcending its local environment, those conditions inevitably changed, along with the affiliated sound and strategies. 'Second wave' centres like London, Bristol, Toronto and New York, while enjoying a similar network of Jamaican sound system and production cultures, did not quite have the same interplay as in Kingston. Many of the sounds in the UK, for example, were initially leery of homegrown product, and playing music from Jamaica was preferred. The interplay between studio and system was never as intensely reciprocal (nor as aggressively competitive) as in

Kingston since there was not an abundant stream of roots reggae songs coming through for engineers to 'version'. Engineers and producers therefore often took Perry's approach of pre-recording their own material to dub or – later – building dubs directly 'from the ground up'.

According to Dennis Bovell, 'On the UK/London scene producers had to convince the sound systems that their product was worthy of a spin.'

> Rarely were the two connected. Being a producer that had a sound system background made it easier for me to approach other sounds all over the UK and invite them to spin Matumbi, Errol Dunkley, Janet Kay, Steel Pulse and other artists I had produced.[6]

Technology was responsible for the birth of dub and has stayed crucial to its development. By the time producers and engineers had started engaging with dub outside Jamaica, they were already using new, or different, equipment and methods compared to their Kingston counterparts. This created a tension between those who viewed dub as a genre specific to 1970s Kingston, and those who believed it should use the new technologies to innovate. This tension continues today.

By the early 1980s, the rise of MIDI, samplers and drum machines led to a new style called 'digidub' (sometimes termed 'neodub'). Music writers such as Simon Reynolds have lamented this movement, stating that 'the difference between classic dub and digital dub is like that between the stained glass window and a computer graphic'.[7]

Perhaps Reynolds was thinking of the so-called coffee-table dub artists around at the time his book *Energy Flash* was published in 1998 (Thievery Corporation and Kruder & Dorfmeister, among others), whose polished blend of ambient chill-out music has very

little in common with Jamaican dub apart from the tempo and a
vaguely exaggerated bassline.

Yet there was another trail of digidub productions that was
started in Britain's sound system scene by Jah Shaka, The Disciples,
Alpha & Omega and others, which maintained a commitment to
root and attempted to reproduce the authentic energy of the
dance hall. The Disciples, for example, started out by attempting
to capture something of Jah Shaka's dances, of which they were
huge fans. Ross Disciple told the *Versionist* that 'I've never been
bogged down in this thing of having to have springs and tape
echos to emulate old school Jamaican dub'.

> Things can be done with digital gear and we were / are in a
> different era, so I always figured do things in our own way . . .
> in between [our] first and second albums I had started looking
> into the MIDI thing . . . I started programming my HRI6 to
> sound like a machine rather than like a live drummer, and
> there was something different about the style of the b-line,
> hard to define in words, maybe just more simple or strict, and
> of course making it with a keyboard bass gives it a next tone
> as well.
>
> I was inspired by the JA productions at the time. Even
> though dancehall was the most prevalent style there was still
> nuff roots vibes as well. The scene was also moving fast and
> in different directions, so I just moved with it. Jamaican music
> never remained static, it always moved on either in style or
> production, like how Scientist redefined the sound of dub
> away from Tubby's. For me it was mixing the old school
> roots vibes with the JA/UK digi vibe, but we was still making
> just instrumental / dubs, and the JA digi style of riddim was
> made more for vocals, so we had to come with a slightly
> different style that could work on its own.[8]

The debate between analogue and digital dub has raged ever since, with new school producers like Mossman and Twilight Circus considering a human touch as essential for an authentic dub recording. Mossman says that

> The main thing, to me at least, is the difference between producer, mixer and musician. Some people that make dub are good at all three of these things . . . but most are only good at one, and it takes all three to make a good dub recording, whether it's new or old. It seems a lot of the new stuff is really lacking as far the musicianship, at least in comparison to the dubs of the '70s and '80s.[9]

Scott Monteith (Deadbeat) argues that the current array of software available makes good dub more than possible.

> From a technical perspective a lot of the same effects [delays reverbs, phasers, extreme filtering] people like Tubbys and Scratch were using in the mid-'70s are the same as those used now, albeit in software form a good deal of the time.
>
> At the end of the day though, a dub is only as good as the material being fed into said effects. Perry and Tubby had some of the best musicians who have ever walked the earth at their disposal writing some of the heaviest grooves ever heard. While in my opinion those players will never be matched, the virtualization of instruments, vastly intelligent sequencers, and near one-to-one copies of nearly every vintage piece of hardware known to man offers at the very least the potential for new generations to write some bloody heavy grooves indeed.[10]

The analogue–digital debate has even lured old school producers such as Clive Chin back into the studio. In 1998 he began working with New York-based band The Slackers, and around the same time began a rescue mission for the 'lost archives' stored in Randy's old studio at studio 17 North Parade in Kingston. With the assistance of the Experience Music Project (EMP and Microsoft co-founder Paul Allen, Chin went back to Kingston in 1999 and unearthed all of the original master tapes, including material from Bob Marley, Peter Tosh, Alton Ellis, John Holt, U-Roy, and Augustus Pablo. These tapes were then digitized and catalogued for the first time by Chin and producer/engineer Billy 'Prince Polo' Szeflinski.[11]

Troubled by the apparent 'lack of gravity' in modern digital productions, Chin gave a lecture at the Red Bull Music Academy in South Africa in 2003, and has subsequently travelled the world giving lectures and workshops on the benefits of analogue equipment (and how to use it). Chin claims that Digital 'just doesn't sound as pure and warm as analogue. When you capture from tape, it's pure'.[12]

However, dub was not only just about technology. It was also about improvisation – 'jazz at the mixing board' – and the personality that the first producers like Perry, Tubby, Jammy and Scientist gave to the music. King Jammy's thinks that

> dub music on the whole is experimental sound. And the feeling you have at the time, you create things about the feeling that come across you when you do the mix. Dub is not something you plan to do this way or that way – it can never come out authentic if you do it that way. It has to be spot on at the time, the creativeness you put into it at the time, that's dub music, real dub music.[13]

One of the criticisms levelled at computers is that they do not have the same ability to be spontaneous, nor can they be abused in the same way. In the documentary *Dub Stories* (2006), Mad Professor states that the worst thing is that the technology right now doesn't really lend itself to dub. Because a lot of the spontaneous elements of dub music are lost. Now with a computer a man will try seh . . . oh let me put an echo here . . . and yes after I put that echo here I'll measure it . . . hmmm it's 5 seconds . . . and then I'll put a reverb there . . . It's too predetermined. Dub isn't supposed to be like that.[14]

This perhaps goes some way to explaining the development in the 'clicks & cuts' scene of the 1990s (see, for example, Pole and the broader work of the German Mille Plateaux label), which utilized randomized glitches and additional surface crackle to introduce arbitrary or analogue feels into the music. Interestingly, one of the best known German digidub labels of the noughties, Jahtari, has recently switched back to analogue. Jan Gleichmar recalls that when he started out,

I only had a laptop and a MIDI keyboard to play the laptop's internal VST synths. When you're alone, you're also the only musician around and you have to play everything by yourself and record those notes into the program: drums, bass, skanks. I always tried to avoid using samples to build the core riddim, and use them more for effects, like speech from Sci Fi movies, etc. But I always played basslines, skanks and the rest pretty much the same like I do now, but with gear. The main difference is shaping the sound: instead of clicking on the on-screen-knobs with the mouse, now there are real knobs, which is way more fun. I spend much more time actually shaping and creating sounds from scratch rather than clicking through existing presets in the computer. This way you stumble over things by accident you'd never do on a computer. I used to program drums 'visually' in the laptop but now we build all out basic riddims in the MPC now, by playing them live. It's still a very different approach to the classic dub producers, more like a '90s hip hop machine. Making reggae with a box like that adds something new.[15]

While dubstep producers like Mala manage to produce convincing dub recordings on digital equipment – including reverbs, delays, flangers, phasing – he maintains strong connections to the analogue side of the industry. He's one of the last dubstep producers to cut his tracks to dubplates, insisting that the process teaches him a about his music and helps him to raise the standards of his work. Mala laments the decline of cutting houses, which he sees as community centres, as well as the lack of technical knowledge available in the larger club music infrastructure.[16]

> Everything comes from a digital background nowadays. Digital EQS, digital compression, digital limiting . . . all played on digital sources like laptops, CDS and MP3S. Even when clubs have good sounds, the promoters think our music just needs extra subwoofers, without realising that we also need the tops and mids to be translated. It's about balance. When you think about it, technology should have enhanced the quality of sound three or four times more than how it was in the '70s. But it hasn't. The dynamic range is more limited, the quality of musicianship too. In many ways it's gone backwards.[17]

Interestingly, Scientist, who is arguably the last remaining original dub engineer apart from King Jammy (Perry and Chin are first and foremost producers), is committed to digital. He holds that 'Analogue is dead and people just have to wake up and realize that'. Yet he similarly sees a problem with a lack of technical knowledge in the music industry more generally.

We all have access to the same technology and always have had. Yet why does a drum on a Jamaican mix sound better and more powerful than one on a Righteous Brothers or Beatles song? I have been teaching people since my days at Studio One that music should be recorded in a certain way to bring out the best quality. That is what dub is about. I used the console far more than King Tubby and what I did in Jamaica and Channel One in terms of high-fidelity recording is what started what we all have now.

It wasn't musicians who designed the pre-amps. It was us technicians who were testing our amps that pushed for better sound. It was Jamaican technicians that built the speakers to test that sound. We were the first ones to replace paper inside the speaker cones with different materials to make it louder and better, something that would become a standard procedure several years later. Jamaica set the standard for high-fidelity recording. People think reggae production is the easiest but it's the hardest. If you put a Jamaican engineer next to a rock and roll one it will show up their weaknesses immediately.[18]

To prove his point, Scientist took part in an experiment to remix the original tapes of Marvin Gaye's soul classic 'What's Going On' and brought out all of its previously muddied parts – hi-hats, drum sounds and vocals – in just 45 minutes. To watch the short clip of the project available online is to be reminded of dub's capacity to turn songs inside out – and to bring them to life.[19]

DUB AND THE REMIX

Dub's strategies also live on in the concept of the remix. As noted in the Introduction, the idea of cutting up and rearranging music goes back at least to the days of tape editing. In terms of dub, it was multitrack recording that allowed songs to be broken into fragments and reassembled in various ways. Although this technology was available across Europe and North America, Jamaica's unique application of it rests on several key 'advantages'. First, having access to studios was generally easier in Jamaica than it was for u.s. musicians and artists, owing to cheaper running costs and a tighter-knit social scene. Since producers tended to own as well as operate their studios, they also enjoyed unrestricted access to their master tapes. In contrast, in America the masters were owned and closely guarded by the record companies. A relative lack of copyright law (or at least enforced copyright law) in Jamaica also meant that producers owned the songs, rather than the musicians who were generally paid by the session, rather than by the song. As such, Jamaican producers and engineers could do what they wanted with the songs. As Paul D. Miller (DJ Spooky) has put it, 'You can think of the whole culture as a shareware update, a software source for the rest of the world to upload.'[20]

As we saw in chapter Four, the culture of the remix occurred within the context of the disco scene, and was tied in with the advent of the twelve-inch single. The aim for the disco remix pioneer Tom Moulton was not to alter the track's essence though, but simply to edit it. Whereas radio edits involved removing a piece of a composition to make it shorter for radio play, Moulton was interested in adding material in order to make a track longer. This was quite a radical approach at the time, given that it would immediately destroy any chances of airplay. In addition, the producers were not too keen to have their work played with either.

As we have seen, disco remixers got their own way and they did not stop at simple edits. Once they had the know-how to change tracks, Gibbons, Levan, Russell and others also set about applying similar experimental methodologies as dub. However, any specific influence of dub on disco remixers has been difficult to prove. Despite Moulton travelling to Jamaica around this time and hanging out at Studio One (see chapter Four), the disco remix appears to have developed in complete isolation from the dub 'version', as Tim Lawrence describes:

> New York remixers . . . weren't really influenced by Jamaica, in part because New York dance crowds demanded music that was much more up-tempo than reggae and dub. Jamaican remixes usually involved the producer-DJs taking out elements from the original track and placing greater emphasis on the drums and the bass via a process of subtraction, but the records weren't extended. New York remixers would also strip records down, but they were also focused on drama and an idea of a journey, so they would often retain complete elements from the original and would then take the record 'somewhere else' by stripping out certain sections and extending others. New Yorkers developed their own remix technique in almost complete isolation and apparently without outside influence for something like seven years.[21]

Eduardo Navas, author of *Remix Theory: The Aesthetics of Sampling* (2012), also states that

> the early form of remix from Jamaica known as 'version' is not a remix in the popular sense. The remix of NYC was developed in large part due to commercial interests to promote specific songs in a growing consumerist market thriving on the wings of disco and hip hop subcultures. Yet historically, it is agreed that the basic concept of remixing that was defined in NYC was already at play in Jamaica. When considering this, one should keep in mind that the type of consumption that took place in Jamaica's culture is very different from what took place in popular culture in the United States and other places of the world, and that this does affect the different

names that acts of appropriation attain. In short, there are cultural and political reasons why Jamaican musicians called their remixes 'versions' and not 'remixes'.[22]

It is not generally contested that Jamaica arrived at the idea of using multitrack technology to rearrange tracks first in this sense. As John Bush has remarked, '[dub] was certainly the first to fully embrace the idea that artistic success could be achieved by rearranging pre-recorded music'.[23] Of course, DJ Kool Herc was already editing tracks via his beat-juggling to achieve the same goals as Moulton, that is, to extend the breaks so the audience would dance for longer. It was when these techniques became commonplace in American recording studios that the remix took off, specifically in the genres of disco and hip hop.

Navas, who has defined a music remix as a 'reinterpretation of a pre-existing song, meaning that the "aura" of the original will be dominant in the remixed version', outlines three basic forms.

> The first remix is extended, that is a longer version of the original song containing long instrumental sections making it more mixable for the club DJ . . . the second remix is selective; it consists of adding or subtracting material from the original song; this is the type of remix which made DJs popular producers in the music mainstream . . . the third remix is reflexive; it allegorizes and extends the aesthetic of sampling, where the remixed version challenges the aura of the original and claims autonomy even when it carries the name of the original; material is added or deleted, but the original tracks are largely left intact to be recognizable.[24]

Navas gives Walter Gibbons's remix of Double Exposure's 'Ten Percent' (1976) as an example of the extended remix. For the selective remix, he cites Coldcut's remix of Eric B. & Rakim's

'Paid in Full' (1987), and Mad Professor's mix of Massive Attack's *Protection* album (*No Protection*) for the reflexive.

> In this [third] case both albums, the original and the remixed versions, are considered works on their own, yet the remixed version is completely dependent on Massive Attack's original production for validation. The fact that both albums were released at the same time in 1994 further complicates Mad Professor's allegory. This complexity lies in the fact that Mad Professor's production is part of the tradition of Jamaican dub, where the term 'version' was often used to refer to 'remixes' which due to their extensive manipulation in the studio pushed for autonomy.[25]

Dub, at least according to this theory, has therefore more in common with the reflexive remix, that is, the more radical of the three elements proposed. For Navas,

> The creative drive behind dub was successful and has become assimilated into what is known as remix culture . . . [partly because] it allows the individual to thrive alone in his studio with proper sound equipment, to then quickly disseminate the composition in the community, and often allow others to create other versions of the composition. Dub was the first activity in electronic music and Remix Culture to make the most of individual input in large part dependent on technologies of post-production, while also making it efficiently available to others for further development, and input, when the time was appropriate.[26]

According to Discogs.com, around 800 remixes were released in 1983. By 2010, there were 22,750 remixed releases. Remixes have also have come to represent a much larger share of what is being released: in 1983, they accounted for 2 per cent of all releases; 7 per cent in 1990; 17 per cent in 2000; by 2010, a staggering 20 per cent of all releases were remixes.[27]

These statistics suggest that there are too many remixes in the world and not enough innovation. Enter the art of 'versioning', which suddenly seems like an even more creative possibility than before, in the sense that it allows at least a degree of improvisation. Fortunately, the original spirit of 'versioning' is indeed alive and well, and not only in reggae or neo-reggae/dub. From Mad Professor's remixing of Massive Attack's *Protection* (*No Protection*) to Mark Stewart's pillaging of his own album *Politics of Envy*, the strategies are still very much in practice.

Almost 25 years after their initial experiments, Killing Joke also finally released *Dub* (2012) a long-awaited compilation of dub remixes. One disc has remixes by Glover, while the second features remixes by Nine Inch Nails and the Bloody Beetroots and a highlight on the third disc is a remix by The Orb. Even contemporary underground bands like California-based Peaking Lights draw on dub as an influence, not only as a sound to anchor their mix of styles, but as a process. This is evident in their 'version' album *Lucifer in Dub*, a stripped-down take on the album *Lucifer* (2012), for example.

All of this is very impressive for a genre that came about by mistake. As Chris Lane of Fashion Records once said, 'The most important musical development of the late twentieth century was born out of simple economy (and a certain amount of laziness) and created by a handful of people who had no idea of the impact their music would have on the rest of the world.'[28] Or, as a Jamaican might put it, 'every spoil is a style'.

REFERENCES

INTRODUCTION

1 Ian Penman, sleeve notes to *Macro Dub Infection vol. 1*, quoted in Emily
   Berquist, 'Dub Devours the Music World', *Miscellany News*, cxxiv / 17
   (22 March 1996).
2 Lloyd Bradley, *This is Reggae Music: The Story of Jamaica's Music* (New York,
   2000), p. 312.
3 Ibid.
4 Erik Davis, 'Dub, Scratch, and the Black Star: Lee Perry on the Mix' (1997),
   www.techgnosis.com / ubhtml.
5 Christopher Partridge, *Dub in Babylon* (London, 2010), p. 138.
6 Simon Reynolds, 'Feed Your Head: 'Lie Down and Be Counted', in *Energy
   Flash: A Journey through Rave Music and Dance Culture* (London, 1998).
7 Jah Wobble quoted by Peter Shapiro, 'Bass Invader: Jah Wobble', *The Wire*,
   140 (October 1995), pp. 32–5.

1 THE KINGSTON CONTEXT

1 Kevin O'Brien Chang and Wayne Chen, 'From Zinc Shack to 16-Track:
   Early Jamaican Recording Studios', in *Reggae Routes: The Story of Jamaican
   Music* (Philadelphia, 1998), p. 19.
2 Norman Stolzoff, '"Talking Blues": The Rise of the Sound System', in *Wake
   the Town and Tell the People: Dancehall Culture in Jamaica* (Durham, NC, 2000),
   p. 41.
3 Lloyd Bradley, *Bass Culture: When Reggae Was King* (London, 2001), p. 34.
4 Heather Marie Saunders, 'An Exploration of the Dubbers, Deejays and
   Toasters of the Late 1960s–1980s Jamaican Style Music',
   www.debate.uvm.edu / dreadlibrary / saunders.html, April 1998.
5 David Katz, 'Obituary: Clement 'Sir Coxone' Dodd', *The Guardian*
   (6 May 2004).

6　O'Brien Chang and Chen, *Reggae Routes*, p. 30. According to O'Brien Chang
　　and Chen, 'the music simply evolved as the subtle difference from Rhythm
　　& Blues became progressively more pronounced. No one can say when the
　　first ska record was created, but it became progressively more obvious that
　　the music the session men were playing just didn't sound like regular r & b
　　anymore.'

7　Stolzoff, *Wake the Town*, p. 89.

8　Ibid.

9　Michael E. Veal, *Dub: Soundscapes and Shattered Songs in Jamaican Reggae*
　　(Middletown, CT, 2007), p. 52.

10　Bunny Lee, in interview in March 2002, quoted by Veal, 'Dub Plates &
　　Rhythm Versions', in *Dub*, p. 52.

11　David Katz, *People Funny Boy: The Genius of Lee 'Scratch' Perry*
　　(London, 2000), p. 65.

12　Ibid.

13　Saunders, 'Dubbers, Deejays and Toasters'.

14　Lloyd Bradley, *Bass Culture*, p. 293.

15　Stephen David quoted by Dick Hebdige, in *Cut 'n' Mix: Culture, Identity
　　and Caribbean Music* (London, 1987), p. 84.

16　Interview with the author, 2012.

17　Interview with the author, 2012.

2 KINGSTON'S DUB PIONEERS

1　Steve Barrow and Peter Dalton, *The Rough Guide to Reggae* (London, 2001),
　　p. 202.

2　Ibid., p. 246.

3　Michael E. Veal, *Dub: Soundscapes and Shattered Songs in Jamaican Reggae*
　　(Middletown, CT, 2007), p. 98.

4　Ibid., *Dub*, pp. 102–5.

5　Interview with the author, 2012.

6　Interview with the author, 2012

7　David Katz, *People Funny Boy: The Genius of Lee 'Scratch' Perry* (London, 2000),
　　p. 165.

8　Ibid.

9　Ibid.

10　Ibid.

11　Interview with the author, 2012.

12　Erik Davis, 'Dub, Scratch, and the Black Star', *21C*, 24 (1997).

13 David Toop, *Ocean of Sound: Aether Talk, Ambient Sound and Imaginary Worlds* (London, 1995), p. 129.

14 Veal, *Dub*, p. 161.

15 Jean-Paul Lapp-Szymanski, 'Technology Inna Rub-a-Dub Style: Technology and Dub in the Jamaican Sound System and Recording Studio', MA thesis, McGill University, 2005, p. 151, www.mcgill.ca/library.

16 Barrow and Dalton, *Rough Guide*, p. 232.

17 Veal, *Dub*, p. 52.

18 Lloyd Bradley, *Bass Culture: When Reggae was King* (New York, 2000), p. 320.

19 Barrow and Dalton, *Rough Guide*, p. 225.

20 Beth Lesser, 'The Sound and the Fury', *The New Inquiry* (9 October 2012), pp. 21–31.

21 Andrea Seddon, 'King Tubby's Reign', http://debate.uvm.edu/dreadlibrary/seddon, citing Stephen Davis and Peter Simon, *Reggae International* (New York, 1982).

22 Interview with the author, 2012.

23 Ibid.

24 Ibid.

3 LONDON: SOUND SYSTEM CULTURE, DIGIDUB AND POST-PUNK

1 Bill Brewster and Frank Broughton, *Last Night a DJ Saved My Life* (New York, 1999), p. 121.

2 Trevor Munroe, *The Politics of Constitutional Decolonization: Jamaica, 1944–62* (Mona, 1972), p. 102.

3 Stephen Pollard, *Ten Days That Changed the Nation: The Making of Modern Britain* (eBook, 2009), 'Immigration: 22 June 1948'.

4 John Eden, 'Shaking The Foundations: Reggae Soundsystem Meets "Big Ben British Values" Downtown', *Datacide*, 11 (October 2008).

5 Lloyd Bradley, *Bass Culture: When Reggae was King* (London, 2001), p. 115.

6 *Duke Vin and the Birth of Ska*, dir. Gus Berger (DVD, 2008).

7 Ibid.

8 Neil Spencer, 'Reggae: The Sound that Revolutionised Britain', *The Observer* (30 January 2011).

9 Bradley, *Bass Culture*, p. 121.

10 David V. Moskowitz, *Caribbean Popular Music: An Encyclopedia of Reggae, Mento, Ska, Rock Steady* (Westport, CT, 2006), p. 72.

11 'Sir Coxone Outernational', *New Musical Express* (February 1981).

12 *Musically Mad: A Documentary on uk Reggae Sound Systems*, dir. Karl Folke (DVD, 2009).

13 'The Big Sound System Splashdown: Directory of Sounds', *New Musical Express* (February, 1981).

14 Interview with the author, 2012.

15 Seb Wheeler, 'Lewisham: Home of Sound-system Culture', www.eastlondonlines.co.uk, 22 December 2010.

16 Jah Warrior, 'Jah Shaka the Dub Warrior', www.dubclub.com, April 2003.

17 Pete Murder Tone, 'Disciples Interview', www.theversionist.com, February 2006.

18 Gregory Mario Whitfield, 'Aba Shanti Interview', www.uncarved.org, January 2002.

19 Pete Murder Tone, 'Disciples Interview'.

20 John Street, *Rebel Rock* (Oxford, 1986), pp. 74–5.

21 Steve Barrow and Peter Dalton, *The Rough Guide to Reggae* (London, 1997), p. 330.

22 Ashley Dawson, 'Love Music, Hate Racism': The Cultural Politics of the Rock Against Racism Campaigns, 1976–1981' (New York, 2005), p. 18.

23 Vivien Goldman, 'Liner Notes', *Wild Dub: Dread Meets Punk Rocker Downtown* (CD booklet, Germany, 2003).

24 John Lydon, *No Irish, No Blacks, No Dogs* (London, 1993), p. 1.

25 Greg Whitfield, 'Bass Cultural Vibrations: Visionaries, Outlaws, Mystics and Chanters', www.3ammagazine.com, 2002.

26 Keith Levene, 'Albatross Soup', *The Wire*, 226 (December 2002), p. 26.

27 Jah Wobble, 'Epiphanies', *The Wire*, 203 (January 2001), p. 98.

28 Robin Murray, 'Jah Wobble Dissects Metal Box', *Clash Magazine* (April 2004).

29 Alex Ogg, 'Dodge the Bullets: An Interview with Killing Joke', www.thequietus.com, 25 October 2010.

30 Vivien Goldman, 'Spiky Dread' compilation sleeve notes (2012).

31 Interview with the author, 2012.

32 Ibid.

33 Ibid.

34 Ibid.

35 JD Twitch, 'JD Twitch Meets Adrian Sherwood (Part 1)', www.racketracket.co.uk, 7 May 2012.

36 Interview with the author, 2012.

37 Steve Barker, 'African Head Charge', www.skysaw.org, accessed November 2012.

38 JD Twitch, 'JD Twitch Meets Adrian Sherwood (Part 2)', www.racketracket.co.uk, 20 May 2012.

39 Interview with the author, 2012.

40 Ibid.

41 Ibid.

42 Ibid.

43 Ibid.

44 Ibid.

45 Ariwa Studios, 'Interview with Mad Professor', www.youtube.com, accessed August 2011.

4 NYC: DUB, RAP, DISCO AND ILLBIENT

1 Robert Pastor, 'The Impact of u.s. Immigration Policy on Caribbean Emigration: Does it Matter?', in *The Caribbean Exodus*, ed. Barry B. Levine (Westport, CT, 1987), p. 248.

2 N. Samuel Murrell, 'Jamaican Americans', *Every Culture* (August 2006).

3 Lloyd Barnes interviewed in 1996 by Ray Hurford and Colin Moore, 'Wackies House of Music', www.smallaxepeople.com.

4 Niko Koppel, 'New Roots in the Bronx for a Lion of Reggae', *New York Times* (12 April 2009).

5 As Hebdige points out, rap was exported: Dick Hebdige, *Cut 'n' Mix: Culture, Identity and Caribbean Music* (London, 1987), p. 136.

6 Jeff Chang, *Can't Stop Won't Stop: A History of the Hip-Hop Generation* (New York, 2005), p. 73.

7 Frank Broughton, 'Interviews: Afrika Bambaataa', www.djhistory.com, 6 October 1998.

8 Wayne Marshall, 'Kool Herc', in *Icons of Hip Hop: An Encyclopedia of the Movement, Music, and Culture, Volume 1*, ed. Mickey Hess (Westport, CT, 2007), p. 2.

9 Chang, *Can't Stop Won't Stop*, p. 22.

10 Tim Lawrence, 'Disco Madness: Walter Gibbons and the Legacy of Turntablism and Remixology', *Journal of Popular Music Studies* (March 2008), pp. 276–329.

11 Kounter Kulture, 'Hip Hop History: Part II', *Zulu Nation* (June 2005).

12 Interview with the author, 2012.

13 Ibid.

14 John Wilson, Nile Rodgers Interview, *Front Row*, BBC *Radio 4* (6 January 2005).

15 Mike Alleyne, 'Nile Rogers: Navigating Production Space', *Journal on the Art of Record Production*, 2 (October 2007).

16 Dennis Howard, 'From Ghetto Laboratory to the Technosphere: The Influence of Jamaican Studio Techniques on Popular Music' (2008), mona-uni.academia.edu/Dennis Howard.

17 Bill Brewster, 'Interviews: Tom Moulton', www.djhistory.com, (September 2008).

18 Peter Shapiro, *Turn the Beat Around: The Rise and Fall of Disco* (New York, 2005), p. 44.

19 Interview with the author, 2012.

20 Peter Shapiro, ed, *Modulations: A History of Electronic Music – Throbbing Words on Sound* (New York, 2000), p. 70.

21 Interview with the author, 2012.

22 Ibid.

23 Ibid.

24 Ibid.

5 LONDON II: UK RAP AND THE DUBCORE CONTINUUM

1 Sound System History: Saxon vs Coxsone – Soundsystem History pt 1, dir. DJ Senior P, www.genesisradio.co.uk.

2 Ibid.

3 Holy Roller, Two Big Sound, Part One: 7 Nights a Week, www.hollyrollerproductions.com, 26 August 2011.

4 Ibid.

5 Interview with the author, 2013.

6 Max lx of Mastermind Sound quoted by Matthew Bennett, 'Hackney Soldiers: The Birth of Jungle', *Clash Magazine* (April 2011).

7 Interview with the author, 2012.

8 Ibid.

9 Ibid.

10 Ibid.

11 Ibid.

12 Ibid.

13 Bill Brewster and Frank Broughton, *Last Night a DJ Saved My Life: The History of the Disc Jockey* (New York, 1999), p. 65.

14 Simon Reynolds, 'Roots 'n' Future: B-Boy Meets Rude Boy', *Energy Flash: A Journey through Rave Music and Dance Culture* (New York, 1999).

15 Interview with the author, 2013.

16 Lloyd Bradley, 'Jammer: Who Needs a Record Deal', *The Guardian*
    (11 July 2010).
17 Ibid.
18 Gervase de Wilde and Gabriel Myddelton, *An England Story*, sleeve notes
    (2008).
19 Interview with the author, 2012.
20 Ibid.
21 Ibid.
22 Derek Walmsley, 'Kode 9', *The Wire*, 303 (May 2009).
23 John Eden, 'Interview with The Bug: The Psychopathy of Kevin Martin',
    www.uncarved.org, 2003.

6 THE BRISTOL SOUND

 1 Ken Pryce, *Endless Pressure: A Study of West Indian Life-Styles in Bristol*
    (Bristol, 1979), p. 153.
 2 Port Cities, 'Bristol's Music Scene', www.discoveringbristol.org.uk, 29 January
    2012. Nachema Marchal, 'Sound of the Underground: Bristol's Music Scene',
    www.epigram.org.uk, 19 November 2012.
 3 John Eden, 'The First Taste of Hope is Fear', www.uncarved.org,
    1 July 2002.
 4 Vivien Goldman, 'Local Groove Does Good: The Story of Trip-Hop's Rise
    from Bristol', www.npr.com, 31 January 2012.
 5 Interview with the author, 2012.
 6 Ibid.
 7 Ibid.
 8 Ibid.
 9 Ibid.
10 Ibid.
11 Ibid.
12 Ibid.
13 Adam Burrows, '20 Years of 2 Kings: Blood Red Sounds Meets Henry
    & Louis Uptown', www.bloodredsounds.com, 17 September 2010.
14 Ronnie Randall, 'The Sound of Now', *Jocks* (February 1991).
15 Ibid.
16 Ibid.
17 Andy Pemberton, 'Trip Hop', *Mixmag* (June 1994).
18 Ian Penman, 'Tricky: Black Secret Tricknology', *The Wire*, 133
    (March 1995).

19 Jared Wilson, 'Roni Size Interview', www.leftlion.co.uk, 12 February 2008.
20 Richard Carnes, 'Peverelist: Punch Drunk Love', www.residentadvisor.net, 8 February 2009.
21 Interview with the author, 2012.
22 Ibid.
23 Ibid.

7 BERLIN: GLITCH AND TECHNO

1   Interview with the author, 2012.
2   Torsten Schmidt, 'Moritz Von Oswald: Treading on the Detroit-Kingston-Berlin Axis', Red Bull Music Academy, 2008.
3   Interview with the author, 2012.
4   Schmidt, 'Moritz Von Oswald'.
5   Interview with the author, 2012.
6   Interview with the author, 2011.
7   Ibid.
8   Ibid.
9   Ibid.
10 Ibid.
11 Ibid.
12 Ibid.
13 'Nonplace 10th Anniversary, a Compilation of Fourteen Exclusive Cuts from Burnt Friedman's Nonplace Label', *Fact* (April 2010).
14 Interview with the author, 2013.
15 Ibid.
16 Ibid.
17 Ibid.

8 CANADA'S DUB POETRY AND DANCEHALL

1   George J. Borjas, 'Immigration Policy, National Origin, and Immigrant Skills: A Comparison of Canada and the United States', *NBER Working Paper Series: No. 3691* (Cambridge, MA, April 1991), pp. 3–5.
2   'Messenjah', www.thecanadianencyclopedia.com, accessed 22 October 2008.
3   Eric Doumerc, 'Jamaica's First Dub Poets', PhD thesis, University of Birmingham, 2007.
4   Interview with the author, 2013.
5   Ibid.

6 See http://dubpoetscollective.blogspot.de/2006/08/dub-poets-collective-reading-series.html.
7 Ibid.
8 See http://northsidehiphop.ca/audio/classic-material/street-beat-compilation-1987.
9 Beatrice Ekwa Ekoko, 'Michie Mee: Canada's Queen of Hip Hop', www.more.ca, 2 April 2012.
10 HHC, 'Austin "Watt's" Garrick: [Interview]', www.hiphopcanada.com, 7 August 2007.
11 Interview with the author, 2013.
12 See www.inktalks.com/discover/283/d-bi-young-anitafrika-we-women-are-warriors.
13 Ibid.
14 Ibid.
15 See http://dbi333.com.
16 Ibid.
17 Ibid.
18 Ibid.
19 Ibid.
20 Ibid.
21 Ibid.

CONCLUSION

1 Interview with the author, 2013.
2 Ibid.
3 See http://pathogenomics.bham.ac.uk/Dub/dub.html.
4 Ibid.
5 The Genomic Dub Collective, 'Manifesto', www.pathogenomics.bham.ac.uk.
6 Interview with the author, 2012.
7 Simon Reynolds, 'Feed Your Head', *Energy Flash: A Journey Through Rave Music and Dance Culture* (London, 1998).
8 Pete Murder Tone, 'Disciples Interview', http://articles.dubroom.org/pmt/parto1.htm.
9 Interview with the author, 2013.
10 Ibid.
11 'Clive Chin's Lost Archives of 17 N. Parade', midnightraverblog.com.
12 Ibid.
13 David Dacks, 'Interviews: King Jammy', www.exclaim.ca, October 2007.

14 Dubbhism, 'Dub Equipment and Dub Philosophy', www.dubbhism.com, 12 November 2008.

15 Interview with the author, 2013.

16 Interview with the author, 2012.

17 Interview with the author, 2012.

18 Interview with the author, 2012.

19 'LargeUp Exclusive: Scientist x Marvin Gaye + Rare Interview', www.okayplayer.com, 15 October 2012.

20 Scott Thill, 'DJ Spooky: How a Tiny Caribbean Island Birthed the Mashup', www.wired.com, 7 December 2007.

21 Mike Barthel, 'When Did the Remix Become a Requirement', www.theawl.com, 24 January 2012.

22 Eduardo Navas, 'Remix Defined', www.remixtheory.net, 16 January 2009.

23 John Bush, 'Dub Revolution: The Story of Jamaican Dub Reggae and its Legacy', www.debate.uvm.edu, 17 April 2000.

24 Eduardo Navas, 'Remix Defined'.

25 Eduardo Navas, 'Dub, B Sides and their [Re]Versions in the Threshold of Remix', Digital Dub Issue, www.vagueterrain.com, 3 August 2008.

26 See http://remixtheory.net/?p=345.

27 Barthel, 'When Did the Remix Become a Requirement?'.

28 Chris Lane, 'A Musical Revolution', *Natty Dread*, 19 (June–July 2003).

BIBLIOGRAPHY

Adjaye, Joseph K., and Adrianne R. Andrews, eds, *Language, Rhythm
  and Sound: Black Popular Cultures into the Twenty-First Century*
  (Pittsburgh, 1997)
Alleyne, Mervyn C., *Roots of Jamaican Culture* (London, 1988)
Austin, Diane J., *Urban Life in Kingston, Jamaica: The Culture and Class Ideology
  of Two Neighborhoods* (New York, 1984)
Back, Les and John Solomos, *Race, Politics, and Social Change* (London, 1995)
Barrow, Steve, and Peter Dalton, *The Rough Guide to Reggae* (London, 1997)
Bayer, Marcel, *Jamaica: A Guide to the People, Politics and Culture* (London, 1993)
Belle-Fortune, Brian, *All-Crews: Journey's through Jungle / Drum & Bass Culture*
  (London, 2005)
Borjas, George J., 'Immigration Policy, National Origin, and the Immigrant
  Skills: A Comparison of Canada and the United States', NBER *Working Paper
  Series: No. 3691* (Cambridge, MA, April 1991)
Bradley, Lloyd, *Bass Culture: When Reggae was King* (London, 2001)
——, *This is Reggae Music: The Story of Jamaica's Music* (New York, 2000)
Bradshaw, Paul, 'Smiley Culture remembered by Dennis Bovell and David
  Rodigan', *The Guardian* (March 2011)
Brennan, Ally, 'Rhetoric of Reggae: Sound, Rhythm, and Power: Legends of Dub
  Poetry', *Dread Library* (December, 2009)
Brewster, Bill, 'Interviews: Tom Moulton', *dj History* (September 2008)
——, and Frank Broughton, *Last Night a DJ Saved My Life: The History
  of the Disc Jockey* (New York, 1999)
Carr, Brenda, '"Come Mek Wi Work Together": Community Witness and Social
  Agency in Lillian Allen's Dub Poetry', *A Review of International English
  Literature*, XXIX/3 (July 1998)
Chamberlain, Joshua, 'So Special: The Evolution of the Jamaican Dubplate',
  Jamaica Journal, 33 (2010)

Chang, Jeff, *Can't Stop Won't Stop: A History of the Hip Hop Generation*
    (New York, 2005)
Chang, Kevin O'Brien, and Wayne Chen, *Reggae Routes: The Story of Jamaican
    Music* (Philadelphia, 1998)
Chevannes, Barry, *Rastafari: Roots and Ideology* (Syracuse, NY, 1994)
Chude-Sokei, Louis, 'Dr Satan's Echo Chamber': Reggae Technology and the Diaspora
    Process* (Mona, 1997)
Connell, John, and Chris Gibson, *Sound Tracks: Popular Music, Identity and Place*
    (London, 2002)
Dacks, David, 'Interviews: Deadbeat', *Exclaim!* (October 2007)
Davis, Stephen, *Reggae Bloodlines: In Search of the Music and Culture of Jamaica*
    (Boston, 1979)
——, and Peter Simon, *Reggae International* (New York, 1982)
Dooley, Jin, *The Small Axe Guide to Dub* (London, 2010)
Doyle, Peter, *Echo and Reverb: Fabricating Space in Popular Music Recording,
    1900–1960* (Middletown, CT, 2005)
Drozdowski, Ted, 'Reverb: Echo Chambers to Digital Stomp Boxes', *Gibson*
    (June 2012)
During, Elie, Edward George and Francisco Lupez et al., *Sonic Process*
    (Barcelona, 2002)
Durston, Tom, 'Deadbeat', *Inverted Audio* (April 2012)
Eden, John, 'The First Taste of Hope is Fear', *Uncarved* (March 2002)
——, 'Shaking The Foundations: Reggae Soundsystem Meets "Big Ben British
    Values" Downtown', *Datacide* (October 2008)
Edmonds, Ennis Barrington, *Rastafari: From Outcasts to Culture Bearers*
    (Oxford, 2003)
Ekoko, Beatrice Ekwa, 'Michie Mee: Canada's Queen of Hip Hop', *More*
    (April 2012)
Floyd, Barry, *Jamaica: An Island Microcosm* (New York, 1979)
Forman, Murray, and Mark Anthony Neal, eds, *That's the Joint! The Hip Hop
    Studies Reader* (New York, 2004)
Frith, Simon, ed., *Popular Music: Critical Concepts in Media and Cultural Studies,
    Volume Four* (Abingdon, 2004)
Gilroy, Paul, *There Ain't No Black in the Union Jack: The Cultural Politics of Race and
    Nation* (Chicago, 1987)
Goldman, Vivien, 'Local Groove Does Good: The Story of Trip-Hop's Rise from
    Bristol', *NPR* (January 2012)
Goodyer, Ian, 'Rock Against Racism: Multiculturalism and Political Mobilization,
    1976–1981', *Immigrants and Minorities*, XXII (2003)

Hebdige, Dick, *Subculture: The Meaning of Style* (New York, 1979)

Hiro, Dilip, *Black British, White British* (London, 1971)

Hitchcock, Peter, '"It Dread Inna Inglan": Linton Kwesi Johnson, Dread, and Dub Identity', *Postmodern Culture*, IV/I (September 1993)

Johnson, Phil, *Straight Outa Bristol* (London, 1996)

Jones, Simon, *Black Culture, White Youth: The Reggae Tradition from JA to UK* (Basingstoke, 1988)

Katz, David, *People Funny Boy: The Genius of Lee 'Scratch' Perry* (London, 2000)

Knoff, Kerstin, 'Oh Canada: Reflections of Multiculturalism in the Poetry of Canadian Women Dub Artists', *Views of Canadian Cultures*, III/2 (2005)

Knott, Gordon, 'Monsieur Kevorkian', *DJ*, III (1994)

Koppel, Niko, 'New Roots in the Bronx for a Lion of Reggae', *The New York Times* (April 2009)

Kun, Josh, *Audiotopia: Music, Race, and America* (Berkeley, CA, 2005)

Lane, Chris, 'A Musical Revolution', *Natty Dread Magazine* (2001)

Lapp-Szymanski, Jean-Paul, 'Technology Inna Rub-a-Dub Style: Technology and Dub in the Jamaican Sound System and Recording Studio', MA thesis, McGill University, 2005

Lawrence, Tim, *Love Saves the Day: History of American Dance Music Culture, 1970–1979* (Durham, NC, 2004)

——, 'Disco Madness: Walter Gibbons and the Legacy of Turntablism and Remixology', *Journal of Popular Music Studies*, XX/3 (September 2008), pp. 278–329

Letts, Don, *Culture Clash: Dread Meets Punk Rockers* (London, 2008)

Levene, Keith, 'Albatross Soup', *The Wire* (December 2002)

Lydon, John, *No Irish, No Blacks, No Dogs* (London, 1993)

Mallinder, Stephen, *Movement: Journey of the Beat* (Murdoch, WA, 2011)

Manuel, Peter, with Kenneth Bilby and Michael Largey, *Caribbean Currents: Caribbean Music from Rumba to Reggae* (Philadelphia, 1995)

Marchal, Nahema, 'Sound of the Underground: Bristol's Music Scene', *Epigram* (19 November 2012)

Marcus, Greil, *Lipstick Traces: A Secret History of the Twentieth Century* (Cambridge, 1989)

Marshall G, *Spirit of '69: A Skinhead Bible* (Dunoon, 1991)

Maysles, Philip, 'Dubbing the Nation', *Small Axe* (March 2002)

Mickiewicz, Maksymilian Fus, 'Scientist: Interview with the Forefather of Dubstep', *Don't Panic* (23 November 2010)

Moskowitz, David V., *Caribbean Popular Music: An Encyclopedia of Reggae, Mento, Ska, Rock Steady* (Westport, CT, 2006)

Munroe, Trevor, *The Politics of Constitutional Decolonization: Jamaica, 1944–62*
      (Mona, 1972)

Murray, Robin, 'Jah Wobble Dissects "Metal Box"', *Clash Magazine* (April 2004)

Murrell, Nathaniel Samuel, ed., *Chanting Down Babylon: The Rastafari Reader*
      (Philadelphia, 1998)

Navas, Eduardo, *Remix Theory: The Aesthetics of Sampling* (New York, 2012)

Ogg, Alex, and David Upshal, *The Hip Hop Years: A History of Rap* (London, 1999)

Olsen, Dale A., and Daniel E. Sheehy, *South America, Mexico, Central America,*
      and the Caribbean (Garland Encyclopedia of World Music, Volume 2)
      (New York, 1998)

Partridge, Christopher, *Dub in Babylon: Understanding the Evolution and Significance*
      of Dub Reggae in Jamaica and Britain from King Tubby to Post-Punk
      (London, 2010)

Pemberton, Andy, 'Trip Hop', *Mixmag* (June 1994)

Penman, Ian, 'Tricky: Black Secret Tricknology', *The Wire*, 133 (March 1995)

Potash, Chris, ed., *Reggae, Rasta, Revolution: Jamaican Music from Ska to Dub*
      (New York, 1997)

Pryce, Ken, *Endless Pressure: A Study of West Indian Life-Styles in Bristol* (Bristol, 1979)

Randall, Ronnie, 'The Sound of Now', *Jocks* (February 1991)

Reynolds, Simon, *Energy Flash: A Journey through Rave Music and Dance Culture*
      (London, 1998)

——, *Rip it Up and Start Again: Post-Punk, 1978–1982* (London, 2005)

Rose, Tricia, ed., *Microphone Fiends: Youth Music & Youth Culture* (London, 1994)

Rothlein, Jordan, 'Little White Earbuds Interviews Mala', www.littlewhiteear-
      buds.com, 2 March 2011

Salewicz, Chris, and Adrian Boot, *Reggae Explosion: The Story of Jamaican Music*
      (London, 2001)

Saunders, Heather Marie, 'An Exploration of the Dubbers, Deejays and
      Toasters of the Late 1960's–1980's Jamaican Style Music', *Dread Library*
      (April 1998), http://debate.uvm.edu/dreadlibrary/saunders.html

Shapiro, Peter, *Turn the Beat Around: The Rise and Fall of Disco* (New York, 1995)

——, ed., *Modulations: A History of Electronic Music: Throbbing Words on Sound*
      (New York, 2000)

Stolzoff, Norman C., *Wake the Town and Tell the People: Dancehall Culture in*
      Jamaica (Durham, NC, 2000)

Sword, Harry, 'Subliminal Frequencies: An Interview with Pinch', *Quietus*
      (January 2012)

Terho, H., ed., *Looking Back, Looking Ahead: Popular Music Studies 20 Years Later*
      (Turku, 2002)

Toop, David, *Ocean of Sound: Aether Talk, Ambient Sound and Imaginary Worlds*
  (London, 1995)
Veal, Michael E., *Dub: Soundscapes and Shattered Songs in Jamaican Reggae*
  (Middletown, CT, 2007)
Walker, Klive, *Dubwise: Reasoning from the Reggae Underground* (Toronto, 2005)
Waters, Mary C., *Black Identities: West Indian Immigrant Dreams and American
  Realities* (New York, 1999)
Webb, Peter, *Exploring the Networked Worlds of Popular Music: Milieu Cultures*
  (New York, 2007)
Whitfield, Greg, 'Bass Cultural Vibrations: Visionaries, Outlaws, Mystics and
  Chanters', www.fodderstompf.com, October 2002
Widgery, David, *Beating Time: Riot 'n' Race 'n' Rock 'n' Roll* (London, 1986)

FILMOGRAPHY

Duke Vin & the Birth of Ska, dir. Gus Berger (2008)
DJ Senior P, *Sound System History: Saxon vs Coxsone – Soundsystem History pt 1*
(2007)
Musically Mad: A Documentary on UK Reggae Sound Systems, dir. Karl Folke (2009)
The Harder they Come, dir. Perry Henzel (1972)
Two Big Sound, Part One: Seven Nights a Week, dir. 'Schottsman' (2011)
The Heatwave presents Showtime! History of UK Dancehall Live On Stage, dir. Rollo
Jackson (2010)
Dub to Jungle, dir. Chris Jones (2011)
Sound System, dir. Enda Murray (2010)
Dub Echoes, dir. Bruno Natal (2009)
Moritz Von Oswald: Treading on the Detroit-Kingston-Berlin Axis, filmed at the Red
Bull Music Academy (2008)
Babylon, dir. Franco Rosso (1980)
Dub Stories (2006)
A London Someting Dis, dir. John Vanderpuije (1994)

SELECT DISCOGRAPHY

Africa Bambaataa & The Soul Sonic Force, *Planet Rock* (Tommy Boy, 1982)

——, *Looking for the Perfect Beat* (Tommy Boy, 1982)

Africa Bambaataa, *Death Mix* (Paul Winley, 1983)

African Head Charge, *My Life in a Hole in the Ground* (On U Sound, 1981)

——, *Environmental Studies* (On U Sound, 1982)

——, *Drastic Season* (On U Sound, 1983)

——, *Off the Beaten Track* (On U Sound, 1986)

——, *Songs of Praise* (On U Sound, 1990)

Lillian Allen, *Revolutionary Tea Party* (Redwood, 1986)

——, *Conditions Critical* (Redwood, 1987)

Aswad, *A New Chapter of Dub* (Mango, 1982)

Augustus Pablo, *Ital Dub* (Starapple, 1974)

Augustus Pablo & King Tubby, *King Tubby Meets Rockers Uptown* (Shanachie, 1976)

Augustus Pablo, *East of the River Nile* (Message/Shanachie, 1977)

——, *Original Rockers* (1979)

——, *Rockers Meets King Tubby in a Firehouse* (1980)

Automaton, *Dub Terror Exhaust* (Strata, 1994)

The Beatles, *Sgt Pepper's Lonely Hearts Club Band* (Parlophone/Capitol, 1967)

Big Youth, *Dreadlocks Dread* (Klik, 1978)

Bigga Bush, *Bigga Bush Free* (Stereo Deluxe, 2004)

Black Roots, *Black Roots* (Kick, 1983)

——, *Ina Different Style* (Nubian, 1987)

——, *All Day All Night* (Nubian, 1987)

Black Uhuru, *The Dub Factor* (Island, 1983)

Blackbeard, *Strictly Dub Wize* (Tempus, 1978)

——, *I Wah Dub* (More Cut/EMI, 1980)

Dennis Bovell & Steve Mason, *Ghosts Outside* (Domino, 2011)

——, *Mek it Run* (Pressure Sounds, 2012)

The Bug, *London Zoo* (Ninja Tune, 2008)

Bullwackies All Stars, *Creation Dub* (Wackie's, 1977)

Bunny Lee, *King of Dub* (Clock Tower, 1978)

Burnd Friedmann & The Nu-Dub Players, *Just Landed* (~Scape, 2000)

Burning Spear, *Living Dub Volume 1* (Burning Music, 1979)

——, *Living Dub Volume 2* (Burning Music, 1982)

——, *Garvey's Ghost* (Island, 1976)

Prince Buster, *Ten Commandments* (Bluebeat, 1963)

Cabaret Voltaire, *Extended Play* (Rough Trade, 1979)

——, *Digital Rasta* (Some Bizarre / Virgin Records 1984)

Michael Campbell, *African Anthem Dubwise* (Cruise, 1979)

Can, *Future Days* (United Artists, 1973)

Choclair, *Ice Cold* (Priority / Virgin, 1999)

The Clash, *London Calling* (CBS, 1979)

——, *Sandinista!* (CBS, 1980)

Kit Clayton, *Nek Sanalet* (Scape, 1999)

Jimmy Cliff, *The Harder they Come* (Island, 1972)

The Congos, *Heart of The Congos* (Black Art, 1977)

Carl Craig & Moritz von Oswald, *ReComposed* (Deutsche Grammophon)

Creation Rebel, *Dub from Creation* (Hit Run, 1977)

——, *Close Encounters of the 3rd World* (Hit Run, 1978)

——, *Rebel Vibrations* (Hit Run, 1979)

——, *Starship Africa* (Hit Run, 1980)

——, *Psychotic Jonkaroo* (Hit Run, 1981)

Culture, *Two Sevens Clash* (Joe Gibbs, 1977)

DJ Shadow, *Endtroducing* (Mo Wax, 1996)

DJ Spooky, *Songs of a Dead Dreamer* (Asphodel, 1996)

D Train, *Keep On* (Prelude, 1982)

Deadbeat, *Wild Life Documentaries* (~scape, 2002)

——, *Something Borrowed, Something Blue* (~scape, 2004)

——, *Roots and Wire* (Wagon Repair, 2008)

Dennis Alcapone, *Forever Version* (Studio One, 1971)

Digital Mystikz, *Return II Space* (DMZ, 2010)

The Disciples & Jah Shaka, *Commandments of Dub 6 – Deliverance* (Jah Shaka Music, 1987)

Disrupt, *Foundation Bit* (Werk Discs, 2007)

Dizzee Rascal, *Boy in Da Corner* (XL, 2003)

——, *Maths and English* (XL, 2007)

Dread & Fred, *Ironworks* (Jah Shaka Music, 1991)

Dub Syndicate, *The Pounding System* (On U Sound, 1982)

——, *Tunes from the Missing Channel* (On U Sound, 1985)

——, *Fear of a Green Planet* (On U Sound, 1998)

——, *Overdubbed* (Collision, 2006)

Earth, Roots & Water, *Innocent Youths* (Summer, 1977)

Easy Star All-Stars, *Dub Side of the Moon* (Easy Star, 2003)

——, *Radiodread* (Easy Star, 2006)

——, *Easy Star's Lonely Hearts Dub Band* (Easy Star, 2009)

Winston Edwards, *Natty Locks Dub* (Fay Music, 1974)

—— and Blackbeard, *At 10 Downing Street Dub Conference* (Celluloid/Studio 16, 1980)

Noel Ellis, *Noel Ellis* (Summer Records, 1983)

Brian Eno & David Byrne, *My Life in the Bush of Ghosts* (Sire, Warner Bros., 1981)

Fat Freddy's Drop, *Based on a True Story* (The Drop, 2005)

Fingers Inc., *Can You Feel It* (Trax, 1986)

——, *Feelin' Sleazy* (Jack Trax, 1988)

Flanger, *Outer Space/Inner Space* (Ninja Tune, 2001)

Funky Lowlives, *Cartouche* (Stereo Deluxe, 2003)

Joe Gibbs & The Professionals, *African Dub All Mighty Chapter One* (Lightning, 1973)

——, *African Dub All Mighty Chapter Two* (Lightning, 1974)

——, *Tribesman Rockers, African Dub Chapter Three* (Lightning, 1978)

——, *African Dub Chapter 4* (Joe Gibbs, 1979)

Grandmaster Flash, *Adventures of Grandmaster Flash on the Wheels of Steel* (Sugarhill, 1981)

A Guy Called Gerald, *Black Secret Technology* (Juicebox, 1995)

Richie Hawtin, *Decks EFX & 909* (Novamute, 1999)

Henry & Lewis, *Rudiments* (More Rockers, 1995)

—— Meet Blue & Red, *Time Will Tell* (BSI, 2001)

Herman Chin Loy, *Aquarius Dub* (Aquarius, 1973)

Gil Scott Heron, *The Bottle* (Old Gold, 1988)

Horace Andy, *In the Light Dub* (Hungry Town, 1977)

——, *Dance Hall Style* (Wackies, 1982)

——, *Good Vibes* (Blood & Fire, 1997)

——, *Skylarking* (Melankolic, 1997)

——, *Living in the Flood* (Melankolic, 2000)

—— Meets Mad Professor, *From the Roots* (RAS, 2004)

Keith Hudson, *Pick a Dub* (Mamba/Klik/Atra, 1974)

——, *Flesh of My Skin, Blood of My Blood* (Mamba /Atra, 1974)

——, *Rasta Communication* (Joint International, 1978)

——, *Playing it Cool & Playing it Right* (Joint International, 1981)

Impact All Stars, *Java Java Java Java* (Impact!, 1973)

Inner Zone Orchestra, *Bug in the Bassbin* (Planet E, 1996)

Ishan People, *Roots* (GRT, 1976)

I Roy, *Presenting I Roy* (Trojan, 1973)

——, *Don't Check Me With No Lightweight Stuff, 1972–75* (Blood & Fire, 1997)

Jah Shaka, *The Commandments of Dub* (Jah Shaka Music, 1982)

——, *Revelation Songs* (Jah Shaka Music, 1983)

——, *Meets Mad Professor at Ariwa Sounds* (Ariwa, 1984)

——, *Meets Aswad in Addis Ababa Studio* (Jah Shaka Music, 1985)

Jammer, *Jahmanji* (Big Dada, 2010)

The Jimi Hendrix Experience, *Axis: Bold as Love* (Track, 1967)

Joe Gibbs & The Professionals, *African Dub Almighty Chapter 3* (Gibbs Record Globe, 1975)

Johnny Osbourne, *Truths and Rights* (Studio One, 1980)

Killing Joke, *Killing Joke* (E.G., 1980)

King Culture, *King Culture in Cultural Mood* (King Culture, 1981)

King Midas Sound, *Waiting for You* (Hyperdub, 2009)

——, *Without You* (Hyperdub, 2011)

King Tubby, *Dub from the Roots* (Total Sounds, 1974)

King Tubby & Lee Perry, *King Tubby Meets Upsetter at the Grass Roots of Dub* (Fay/Total, 1974)

King Tubby, *The Roots of Dub* (Total Sounds, 1975)

——, *Surrounded by the Dreads at the National Arena 26th September 1975* (Fay, 1976)

—— & Friends, *Dub Like Dirt – 1975–77* (Blood & Fire, 1994)

——, *Dub Gone Crazy: The Evolution of Dub at King Tubby's 1975–79* (Blood & Fire, 1994)

—— Meets Soul Syndicate, *Freedom Sounds in Dub* (Blood & Fire, 1996)
—— & Scientist, *Greenwich Farm Rub A Dub* (Blood & Fire, 1996)
Kode9 & Spaceape, *Memories of the Future* (Hyperdub, 2006)

The Last Poets, *The Last Poets* (Douglas, 1971)
Barrington Levy, *Bounty Hunter* (Jah Life, 1979)
——, *Englishman* (Greensleeves, 1979)
Linton Kwesi Johnson, *Dread Beat an' Blood* (Frontline, 1978)
——, *Forces of Victory* (Mongo, 1979)
——, *LKJ in Dub* (Island, 1980)
——, *Bass Culture* (Island, 1980)
——, *Dread Beat an' Blood* (Virgin, 1981)
——, *Tings an' Times* (LKJ, 1991)

Mad Professor, *Dub Me Crazy* (Ariwa, 1982)
——, *In a Rub a Dub Style* (Blue Moon, 1983)
—— & Lee Perry, *Experryments at the Grass Roots of Dub* (Ariwa, 1995)
Mad Professor, *The Roots of Dubstep* (Ariwa, 2011)
Maddslinky, *Make Your Peace* (Laws of Motion, 2003)
Mala, *Mala in Cuba* (Brownswood, 2012)
Ahdri Zhina Mandiela, *Step into My Head* (Bushooman Rag, 1995)
Bob Marley & Lee Perry, *Punky Reggae Party* (Island Records, 1977)
Massive Attack, *Blue Lines* (Wild Bunch Records, 1991)
——, *Protection* (Circa/Virgin, 1994)
Massive Attack v. Mad Professor, *No Protection* (Circa/Virgin, 1995)
Matumbi, *After Tonight* (Trojan, 1976)
Max Romeo and The Upsetters, *War Ina Babylon* (Island, 1976)
Messenjah, *Jam Session* (Warner Music Canada, 1984)
Microphone Attack, *Niney The Observer, 1974–78* (Blood & Fire, 2003)
Michie Mee and L. A. Luv, *Jamaican Funk – Canadian Style* (Atlantic, 1991)
Mighty Diamonds, *Right Time* (Well Charge, 1976)
Jackie Mittoo, *Wishbone* (Summus, 1971)
——, *Reggae Magic* (CTL, 1972)
——, *Champion in the Arena, 1976–1977* (Blood & Fire, 2003)
Monolake, *Interstate* (Monolake/Imbalance Computer Music, 1999)
——, *Silence* (Monolake/Imbalance Computer Music, 2009)
Moritz von Oswald Trio, *Vertical Ascent* (Honest Jon's, 2009)
——, *Horizontal Structures* (Honest Jon's, 2010)
Sylvan Morris, *Morris on Dub* (Jaywax, 1975)

Mossman, *Message in the Dub* (Dispension, 2004)
Muddy Waters, *Folk Singer* (Chess, 1964)
Hugh Mundell, *Africa Must be Free by 1983* (Message, 1978)

Nightmares on Wax, *Smokers Delight* (Warp Records 1996)
Niney the Observer, *Dubbing with the Observer* (Trojan, 1975)
Burnt Friedman & The Nu-Dub Players, *Just Landed* (~scape, 2000)

Oku Onuora, *Reflection in Red* (56 Hope Road, 1979)
Johnny Osbourne, *Truth and Rights* (Studio 1, 1980)

Peech Boys, *Don't Make Me Wait* (West End, 1982)
Lee Perry, *The Upsetter* (Trojan, 1969)
——, *Cloak and Dagger* (Rhino, 1973)
——, *Revolution Dub* (Lagoon, 1975)
——, *Megaton Dub* (Seven Leaves, 1983)
——, *Time Boom X De Devil Dead* (Syncopate, 1987)
——, *Black Ark in Dub* (Lagoon, 1991)
——, *Upsetter in Dub* (Heartbeat, 1997)
——, *From the Secret Laboratory* (Universal/Island, 1997)
——, *Repentance* (Narnack Records, 2008)
——, *The Mighty Upsetter* (Egea, 2008)
—— & Mad Professor, *Black Ark Experryments* (Ariwa, 1995)
—— & Adrian Sherwood, *Dubsetter* (On U Sound, 2009)
—— & The Upsetters, *Blackboard Jungle Dub* (Upsetter, 1973)
——, *Double Seven* (Trojan, 1974)
——, *Super Ape* (Island, 1976)
—— & Mad Professor, *Super Ape inna Jungle* (DIP, 1995)
—— & The Upsetters, *Sound System Scratch* (Pressure Sounds, 2010)
Phase Selector Sound, *Disassemble Dub* (ROIR, 1999)
Phuturistix, *Feel it Out* (Hospital, 2003)
Pinch, *Underwater Dancehall* (Tectonic, 2007)
—— & Shackleton, *Pinch & Shackleton* (Honest Jon's, 2011)
Poet & The Roots, *Dread Beat an' Blood* (Heartbeat/Virgin, 1978)
Pole, *1 / 2 / 3* (Kiff SM/PIAS Germany, 1998/1999/2000)
——, *R* (~scape, 2001)
——, *Pole* (Mute, 2003)
The Pop Group, *Y* (Radar, 1979)
——, *For How Much Longer do we Tolerate Mass Murder?* (Rough Trade, 1980)

Portishead, *Dummy* (Go! Discs, 1994)

Prince Buster, *The Message Dubwise* (Prince Buster, 1972)

Prince Far I, *Dub to Africa* (Pressure Sounds, 1987)

——, *Cry Tough Dub Encounter Chapter 1* (Cry Tuff, 1978)

——, *Cry Tough Dub Encounter Chapter 2* (Cry Tuff, 1979)

——, *Voice of Thunder* (Trojan, 1981)

Prince Jammy, *In Lion Dub Style* (Jammy's, 1978)

——, *Kamikaze Dub* (Trojan, 1979)

The Prophets, *King Tubby's Prophecies of Dub* (Prestige, 1976)

Public Image Limited, *First Issue* (Virgin, 1978)

——, *Metal Box* (Virgin 1979)

Q-Bert, *Q-Bert Live* (Mo Wax, 1997)

Rebel MC, *Black Meaning Good* (Desire, 1991)

Steve Reich, *Music For 18 Musicians* (ECM 1978)

Renegade Soundwave, *In Dub* (Mute, 1991)

Reprazent / Roni Size, *New Forms* (Talkin' Loud, 1997)

The Revolutionaries, *Revival Dub Roots Now* (Well Charge, 1976)

Rhythm & Sound, *See Mi Yah* (Burial Mix, 2005)

Roots Manuva, *Brand New Second Hand* (Big Dad, 1999)

——, *Badmeaningood* (Ultimate Dilemma, 2001)

——, *Duppy Writer* (Big Dada, 2010)

RSD, *Good Energy* (Punch Drunk, 2009)

Salmonella Dub, *Dub for Straights* (EMI 1, 1993)

——, *Outside the Dubplates* (Salmonella Dub, 2002)

Scientist, *Scientist Heavyweight Dub Champion* (Greensleeves, 1980)

——, *Scientist Meets the Space Invaders* (Greensleeves, 1981)

——, *Scientific Dub* (Clock Tower, 1981)

——, *Scientist Rids the World of the Evil Curse of the Vampires* (Greensleeves, 1981)

——, *Scientist Encounters Pac-Man* (Greensleeves, 1982)

——, *Dub in the Roots Tradition, 1976–79* (Blood & Fire, 1996)

——, *Scientist Launches Dubstep into Outer Space* (Techtonic, 2010)

Sex Pistols, *Never Mind the Bollocks, Here's the Sex Pistols* (EMI, 1977)

Shackleton, *Three EPS* (Perlon, 2009)

Sir Coxone Sound, *King of the Dub Rock Pt. 1* (Safari, 1975)

The Skatalites Meet King Tubby, *Heroes of Reggae in Dub* (Motion, 1999)

Skream, *Skream!* (Tempa, 2006)

The Slits, *Cut* (Island, 1978)

Smith & Mighty, *Bass is Maternal* (More Rockers, 1995)
Michael Smith, *Mi Cyaan Believe It* (Island/Mango, 1982)
Wayne Smith, *Under Mi Sleng Teng* (Jammy's Records, 1985)
Soul II Soul, *Club Classics Volume One* (Virgin, 1989)
Mark Stewart & The Maffia, *Learning to Cope with Cowardice* (On U Sound,
    1983)
Mark Stewart, *As the Veneer of Democracy Starts to Fade* (On U Sound, 1985)
——, *Mark Stewart* (Mute, 1987)
——, *Kiss the Future* (Soul Jazz, 2005)
——, *Edit* (Crippled Dick Hot Wax!, 2008)
——, *Politics of Envy* (Future Noise, 2012)
The Sugarhill Gang, *Rapper's Delight* (Sugarhill Records, 1979)

Talisman, *Takin' the Strain* (Embryo, 1984)
Talking Heads, *Fear of Music* (Sire, 1979)
——, *Remain in Light* (Sire, 1980)
Max Tannone, *Mos Dub* (self-released, 2010)
Tricky, *Maxinquaye* (Island, 1995)
Twilight Circus, *In Dub Volume 1* (M Records, 1995)

Unitone HiFi, *Wickedness Increased* (Incoming!, 1995)
——, *Rewound & Rerubbed* (Incoming!, 1995)
——, *Boomshot* (Incoming!, 1996)
The Uplifters, *We are Moving* (King Culture, 1983)
The Upsetters, *Return of the Django* (Trojan, 1969)
——, *Corn Fish Dub* (Trojan, 2007)
U Brown, *Satta Dread* (Kilk, 1976)
——, *Train to Zion* (Blood & Fire, 1997)
U-Roy, *Dread in a Babylon* (Virgin, 1975)
——, *With a Flick of my Musical Wrist: Jamaican Deejay Music, 1970–1973* (Trojan,
    1994)

various artists, *Java Java Dub*
——, *Break'n Out* (Up Your, 1987)
——, *Wackie's Selective Showcase Vol. 1* (Wackie's, 1980)
——, *Raiders of the Lost Dub* (Island/Mango, 1981)
——, *A Whole New Generation of DJs* (Greensleeves, 1981)
——, *Jamaican Dancehall Volcano Hi-power* (Volcano, 1983)
——, *Great British MC's* (Fashion, 1985)

——, *The House Sound of Chicago Volume III* (FFRR, 1987)

——, *Live at Soul All Dayer of the Century* (LGR, 1987)

——, *Tresor II – Berlin & Detroit – A Techno Alliance* (NovaMute, 1993)

——, *Wild Dub Meets Punk Rocker* (Select, 1993)

——, *bcd* (Basic Channel, 1995)

——, *Jungle Book: Intelligent Minds of Jungle Volume 1* (Reinforced, 1996)

——, *If Deejay was your Trade: The Dreads at King Tubby's, 1974–1977* (Blood & Fire, 1996)

——, *17 North Parade* (Pressure Sounds, 1997)

——, *Tuff Jam Presents: Underground Frequencies Volume 1* (Satellite, 1997)

——, *Forward the Bass: Dub from Randy's, 1972–75* (Blood & Fire, 1998)

——, *Larry Levan Live at the Paradise Garage* (Strut, 2000)

——, *Docking Sequence* (BSI, 2000)

——, *Now Thing* (Mo'Wax, 2001)

——, *Rhythm & Sound* (Burial Mix, 2001)

——, *The Biggest Dancehall Anthems, 1979–82* (Greensleeves, 2002)

——, *The Wild Bunch: Story of a Sound System Mixed by DJ Milo* (Strut, 2002)

——, *Wild Dub: Dread Meets Punk Rocker* (Select Cuts, 2003)

——, *Rhythm & Sound w/The Artists* (Burial Mix, 2003)

——, *Boozoo Bajou Remixes* (Stereo Deluxe, 2003)

——, *Glory, Dominion, Majesty, Power* (Honest Jon's, 2003)

——, *Rodigan's Dub Classics: Serious Selections Volume 1* (Rewind Selecta, 2004)

——, *Stereo Deluxe 2* (Stereo Deluxe, 2004)

——, *Difficult Easy Listening* (Non Place, 2004)

——, *King Culture & I&I Records Present Roots & Culture (Inna De Dance)* (Drums & Bass, 2005)

——, *Run the Road* (679, 2005)

——, *Jamaica to Toronto: Soul Funk & Reggae, 1967–1974* (Light in the Attic, 2006)

——, *Summer Records Anthology, 1974 –1988* (Light in the Attic, 2007)

——, *Box of Dub: Dubstep and Future Dub* (Soul Jazz, 2007)

——, *Soundboy Punishments* (Skull Disco, 2007)

——, *An England Story* (Soul Jazz, 2008)

——, *Soundboy's Gravestone Gets Desecrated by Vandals* (Skull Disco, 2009)

——, *Worth the Weight* (Punch Drunk, 2010)

——, *Invasion of the Mysteron Killer Sounds in 3d* (Soul Jazz, 2011)

——, *Spiky Dread Issue 1* (Rongorongo, 2012)

——, *Five Million Rewinds* (Heatwave, 2012)

——, *Dubstep Allstars: Vol. 1–Vol. 09* (Dubstep Allstars, 2004–12)

——, *Spiky Dread: Issue 1* (Rongorongo, 2012)

Vibronics, UK *Dub Story* (Scoops, 2008)

Bunny Wailer, *Dubd'sco* (Solomonic, 1978)
The Wailers, *Soul Rebels* (Trojan, 1970)
Wiley, *Treddin' on Thin Ice* (XL, 2004)

Yabby You, *King Tubby's Prophesy of Dub* (Blood & Fire, 1976)
——, *Chant Down Babylon Kingdom* (Nationwide, 1976)
——, *Deliver Me from My Enemies* (Grove Music, 1977)
——, & Michael Prophet, *Meet Scientist at the Dub Station* (Prophet, 1981)
Yellowman, *Them a Mad Over Me* (Channel One, 1982)
——, *Mister Yellowman* (Greensleeves, 1982)

Tappa Zukie, *In Dub* (Stars, 1979)

LIST OF INTERVIEWS

Adrian Sherwood
Basic Channel (Mark Ernestus)
Bernd Friedmann
Clive Chin
Citizen Sound
Congo Natty
D'bi
Deadbeat
Dennis Bovell
Digital Mystikz (Mala)
DJ Spooky
Fashion Records (Chris Lane)
François Kevorkian
Jahtari (Disrupt)
Lillian Allen
London Posse (Rodney P)

Mad Professor
Mark Stewart / The Pop Group
Mala
Mossman
Pinch
Pole
Roots Manuva
Scientist
Shackleton
Shut Up And Dance (Smiley)
Smith & Mighty (Rob Smith)
Tom Moulton
U Brown
U-Roy
Wrongtom

ACKNOWLEDGEMENTS

I would like to thank Ben Rimmer whose help with research and sustained enthusiasm for this project has been invaluable, and my family and friends for their saintly patience too. I would also like to thank all of the managers and PR representatives who helped facilitate the interviews included in this book. Thanks must of course also go to the artists and musicians discussed here for their time, words of wisdom and for the dub-wise sounds.

ACKNOWLEDGEMENTS

PHOTO ACKNOWLEDGEMENTS

The author and the publishers wish to thank the below sources of illustrative material and/or permission to reproduce it:

With permission from Lillian Allen: pp. 190, 196; Ashes 57: p.142; Beezer: p. 151; with permission from Clive Chin: pp. 22, 36; Chiarra Dom: p. 152; with permission from Bernd Friedmann: pp. 183, 185; with permission from Jan Gleichmar: p. 179; Wayne Hudson: pp. 202, 203; with permission from Chris Lane: pp. 118, 120; Dan Medhurst: p. 129; Giancarlo Minelli: p. 105; with permission from Moss Raxlen: p. 207; RELAXMAX: p. 156; with permission from Scientist: p. 51; with permission from Adrian Sherwood & Rob Ellis: p. 166; with permission from Mark Stewart: p. 85; with permission from Paul Zasky: pp. 210, 211.

INDEX